"Dr. Dockweiler expertly breaks down the advc ... . the most inexperienced advocate will walk away from this book feeling empowered to advocate for school mental health services."

From the foreword by **Kelly Vaillancourt Strobach, PhD,**
Director of Policy and Advocacy,
National Association of School Psychologists

"*Advocating for Mental Health Supports in Schools* is a fantastic resource for stakeholders engaged in student mental health work at all levels of policy making. It touches on collaboration, workforce, and funding priorities and provides a view of the policy landscape that is rarely placed in one resource."

Meghan McCann, JD,
Assistant Director,
Education Commission of the States

"I am excited for *Advocating for Mental Health Supports in Schools* as readers will find it a relatable and practical manual. We have a desperate need for a how-to book on advocacy and policy to inspire change around the topic of school-based mental health and workforce development."

Sara Hunt, PhD, *Assistant Dean of Behavioral Health Sciences at the Kirk Kerkorian School of Medicine at UNLV*

ADVOCATING FOR MENTAL HEALTH SUPPORTS IN SCHOOLS

Advocating for Mental Health Supports in Schools shows readers how to advocate for, and achieve, more mental health supports in schools.

This timely book takes an actionable stance on the mental health issues schools are facing today, offering concrete strategies on how to advocate and what to advocate for. It contains model policy examples and expert advice from policy makers and practitioners across the country who are leaders in advocacy work. The book is divided into three sections. "Advocacy Truths" orients the reader as to what advocacy is and how to do it. "Policy Making" breaks down the complexity of the policy making process using simple terms and language, making it feel accessible and feasible. Finally, "Levels in Action" provides examples of federal, state, and local policy options to increase school-based mental health supports in schools. This section also outlines the ARTERY Pipeline Framework, showing readers how to systemically create workforce solutions to successfully recruit, train, and retain more school-based mental health professionals.

Within this guide, educators; school-based mental health professionals; graduate students in school psychology, counseling, and social work; school board members; policy makers; families and others will find concrete solutions to incorporate into their advocacy work at all levels of policy making.

Katherine A. Dockweiler, EdD, NCSP, is a policy researcher and school psychologist. She is an assistant professor of School Psychology at Nevada State College, a Nevada State Board of Education member, NASP Communications Committee Chair, and creator of the ARTERY Pipeline Framework.

ADVOCATING FOR MENTAL HEALTH SUPPORTS IN SCHOOLS

A Step-by-Step Guide

By Katherine A. Dockweiler

Routledge
Taylor & Francis Group

NEW YORK AND LONDON

Designed cover image: © Getty Images

First published 2023
by Routledge
605 Third Avenue, New York, NY 10158

and by Routledge
4 Park Square, Milton Park, Abingdon, Oxon, OX14 4RN

Routledge is an imprint of the Taylor & Francis Group, an informa business

© 2023 Katherine A. Dockweiler

Library of Congress Cataloging-in-Publication Data
Names: Dockweiler, Katherine A., author.
Title: Advocating for mental health supports in schools : a step-by-step guide / by Katherine A. Dockweiler.
Description: First Edition. | New York : Routledge, 2023. | Includes bibliographical references and index.
Identifiers: LCCN 2022035624 (print) | LCCN 2022035625 (ebook) | ISBN 9781032311890 (Hardback) | ISBN 9781032311883 (Paperback) | ISBN 9781003308515 (eBook)
Subjects: LCSH: Students—Mental health—United States. | Students—Mental health services—United States. | School psychology—United States. | Mental health counseling—United States.
Classification: LCC LB3430 .D63 2023 (print) | LCC LB3430 (ebook) | DDC 371.7/13—dc23/eng/20221014
LC record available at https://lccn.loc.gov/2022035624
LC ebook record available at https://lccn.loc.gov/2022035625

ISBN: 978-1-032-31189-0 (hbk)
ISBN: 978-1-032-31188-3 (pbk)
ISBN: 978-1-003-30851-5 (ebk)

DOI: 10.4324/9781003308515

Typeset in Joanna
by Apex CoVantage, LLC

To Audrey and Beau, may you always use your voice

CONTENTS

About the Author   xi

Foreword   xiii

Preface   xxiii

Acknowledgments   xxv

Section I: Advocacy Truths   **1**

1 The Students Are Not Okay and They Haven't Been
   for a While   3

2 Your Past Led You Here   18

3 Advocacy Is Uncomfortable   29

4 Advocacy Has a Strategic Scope   41

5 Advocacy Is Relationship Building   53

Section II: The Policy Making Process   **63**

6 Boomerang Policy Making Model   65

7 Advocacy Action Phase 1: The Message   78

8 Advocacy Action Phase 2: The Puzzle   91

9 Advocacy Action Phase 3: Puzzle Management   103

Section III: Levels in Action   **113**

10 One State's Policy Journey: Expanding Access to School-
    Based Mental Health Providers From the Federal Level
    to the Classroom   115

11 Federal Engagement   129

12 State Statutes   139

13 State Regulations   151

14 State Education Agencies   161

15 Institutes of Higher Education   169

16 Workforce Development: ARTERY Pipeline Framework   178

17 Local Education Agencies   198

18 School Role With Policies and Implementation   209

19 Getting Started   221

    Glossary   224
    Index   229

ABOUT THE AUTHOR

 Katherine A. Dockweiler, EdD, NCSP is a policy researcher, school psychologist, and assistant professor of School Psychology at Nevada State College. She is the creator of the ARTERY Pipeline Framework to address school-based mental health shortages, and is co-founder of Healthy Minds, Safe Schools, a mental health and school violence prevention program. She is a Member of the Nevada State Board of Education and Chair of the Communications Committee for the National Association of School Psychologists.

FOREWORD

Kelly Vaillancourt Strobach

According to Merriam-Webster, the definition of advocacy is "the act or process of supporting a cause or proposal". By this definition, I, like many of you, have been an advocate for most of my adult life, and certainly in my career as a school psychologist, even if I did not see myself in that way. Advocacy serves as the foundation of the work of many educators, school leaders, school employed mental health professionals, parents, families, and others who care about the healthy development of children, even if they are not aware of it. Each day, collectively, they engage in a variety of actions with the sole purpose of helping children be successful. This includes: designing engaging lessons that build upon the strengths and interests of students; fighting to ensure every student has access to the supports and interventions they need to be successful in school; helping connect students with community resources; nurturing their physical and mental wellness; offering a listening ear when a student is having a bad day; problem solving with building and/or district leaders to address the needs of the school as a whole and specific groups of students; and making sure the school board understands the human and financial resources necessary to support our students.

For many in the general public, "advocacy" is synonymous with politics, working with state and federal elected officials to pass legislation, and what is commonly referred to as lobbying. This was certainly my perception of advocacy for quite some time and is what I spend most of my time on in my current role as the Director of Policy and Advocacy for the National Association of School Psychologists. To be sure, this is one type of advocacy, but it is not the only type of advocacy. And while educators may be seasoned advocates when it comes to fighting for the needs of individual students, for many, advocating for systemic change within their building/district or fighting for legislative changes at the state or federal level can feel daunting and many may shy away from this critical work because they don't know where to start.

I admit that I was once in that place; knowing that I should be using my voice to advocate for meaningful systemic change, but not knowing where to begin. I began my career as a school psychologist shortly after No Child Left Behind was enacted. I grew increasingly frustrated with the overemphasis on accountability and standardized testing at the expense of almost everything else. Mental health services were primary offered to students in special education or in response to a crisis and workforce shortages limited the ability of school psychologists, and my school counselor and school social worker partners, to engage in the prevention and early intervention work we know is so critical. I am grateful that I worked with school and district administrators that understood the importance of comprehensive school mental health services. During my tenure, they successfully advocated for an expanded school mental health workforce and enacted critical systemic changes needed to support sustained delivery of comprehensive school mental health services. However, as I talked to my colleagues in other districts and states, I realized that we were the exception, not the rule. I knew something had to change and I wanted to do my part, but like so many others in education, I was burned out and the thought of adding one more thing to my plate felt overwhelming. But, the beautiful thing about advocacy is that you don't have to do it alone, and there is a path and a role for everyone.

For me, it was clear that my path included a second stint in graduate school, this time to focus on education policy. I continued to work as a school psychologist and I started having conversations with my colleagues and building level administrators about small, but meaningful changes we could make to infuse mental wellness promotion and carve out more time for direct service delivery without sacrificing too much instructional time. I built relationships and eventually helped support district wide initiatives to promote mental health. I didn't want to leave the field of school psychology, and serendipitously, I attended an advocacy training that ultimately led me to my current role. For the last ten years, I have been fortunate to lead the advocacy and policy work of the National Association of School Psychologists in collaboration with the countless dedicated school psychologists working in our schools across the country. Collectively, we have shaped state and federal policy to promote increased access to school mental health services and address the workforce shortages, but we still have a lot of work to do!

If only this book had been available to me 15 years ago. Dr. Katie Dockweiler, an advocate I am proud to call a friend and colleague, expertly breaks down the advocacy process so that even the most inexperienced advocate will walk away from this book feeling empowered to advocate for school mental health services. The expert advice and real-world experiences articulated in this book are invaluable and I wish I had had more access to this kind of information as I began this work. Whether your goals are focused on making change in one school or an entire country, this book will improve your capacity for advocacy and increase your chances of successfully achieving your policy goals.

Importance of This Topic

There has never been a greater sense of urgency to increase access to school mental health services and school employed mental health professionals (e.g. school psychologists, school counselors, school social workers) and ensure that these efforts are sustained. Over the last 20 years or so, interest in and attention to the importance of school mental health services has waxed and waned, with increased attention generally following a horrific event (e.g. 9/11 attack, natural disasters, acts of mass violence). These events tend to galvanize support for increased funding for mental health and expanded school mental health services as a short-term response to a crisis. However, over the last decade, thanks to a tremendous amount of advocacy by countless individuals and organizations, there is a greater understanding that school mental health services are necessary for the well-being of children, both in times of crisis and not. We are at an inflection point where we absolutely must build on this momentum, capitalize on current events and existing policy levers (more on that later) to ensure that every student, no matter where they live, has access to school mental health services.

We simply cannot wait. The situation is so dire that the U.S. Surgeon General issued an unprecedented public health advisory calling for significant action to protect the mental health of our children and youth (Office of the Surgeon General [OSG], 2021). Rates of childhood mental health concerns, including depression, have risen over the past 20 years, with suicide rates at an all-time high (Curtin & Heron, 2019). Research reveals that by seventh grade, 40% of students will have experienced a mental health issue such as anxiety or depression, and that, each year, nearly 20% of school-age youth meet the criteria for a mental health disorder (Centers for Disease Control and Prevention, 2019). The majority of these children and youth do not receive the care they need (Whitney & Peterson, 2019), and of those who do, the overwhelming majority do so in schools (Rones & Hoagwood, 2000). Much attention has been paid to the impact COVID-19 had on children's mental health. And while it is true that the pandemic did have an impact on children's mental health (see NASP, 2021), COVID-19 simply laid bare existing inequities and exacerbated difficulties in children and youth receiving necessary care. This is in large part due to the critical role that schools play in our mental and behavioral health care system. (Phelps & Sperry, 2020) and the Surgeon General explicitly notes the need to increase access to school mental health services, including addressing workforce shortages, as part of a comprehensive strategy (OSG, 2021).

This is one of the many reasons why Dr. Dockweiler's book is so important and timely. Advocacy is a marathon, not a sprint. It took decades of advocacy to get to the point where there is general consensus that comprehensive school mental health services are viewed as an integral component of our public education system. However, we cannot be complacent. It will take decades of continued advocacy to build upon this existing foundation and to address the workforce shortages and other systemic issues that result in inequitable access to comprehensive care.

Comprehensive School Mental and Behavioral Health Services: What Does This Look Like and Why Is It Important?

Before you embark on your advocacy journey, it is critical that you understand exactly what you are advocating for and are able to articulate it in a manner that resonates with your audience. Although we have made tremendous strides in educating the public and policy makers as to what school health services entail, not everyone fully "gets it" and your advocacy must include continued accurate messaging about school mental health. In my 20 years of experience as a school psychologist, advocate, and mental health policy expert I have had to push back against numerous myths and inaccuracies about school mental health services, some of which you may encounter in your work.

Common Myths About School Mental Health Services

- We can only provide mental health services to students with disabilities;
- School counselors, school psychologists, and school social workers aren't mental health providers;
- Our school has a clinical psychologist come twice a month to see students; we don't need anything else;
- Our school doesn't have "mental health problems";
- If we talk about mental health, it will only cause kids to have mental health problems;
- We can't afford to provide school mental health services;
- It is not the school's responsibility to support student mental health because it has no impact on student learning.

In reality, comprehensive school mental health services are foundational to supporting children's healthy development and academic success (Sanchez et al., 2018), improve school climate, improve attendance rates, increase academic achievement, reduce disciplinary issues (e.g. DiGirolamo et al., 2021 and Thompson et al., 2021), and can actually save schools money in the long term (Bradshaw et al., 2021). As Dr. Dockweiler emphasizes, it is imperative that we advocate for comprehensive school mental health services that include: mental wellness promotion for all students (Tier 1), processes to identify and address concerns early; and a continuum of evidence-based targeted (Tier 2) and intensive services (Tier 3) for individual students or groups of students as needed. Underpinning this framework is a multidisciplinary team that uses data-based decision-making processes to connect students with needed supports and monitor their response to specific interventions, adjusting service provision as necessary.

Figure 0.1 is just one of a multitude of visual representations of a comprehensive mental health service delivery system. However, access to adequate staffing of school-employed mental health professionals, such as school psychologists, is essential to the quality and effectiveness of any service delivery model.

My Advocacy Truths

Every single one of us has a role to play in advocating for school mental health services. No action is too small in this fight. If you are reading this book, congratulations, you have taken the first step in acknowledging that your voice is powerful and necessary in creating and sustaining change. This step-by-step guide will give you the necessary tools to advocate for increased access to school mental health services at the local, state, and federal level. This book is filled with a number of "advocacy truths", real-life examples, and sage advice from seasoned advocates. As you dive into this empowering and informative book, I wish to leave you with some of my advocacy truths and unconventional wisdom based on my experiences, which I hope helps you in achieving your goals.

- **Relationships are the foundation of advocacy.** Take time to cultivate professional and personal relationships with your colleagues, policy makers and their staff, key leaders of various organizations, and others who are doing similar advocacy work. Bring them into your work, build upon each other's ideas, and support their unique policy goals as appropriate. The effort you put into developing and cultivating these relationships will be paid back in spades, in time. Once you build that foundation of trust, you will be viewed as a trusted advisor whom key decision makers turn to for advice to help shape major policy decisions.

School Psychologists' Role in Comprehensive School Mental and Behavioral Health Services

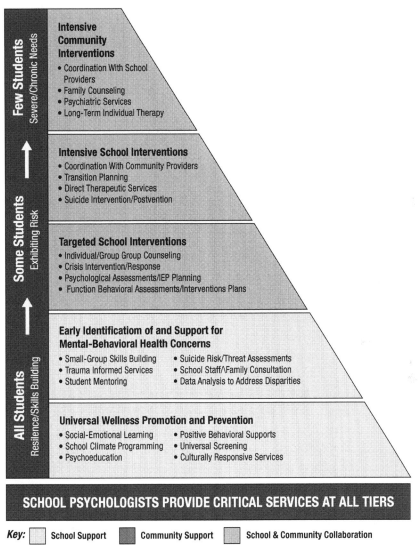

Figure 0.1 Comprehensive School Mental and Behavioral Health Services

Source: National Association of School Psycologists

- **Avoid partisanship.** It can be easy to get caught up in the politics when you are engaged in advocacy, particularly legislative advocacy. However, you are selling yourself, your issue, and ultimately our children, short if you refuse to work with policy makers of a specific political party. I am proud of the many legislative successes I have been a part of over the years – and every single one of them was achieved with bipartisan support.

- **Immerse yourself in the issue.** Take the time to ask questions. Learn the unique history of why a policy has or has not been successful in your community/district/state. What person(s)/organization(s) have typically led the work in this issue? In my experience, advocates who do not take the time to fully understand the nuances of a specific issue or policy can do more harm than good. True and sustainable policy change takes years and it is imperative that you take the time to really understand the issue and the key players before moving ahead with your singular agenda.

- **If you don't have a seat at the table, bring your own chair.** Don't wait for key decision makers to reach out to you. Show up at school board meetings; testify at legislative hearings; proactively reach out to key policymakers. Make yourself known, and make your perspective invaluable.

- **Build diverse coalitions.** Policy and advocacy work is most successful when you have a large group of people with different perspectives who are speaking with one voice. On the issue of school mental health, it is common to see coalitions that include parents, teachers, principals and other school leaders, school psychologists/counselors/social workers, and other professionals (and their respective professional associations) engaged. Consider what critical voices are missing and who has the necessary political capital to advance your issue. Don't be quick to write off organizations or individuals with whom you may not always agree. In my work, I have yet to engage with a coalition where all members agree on every single issue. The success of a coalition is predicated on one simple thing – a commitment to work toward the same goal.

- **Turn crisis into opportunity.** I don't mean that we should exploit every crisis as a political opportunity, but consider how specific events can galvanize support for increased access to school mental health services. In the last decade, the horrific school shootings in Newtown (Connecticut), Parkland (Florida), and Uvalde (Texas) combined with the COVID-19 pandemic and a host of devastating natural disasters created a groundswell of support for school mental health services. We were able to successfully leverage these events into real policy change because of the decades of work we had done to advocate for increased access to services and efforts to address the workforce shortages. Often, policy makers are quick to react to a crisis, and they will look to solutions they are aware of and lean on existing relationships. If you are only engaged in advocacy after a crisis event, you will not be successful. But if you sustain your advocacy, you will be in an excellent position to leverage a current event to secure a win.

- **Many hands make light work**. No one person can or should be expected to carry the full weight of the work. We all have different talents and advocacy requires a diverse set of skills. Utilize your strengths and rely on the specific skills of others to execute your work.
- **Don't let perfect be the enemy of the good.** It is my opinion that the best policy results from compromise. Although this perspective is not shared by all advocates, I believe that sometimes you have to be willing to support some policies that are less than ideal in exchange for what you want. It is also important to understand that change is often incremental. Small steps toward your ultimate goal should be celebrated and built upon.
- **Keep the focus on children and youth.** I assume that you have picked up this book and are committed to advocating for school mental health services because you know this is what is best for kids. If you keep kids at the center of all of your work, you will be taken seriously and will have more success.

Wherever you are in your advocacy journey, Dr. Dockweiler is an excellent guide. I applaud your dedication to improving access to school mental health services, and I sincerely hope our advocacy paths cross in this critical fight.

References

Bradshaw, C. P., Lindstrom Johnson, S., Zhu, Y., & Pas, E. T. (2021). Scaling up behavioral health promotion efforts in Maryland: The economic benefit of positive behavioral interventions and supports. *School Psychology Review, 50,* 99–109. Centers for Disease Control and Prevention.

Centers for Disease Control and Prevention. (2019). *Youth risk behavior survey data.* Retrieved May 10, 2021, from https://www.cdc.gov/yrbs

Curtin, S. C., & Heron, M. (2019). Death rates due to suicide and homicide among persons aged 10–24: United States, 2000–2017. NCHS Data Brief, 352, National Center for Health Statistics.

DiGirolamo, A. M., Desai, D., Farmer, D., McLaren, S., Whitmore, A., McKay, D., Fitzgerald, L., Pearson, S., & McGiboney, G. (2021). Results from a statewide school-based mental health program: Effects on school climate. *School Psychology Review, 50,* 81–98.

Herman, K. C., Reinke, W. M., Thompson, A. M., Hawley, K. M., Wallis, K., Stormont, M., & Peters, C. (2021). A public health approach to reducing the societal prevalence and burden of youth mental health problems: Introduction to the special issue. *School Psychology Review, 50,* 8–16.

Merriam-Webster. (n.d.). Advocacy. In *Merriam-Webster.com dictionary.* Retrieved June 23, 2022, from https://www.merriam-webster.com/dictionary/advocacy

National Association of School Psychologists. (2021). Child and adolescent mental health during the COVID-19 Pandemic [Research summary].

Office of the Surgeon General. (2021). Protecting Youth Mental Health: The U.S. Surgeon General's Advisory [Internet]. US Department of Health and Human Services. PMID: 34982518.

Phelps, C., & Sperry, L. L. (2020). Children and the COVID-19 pandemic. *Psychological Trauma: Theory, Research, Practice, and Policy, 12*(S1), S73–S75. doi:10.1037/tra0000861

Rones, M., & Hoagwood, K. (2000). School-based mental health services: A research review. *Clinical Child and Family Psychology Review, 3,* 223–241.

Sanchez, A. L., Cornacchio, D., Poznanski, B., Golik, A. M., Chou, T., & Comer, J. S. (2018). The effectiveness of school-based mental health services for elementary-aged children: A meta-analysis. *Journal of the American Academy of Child & Adolescent Psychiatry, 57*(3), 153–165.

Whitney, D. G., & Peterson, M. D. (2019). US national and state-level prevalence of mental health disorders and disparities of mental health care use in children. *JAMA Pediatrics, 173,* 389–391.

PREFACE

Have you ever felt lost and no matter which way you turn you can't seem to find the right direction? All the paths seem to look the same, and since you don't know exactly where you are headed, it begins to feel like any choice could be the right choice. Or that no choice might be the right choice. Maybe staying put is the way to go? If you can relate then you are in good company; many of us have been lost at one point or another physically, emotionally, or both.

The beginning phases of mental health advocacy can invoke similar feelings of confusion. Where to start? Which direction to go? Who can help? Sometimes the challenge can seem so daunting that the advocacy never gets off the ground and stalls before it begins. That is where this book comes in. While you contemplate your situation, I invite you to stay put for a moment and read this text to help you chart a path and navigate your mental health advocacy journey. Whether you need a single helpful hint or a comprehensive action plan, this text can help you.

This book is a practical step-by-step guide to help you plan your course. Over the past 20 years I've had the privilege of incredibly diverse experiences related to student mental health, and I present them to you here. These experiences range from consulting with members of Congress and presenting bills to the state legislature, to drafting behavior improvement plans for students and conducting mental health triage for youth in crisis. I've also tied a lot of shoes in the hallways of elementary schools. Proactive prevention is key, from our students' minds all the way down to their toes.

My research and practice have centered around two main themes: school-based mental health and policy frameworks. As a school psychologist, policy maker, higher education professional, and parent I can attest that these roles are all equally important from an advocacy and policy perspective. All voices must be present and ready to do the actionable work that is needed to improve mental health services for students. Advocating for mental health supports is not a burden to be shouldered by any one group; it is an endeavor that must be undertaken by many interested parties to maximize impact for students.

That said, the journey must begin somewhere, and I applaud you for taking the first step, reading this book! My goal is to support you in your advocacy and to share lessons learned. These learned lessons will also include advice and perspectives from colleagues and professionals from across the country, from the national level down to the grassroots advocacy level. Sit back, relax, and enjoy the advocacy journey!

ACKNOWLEDGMENTS

My utmost respect, gratitude, and humility go out to the following individuals for their tenacity and support for student well-being:

- Kelly Vaillancourt Strobach, PhD, NCSP, Director of Policy and Advocacy for the National Association of School Psychologists
- Marilyn Dondero Loop, Nevada State Senator and retired educator
- Jhone Ebert, Nevada Superintendent of Public Instruction
- Felicia Ortiz, Nevada State Board of Education President
- Kari Oyen, PhD, LP, NCSP, Assistant Professor at the University of South Dakota, Chair of the National Association of School Psychologists Government and Professional Relations Committee
- Kristin Barnson, School Counselor and Past President of Nevada School Counselor Association
- Zachary Scott Robbins, PhD, Principal and Author of *Restorative Justice Tribunal*
- Tamara Hudson, National Board Certified Teacher, Nevada State Board of Education Member
- Leslie Baunach, School Psychologist and Hawaii Delegate to the National Association of School Psychologists
- Sondra Cosgrove, PhD, Professor at the College of Southern Nevada, Vice Chair of the Nevada Advisory Committee to the U.S. Commission on Civil Rights

- Sara Hunt, PhD, Assistant Dean of Behavioral Health Sciences at the Kirk Kerkorian School of Medicine at UNLV and Director of the UNLV Mental and Behavioral Health Training Coalition
- Meghan McCann, JD, Assistant Director, Education Commission of the States
- Vicki Schwichtenberg, Retired School Psychologist
- Alison G. Clark, EdS, School Psychologist

SECTION I

ADVOCACY TRUTHS

1

THE STUDENTS ARE NOT OKAY AND THEY HAVEN'T BEEN FOR A WHILE

Learning Concepts

In this chapter, readers will learn:

- The current state of child and adolescent mental health.
- The current state of workforce development for school-based mental health.
- What it means to advocate.
- What encompasses mental health services.
- Who change agents are and where they might be found.

Chapter Keywords

- Epigenetic trauma
- Adverse childhood experience
- School-based mental health providers
- Advocate
- Change agent

DOI: 10.4324/9781003308515-2

State of Emergency in Child and Adolescent Mental Health

In October 2021, the American Academy of Pediatrics, the American Academy of Child and Adolescent Psychiatry, and the Children's Hospital Association declared a State of Emergency in Child and Adolescent Mental Health. This crisis had been bubbling for years, and the strain of the COVID-19 pandemic tipped the scales. Families experienced devastating loss during the pandemic and 140,000 students in America lost their primary or secondary caregiver to COVID-19 (American Academy of Pediatrics, 2021). Children and youth who were experiencing unpredictable life situations, such as food and housing insecurities, or who were navigating unstable home situations with abuse or adult mental health issues, began to experience compound traumas that did not have a chance to recover before the next trauma occurred.

Even students from predictable, stable home environments began to experience tumultuous situations that challenged all that they knew and could count on in their lives. Routine was disrupted and once-grounding forces in children's lives, such as school or sports, were upended. Families were faced with their own traumas and once-stable adults were forced to contend with loss of income, loss of work identity, and loss of family and friends through separation or death. Grief and pandemic fatigue set in, causing unprecedent levels of mental health issues for adults as well as children and adolescents. Structural racism also reared its ugly head and emerged as inextricably linked to the growing mental health crisis (American Academy of Pediatrics, 2021).

Child and adolescent mental health have been in crisis for years. Prior to the COVID-19 pandemic, students were experiencing rising levels of internalized and externalized behaviors such as depression, anxiety, violence, and suicide (Bera et al., 2022; Curtin & Heron, 2019). While all students were impacted during the pandemic in some way, adolescents with pre-existing mental health conditions experienced higher rates of anxiety and depression than their peers without pre-existing conditions (Bera et al., 2022). They also experienced greater risk for emergency room visits for eating disorders, suicidal ideations, and suicide attempts.

From 2000 to 2007 the suicide rate of youths aged 15–19 remained stable; however, from 2007 to 2017 it rose 76% (Curtin & Heron,

2019). Suicide is consistently the second leading cause of death for youths aged 15–19 (Curtin & Heron, 2019) and has now also become the second leading cause of death for children aged 10–14 (Center for Disease Control and Prevention, 2020). Our students are facing more and more pressures at younger and younger ages. In many cases, these young students lack protective factors and do not know how to cope with or regulate their intense emotions. They are turning to extreme solutions to end their pain and may not fully realize the finality of their actions. Suicidal ideations and attempts are on the rise for students aged 10–19 and have not stopped climbing as we transition out of the pandemic.

More and more students are being diagnosed with complex post-traumatic stress syndrome as the daily trauma they experience is compounded and they don't have a chance to heal before the next trauma occurs (Maercker, 2021; Bhatia, 2019). Chronic trauma has significant health impacts for children and their families, physically and mentally. To compound this trauma, our students must also contend with preventable acts of violence such as school shootings.

The study of *epigenetic trauma* and its transgenerational impact is fascinating. Epigenetics is the study of how behavior and environment can impact expressed DNA sequences (Center for Disease Control and Prevention, 2020). For example, students who experience complex post-traumatic stress disorder may have a shift in their expressed DNA sequences that can ultimately be passed on to their children. While their actual DNA sequence doesn't change, how it is expressed does. Transgenerational epigenetic inheritance is the passing down of this effect or change (Heard & Martienssen, 2014). Evidence of this phenomenon has been documented in children conceived during the 1918 influenza pandemic, in the children of Holocaust survivors, and in the children of mothers who experienced PTSD after the World Trade Center collapsed (Senaldi & Smith-Raska, 2020). Child abuse and stress during childhood can affect gene expression, leading to changes in brain development and stress regulation (Senaldi & Smith-Raska, 2020).

These changes in brain development and stress regulation impact how our children learn, problem solve, and respond to their environment. Nearly one in five children aged 6–17 experience a mental health condition with 50% of lifetime mental illness beginning by age 14 (National

Alliance on Mental Illness [NAMI], 2022). Nearly 80% of students with mental health conditions will not receive the services that they need for a variety of reasons, such as access to care or cost (National Association of School Psychologists [NASP], 2021a; Hanchon & Fernald, 2013). Of those who do receive support and intervention, 80% of students will receive it in the school setting (NASP, 2021; Farmer et al., 2003).

Mental health issues may run in families and are not specific to any demographic group or socio-economic class. They occur with fairly similar prevalence across racial groups with higher rates noted for those who identify as multiracial or for those who identify as lesbian, gay, or bisexual (NAMI, 2022).

By the age of 16, more than two-thirds of students report having experienced some sort of trauma or *adverse childhood experience* (ACE) (Substance Abuse and Mental Health Services Administration [SAMHSA], 2022). These ACEs may include, but are not limited to:

- abuse (psychological, physical, sexual)
- witnessing or experiencing domestic violence
- national disasters or terrorism
- sudden or violent loss of a loved one
- neglect
- military family-related stressors
- refugees or war experiences
- serious accidents or life-threatening illness

Given the holistic expanse of stressors happening in the world over the past few years, it is not surprising that so many of our students can report ACEs. Research has consistently demonstrated that it is not the severity of any one ACE that negatively impacts a child's outcomes, but the multitude of ACEs. As students transition from childhood to early adulthood, a history of multiple ACEs is "associated with poorer self-rated health and life satisfaction, as well as more frequent depressive symptoms, anxiety, tobacco use, alcohol use, and marijuana use" (Mersky et al., 2014, p. 917). There are four actions caring adults can do to support children who have experienced ACEs: (1) assure them that they are safe, (2) explain they are not responsible for what happened, (3) be patient, and (4) seek professional help (SAMHSA, 2022).

Let's not forget that mental health issues are not always clinically significant or medically diagnosable. Elementary schools across the country are struggling with students who have been socially isolated and have lacked opportunities to practice good prosocial behaviors and problem-solving skills for almost two years. Kindergarten classrooms are full of five-year-olds who cannot self-regulate or follow routines or directions. A veteran teacher of 27 years from the east coast shared that in all her years of teaching kindergarten, the 2021–2022 school year saw the highest number of students who flipped desks, threw chairs, and hit others.

Similarly, a teacher with 21 years of experience from the west coast shared that the same school year she had the highest number of 3rd graders who cried for Mommy, hid under desks, or just refused to do what was asked of them. She said they acted like much younger children, and it almost felt like she was teaching kindergarten, not 3rd grade. The reports by these teachers about their experiences are not unique and symbolize an entire generation of children across the country, and world, who lack years of typical social-emotional development. This lack of social-emotional maturity impairs their interactions with others, their internal processing, and their academic performance. Without intervention, these seemingly minor mental health issues can escalate into significant mental health issues with devastating impacts. Layered on top of the already existing trend of elevated suicide rates in students aged 10–19, we can anticipate even higher rates as these young children mature – if their mental health needs are not addressed.

As repeatedly documented, the rate of students with mental health issues has been on the rise for years and mental health issues are increasingly impacting students at younger ages. Evidence also supports transgenerational epigenetic inheritance from conditions such as complex PTSD that is impacting student mental health and generations of trauma-exposed families. Finally, issues related to the COVID-19 pandemic are further exacerbating the existing mental health crisis. In addition to all of this, a silent threat to student well-being has been lurking beneath the surface and we have been late to identify or recognize its existence. Turning a blind eye to the structural threat undermining student mental health supports has brought our communities to breaking point. What could this dangerous and silent threat be?

State of Emergency in Workforce Development

To answer the question about underlying threats, I postulate there is also a State of Emergency in Workforce Development and higher education training programs that prepare school-based mental health professionals. These *school-based mental health professionals* include school psychologists, school counselors, and school social workers and there just aren't enough of them. It is no coincidence to me that we are experiencing an inverse relationship between the number of students with mental health needs and the number of trained mental health providers. As the number of mental health occurrences have gone up, access to mental health providers has gone down. The absence of trained mental health providers is the dangerous and silent threat undermining all mental health services, both school-based and community-based.

To properly address children's mental health and the crisis situation we find ourselves in, we need to understand how we got to this point. We need to dig deep and identify systemic sources of the crisis. Through research and field experience I can attest that at its core, our country has a workforce development issue: it does not have enough training programs to produce the number of professionals needed to alleviate the worsening mental health crisis. Ultimately, *having adequate mental health services in schools is predicated on having an adequate number of professionals to deliver the services.*

This theme is woven throughout the book as an underlying problem to delivering mental health supports in schools and is a problem that unequivocally must be solved. Fiscal support, career pipelines, and expanded training programs are all key elements to bolstering workforce development (NASP, 2021; American School Counselor Association [ASCA], 2020). In a report by the U.S. Department of Health and Human Services (2016), the growth for school psychologists was projected to be only 1% through 2025, whereas the attrition rates and demand continually rise higher, at approximately 23%. Similar findings relative to supply, demand, and staffing ratios have been found for school counselors and school social workers (U.S. Department of Health and Human Services, Health Resources and Services Administration, National Center for Health Workforce Analysis, 2019).

Below are the recommended ratios of licensed professionals to students according to their national associations compared to actual ratios nationwide (NASP, 2021; ASCA, 2021; School Social Work Association of America, 2013, 2019):

Table 1.1 Recommended and actual ratios across the three school-based mental health professions

Professional	Recommended Ratio	Actual Ratio
School Psychologists	1:500	1:1211–5000
School Counselors	1:250	1:415
School Social Workers	1:250	1:2106

An ocean of evidence supports the need for additional school-based mental health providers and the negative impact their absences have on students.

Taking a step back and framing the lack of mental health supports and providers from a different angle, there are short-term and long-term solutions that can be implemented simultaneously. The short-term solutions may be small actions that must be taken incrementally to ultimately achieve the long-term solution. Other short-term solutions may be Band-Aid fixes that will keep the wound covered and prevent the crisis from getting worse while the long-term solution is being built.

This book will tackle the workforce challenge head on in Chapters 10–18. Applying the ARTERY Pipeline Framework (Dockweiler, 2019), change agents can evaluate what short- and long-term steps are needed within their unique contexts and can begin action planning goals and next steps. A foundational step is the establishment of student to provider ratios (NASP, 2021). Once target ratios are determined, back mapping, forward mapping, and lateral mapping can occur to achieve these goals. Families, educators, policy makers, or anyone interested in the improvement of mental health services and service providers can help advocate for this comprehensive action planning framework.

In addition to problem solving the State of Emergency in Workforce Development and the lack of mental health service providers, this text will introduce the reader to what advocacy is and how to advocate successfully. Having a goal and the best of intentions will only get you so far. Engaging in effective communication and advocacy will help you build coalition to move your initiative over the goal line.

Advocacy

Advocacy is a major theme of this text, as are mental health supports for students. Before diving into the book, it will be helpful to have a common understanding about what these two terms mean and how they are used within the context of this book. This book is divided into three sections and is written in an easy to digest manner. The first section, *Advocacy Truths*, orients the reader as to what advocacy is and how to get started. The second section, *The Policy Making Process*, breaks down the complexity of the policy making process using simple terms and language, making it feel accessible and feasible. The last section, *Levels in Action*, provides concrete examples of policy options to increase school-based mental health supports in schools from the federal level down to the school level. Feel free to jump to the section that resonates with your level of experience. Or, just keep reading to learn more about each and how they influence each other.

To *advocate* means to promote or support a particular idea. I would argue that at its core, advocacy contains a central element of communication. In this sense, to advocate means to effectively communicate and share information about a particular idea you care about. This is something we can all wrap our head around as we communicate in this manner many times a day. We share information with our children's teachers about how they are progressing in math, and we communicate with the waiter at our local restaurant about our dislike for onions and our desire to have them omitted from our meal. Communication and advocacy go hand in hand, and you won't be a good advocate if you don't use effective communication skills. Throughout this book, when the term advocacy, or to advocate, is used, it may also be paired with communication or have an underlying understanding that effective communication tools are needed when deploying the advocacy message.

Using the term advocacy is intentional as there is an intended outcome that one hopes to achieve, for example, an additional school-based mental health provider at your child's middle school. It may feel more comfortable to identify as being an effective communicator rather than as an advocate. However, these are two distinct skills and while good communication is necessary for advocacy, advocacy is not necessarily required to be a good communicator. Plenty of people advocate poorly with bad communication skills and their initiative usually doesn't go very far. As you will learn more about in Chapter 3, advocacy can feel uncomfortable, and this is okay.

Advocacy does not need to be aggressive. This has been a repeated theme shared with me from across the country, "I can't advocate; I'm not that confrontational or aggressive". Good advocacy work doesn't need to be contentious; it can feel like a coming together of like minds for a united purpose. There will be challenges, don't get me wrong, but if there weren't challenges then there wouldn't be room to improve. I like to think of advocacy challenges as pieces of an advocacy puzzle. Which pieces need to fit together, and when, to make our goal come together? What pieces are missing that we may need to find to complete our puzzle? In this frame, any challenges or setbacks aren't really a problem. As you will learn in Chapter 8, just turn the puzzle piece, try it in a different spot, and keep going.

Mental Health Services

What are mental health services? "Mental health services" is an umbrella term used to encapsulate any resource or service that can support student mental and behavioral well-being. As previously stated, most mental health supports that students receive are provided in the school setting. This may include the implementation of a social-emotional-behavioral multi-tiered system of support program, community-based resources to share with families, direct counseling services for students, or the hiring or training of school-based mental health providers. This is not an exhaustive list and can include supports big and small, universal or targeted. It may include social-skills training for the entire school, or professional learning on Psychological First Aid for staff. Every school and community are different, and the mental health supports they need will vary. Depending on what they've already got in place, School A will need X supports, whereas School B will need Y supports. Or, more holistically, an entire state may need legislation relative to C, D, and E supports.

You will also notice that this book is written in the first person. This is intentional because advocacy is personal and, as explained in Chapter 2, we are each on our own journey. It will look and feel different for each of us and our motivations for why we are engaging in advocacy work are unique. Advocating for more mental health supports for our youth is a personal choice and using the first-person narrative helps us to see ourselves in the work. Advocating for our students is not something that other people do. It is something that we do as parents, educators, and community members.

After attending years of national conferences, meetings, and work-groups for school psychologists, administrators, teachers, school counselors, policy makers, and families I am confident, now more than ever, that our stories matter. They matter in the sense that they help ground our personal mission for advocacy as well as our motivation for joining others to achieve a common purpose. Advocating for change does not always start in a boardroom. More often, conversations with key decision makers will start by chance at a basketball game, at the park, or a parking lot. Knowing your "why" and having conviction about your purpose will strengthen your message to others. Have your elevator speech ready for these chance moments and seize the opportunity! More information about how to craft your key message and engage stakeholders is discussed in Chapter 7.

In Hawaii, Leslie Baunach, school psychologist, shared that the locals use the term *talk stories*. After meetings or gatherings, they will come together to talk stories and catch up on their work or what's happening in their lives. My goal for this book is to talk stories about the advocacy efforts that are happening around the country relative to school-based mental health and the lived experiences of those individuals or groups who are doing the work. Advocacy is truly not just something that other people do. It is what we do, people like you and me, and this book will highlight the work of families, educators, and leaders who are making positive change.

Change Agents

Who are change agents? A *change agent* is someone working to make change. In our context, anyone advocating for mental health services or mental health service providers is a change agent. As outlined in Chapters 4 and 5, the change may be big or little, collective or individual. The agent may be working for change as part of a larger organization or independently. While not an exhaustive list, these agents may be educators, family members, higher education professionals, policy makers, or community members. What hat(s) do you wear? It is important to recognize that a change agent may wear many hats and can leverage their different roles depending on the situation. For example, I wear every single one of the hats listed above and advocate differently depending on the context. Oftentimes, I balance them all on my head at once and advocate through a collective lens of experiences.

What is meant by the term "educator"? For the purposes of this text, an educator is anyone who works in the schools. It might be school counselors, teachers, administrators, or support staff. Use of the broad term educator is not meant to marginalize the uniqueness of any profession; rather, it is used from the perspective that there is strength in shared voice. Each profession has distinct viewpoints, and they support students differently, but as employees of an education system, the term educator is used in the broad collective sense. Oftentimes a particular situation or role may directly align with a targeted profession, and in those cases, I will use the specific title of the profession.

However, this book is not just for educators, but for anyone who wants to speak out for school-based mental health supports. Parents, guardians, and families are the number one advocates for their children. Their voices should be encouraged and honored as critical decision makers for students. A pet peeve of mine is when families are consulted only *after* policies are created and implemented. This is part of a rubber-stamping process to demonstrate "engagement" but lacks willful desire to actually engage families. Rubber-stamping processes often do not offer feedback looping for continuous improvement. Therefore, when families try to engage and offer suggestions, what they hear is, "you should have told us this before we decided X". However, if families don't have access to the meetings where decisions are being made, their voices are not included.

Higher education professionals will also find value in this text and can use it as a tool to expand their own advocacy or to support the advocacy training of their students. It will be especially beneficial to higher education professionals as they look to the ARTERY Pipeline Framework (Dockweiler, 2019) to advocate for expanding or adding higher education training programs for school-based mental health providers. The various pillars of the ARTERY encompass multiple learning environments from high school all the way through graduate school programming.

Community-based organizations who have an interest in education and student well-being are also great advocates and can provide resources not traditionally found in schools. This book can help them navigate the advocacy process and determine where they can best fit and on what issues. Now is an especially unique time as many funding sources are becoming available through federal and state grants. These grants may be offered to entities that are not available to local education agencies. This is great opportunity to link community-based supports with district and school level offerings. By leveraging financial resources, we can maximize supports and services to students.

Elected officials and other education leaders can play a critical role in advocating for school-based mental health supports. They are essential partners when laws need to be passed to ensure these supports are available. As explained in Chapter 6, good policy making is like a Boomerang: it is multi-directional, and the flow of ideas and information goes both ways. It is not like a Frisbee: only going one way and never looping back to the invested parties. How to manage the various puzzle pieces of policy making is outlined in Chapter 9.

Advocate for Mental Health Services and Providers

Determining what types of mental health services are needed can be a daunting task. You may feel that something is needed, but what that something is may be unknown. Or, you may know exactly what your school needs. If your school does not have a school counselor and small group counseling is in high demand, hiring a school counselor would seem to make perfect sense. This book will not tell you exactly what services to advocate for but will provide advocacy strategies and examples from which to learn. Each school, community, and situation is different and will require unique supports that align with its needs. This book will give you an idea of what types of evidence-based services have been successful and how to go about attaining them.

As mentioned earlier, the underlying premise of the book is that *having adequate mental health services in schools is predicated on having an adequate number of professionals to deliver the services*. Without these professionals, where will the support come from? States could have the best policies in place, and the best intentions at the district and school levels, but if there are no school-based mental health providers to deliver the services, how will the students receive them?

In the following chapters we will talk stories about the successes happening across the country and break down how groups were able to achieve more mental health services, more school-based mental health service providers, or both. In doing so, hopefully you can see yourself in doing the work and determine what steps might be needed to achieve success.

Our students are not okay, and they haven't been for a while. Together we can change the course of student mental health and take steps toward improving the current state of emergency.

Based on the key learning objectives, I can now:

- Describe the current state of child and adolescent mental health.
- Explain what is needed relative to workforce development for school-based mental health.
- Define what it means to advocate.
- Explain what mental health services might include in the school setting.
- Identify who change agents are across a variety of contexts.

References

American Academy of Pediatrics (October 19, 2021). *AAP-AACAP-CHA Declaration of a National Emergency in Child and Adolescent Mental Health*. https://publications.aap.org/aapnews/news/17718

American School Counselor Association. (2021). *ASCA Releases Updated Student-to-School Counselor Ratio Data*. https://www.schoolcounselor. org/getmedia/238f136e-ec52–4bf2–94b6-f24c39447022/Ratios-20–21-Alpha.pdf

Bera, L., Souchon, M., Ladsous, A., Colin, V., & Lopez-Castroman, J. (2022). Emotional and behavioral impact of the COVID-19 epidemic in adolescents. *Current psychiatry reports, 24*(1), 37–46. https://doi.org/ 10.1007/s11920-022-01313-8

Bhatia, R. (2019). Agitation in children and adolescents: Diagnostic and treatment considerations. *Current Psychiatry, 18*(6), 19–27. https:// cdn.mdedge.com/files/s3fs- public/CP01806019.PDF

Centers for Disease Control and Prevention. (2020). *National Center for Health Statistics Mortality Data on CDC WONDER: Underlying cause of death, 1999–2019*. US Department of Health and Human Services. https://wonder.cdc.gov/Deaths-by-Underlying-Cause.html

Curtin, S. C., & Heron, M. (2019). *Death rates due to suicide and homicide among persons aged 10–24: United States, 2000–2017* (NCHS data brief, no 352). National Center for Health Statistics. https://www.cdc.gov/nchs/data/databriefs/db352-h.pdf

Dockweiler, K. A. (2019). *School psychologist pipeline framework ARTERY: Active Recruitment, Training, and Educator Retention to serve our Youth*. Nevada Department of Education [Virtual].

Farmer, E. M., Burns, B. J., Philip, S. D., Angold, A., & Costello, E. J. (2003). Pathways into and through mental health services for children and adolescents. *Psychiatric Services, 54*, 60–67. doi:10.1176/appi.ps.54.1.60

Hanchon, T. A., & Fernald, L. N. (2013). The provision of counseling services among school psychologists: An exploration of training, current practices, and perceptions. *Psychology in the Schools, 50*, 651–671. doi:10.1002/pits.21700

Heard, E. & Martienssen, R. A. (2014). Transgenerational epigenetic inheritance: Myths and mechanisms. *Cell, 157*(1), 95–109. https://doi.org/10.1016/j.cell.2014.02.045

Maercker, A. (2021). Development of the new CPTSD diagnosis for ICD-11. *Borderline Personality Disorder and Emotional Dysregulation, 8*(7), 1–4. https://doi.org/10.1186/s40479-021-00148-8

Mersky, J. P., Topitzes, J., & Reynolds, A. J. (2013). Impacts of adverse childhood experiences on health, mental health, and substance use in early adulthood: A cohort study of an urban, minority sample in the U.S. *Child Abuse & Neglect, 37*(11), 917–925. https://doi.org/10.1016/j.chiabu.2013.07.011

National Alliance on Mental Illness (NAMI). (2022). *Mental health by the numbers*. https://www.nami.org/mhstats

National Association of School Psychologists. (2021a). *School psychologists: Qualified health professionals providing child and adolescent mental and behavioral health services* [White paper]. Author.

National Association of School Psychologists. (2021b). *Improving school and student outcomes: The importance of addressing the shortages in school psychology* [Handout]. Author.

National Association of School Psychologists. (2021c). *Shortages in school psychology: Challenges to meeting the growing needs of U.S. students and schools* [Research summary]. Author.

National Association of School Psychologists. (2021d). *Shortages in school psychology: Policies addressing the shortage of school psychologists.* https://www.nasponline.org/research-and-policy/policy-priorities/critical-policy-issues/shortage-of-school-psychologists

Senaldi, L., & Smith-Raska, M. (2020) Evidence for germline non-genetic inheritance of human phenotypes and diseases. *Clinical Epigenetics, 12*(136), 1–12. https://doi.org/10.1186/s13148-020-00929-y

School Social Work Association of America. (2013). *School social workers helping students succeed: Recommended school social worker to student ratios.* https://www.sswaa.org/_files/ugd/426a18_4050422b3c41478f9ee0db83d1bc1f75.pdf

School Social Work Association of America. (2019). *School social workers: Vital resources for student success.* https://www.sswaa.org/_files/ugd/486e55_076e1bbb0b594c27b57c44d4f6f9a55b.pdf

U.S. Department of Health and Human Services. (2016). *National Projections of Supply and Demand for Selected Behavioral Health Practitioners: 2013–2025.* https://bhw.hrsa.gov/sites/default/files/bureau-health-workforce/data-research/behavioral-health-2013-2025.pdf

U.S. Department of Health and Human Services, Health Resources and Services Administration, National Center for Health Workforce Analysis. (2019). *Technical Documentation for HRSA's Health Workforce Simulation Model.* U.S. Department of Health and Human Services. https://bhw.hrsa.gov/sites/default/files/bureau-health-workforce/data-research/technical-documentation-health-workforce-simulation-model-archived.pdf

2

YOUR PAST LED YOU HERE

Learning Concepts

In this chapter, readers will learn:

- What life experiences have impacted their pathway to advocacy.
- How their past led them to where they are today.
- How to frame their experiences as strengths.
- That advocacy is a personal journey.
- How to see themselves as advocates.

Chapter Keywords

- Why
- Lobbyists
- Content experts
- Implicit bias

DOI: 10.4324/9781003308515-3

What led you to be curious about advocacy? It may be that there is something currently happening in your life that is causing you to consider how to go about making a change. Or perhaps there is an external force influencing your interest. No matter what the current force is, your past has played a part in where you are today. This chapter will help you identify your own motivation for engaging in advocacy, or your "why". As you read through the chapter, probing questions are offered to help guide your thinking and to help you identify how your past has led you here.

Identify Your "Why"

When I first envisioned participating in advocacy work, the image that came to my mind was a courtroom. Or a boxing ring. Some location with verbal sparring, physical sparring, or both. I do not come from a political family and my only reference to politics and advocacy is what I have seen on TV. Scenes from *Ally McBeal*, *Homeland*, and *House of Cards* flashed before my eyes. As with most things in life, we don't know what we don't know. Having engaged in advocacy work for quite a while now, I can assure you that advocacy and policy making is not nearly as provocative as seen on television. There are certainly moments that could come from a TV drama, but for the most part these moments are rare.

Starting out with no political background or frame of reference, I had no idea how to begin the advocacy process. I knew that I wanted to improve school-based mental health supports for students, but emailing the Governor seemed a bit extreme. Conversely, starting with fellow parents and educators didn't seem right either. Where was the happy medium? Where was the right entry point? To answer this question, I had to learn a little bit more about myself.

At the most fundamental level, I am a parent. My children are 9 and 10, 3rd and 4th graders, and I want to make school a safer place for them. I am also a school psychologist who has worked in inner-city, high-risk schools and I want to make school a safer place for students. Finally, I am a member of my community, and I want my community to be a safe place for my children and students to thrive. This is as simple as it gets. If I had to venture a guess, I have a feeling that many of you reading this can relate. Whether you are a parent, educator, mental health provider, non-profit member, or caring stakeholder, my guess is that you want the same thing: for this world to be a safe place. This safety starts with the mental and behavioral wellness of our children and youth.

Growing up, my parents were both school psychologists, and I saw how deeply they cared for their students and families. Just as I did not come from a political background, neither did my parents. They both came from farming families and were first generation college students. Political capital and prowess were as foreign to our family as aeronautical engineering or cardiovascular surgery.

I grew up in a small town where everyone seemed to know everyone. Identifying who the decision makers were and what community supports were available was pretty easy. While political navigation still existed, oftentimes getting extra support for a student or family was as simple as a phone call. In larger systems, it might take ten phone calls, five emails, and a surprise drop-in. That's not to say that small school systems do not face challenges – they do; or that larger systems are not navigable – they are. Bureaucracy and red tape exist in all sizes of systems that must be circumvented or removed.

- What has been your experience with politics and navigating bureaucracies?
- What has been your experience with the creation of laws and the policy making process?
- Are political navigation and policy making familiar environments for you?

I was a very stubborn and determined child. "Strong-willed" is a term I heard my parents use often. If I was told "no" I would find a way to turn it into a "yes". Recently I was talking to my mom about some piece of advocacy I was working on and how determined I was to get it right. Something about my tone or demeanor must have struck a memory because she started laughing and said, "Now can you see how challenging it was to parent you? You always had your own sense about how things should be done!" It was funny to hear this willfulness come full circle, and I'm glad I can use this superpower to help make things better for others.

In college I was very interested in political science but not having any family or friends who worked in the profession I did not "see" myself in that world. As a result, I did not pursue this degree program. Eventually I ended up in a field where I did have family, and where I could see myself – as a school psychologist. Certain interests never seem to go away, though, and eventually I pursued my doctorate degree in Educational Leadership with an emphasis in Policy Studies. It was the perfect marriage of my passion for school-based mental health and advocacy. In this sense, my past lead me to where I ended up.

In exploring your own past there are probably moments or experiences that helped to inform certain decisions in your life. Life experiences, interests, and external influences all shape the path of our life. Within this path, there are probably certain circumstances that led you to advocate for yourself, or someone else. Were you bullied as a child? Did you experience adverse childhood experiences? Was there a caring adult or peer who stuck up for you and helped make your path easier? As you read through this book, I challenge you to explore your own past and how your journey has led you here, to this point where you are ready to be an advocate for students and mental health.

- What characteristics do you possess that could be an asset in the advocacy process?
- What characteristics would you anticipate that could hinder your advocacy?
- How can you turn these perceived hindrances into strengths?

What Does It Mean to Advocate?

On the surface, it seemed like I might be entering into a very aggressive realm, a world vastly different from the one I knew as a humble educator. In my limited experience, mostly from watching those TV dramas, advocates spoke with such assurance and conviction that they induced confidence in their proposed initiatives just by the tone of their voice. Could I ever speak with such confidence? Would I ever have the courage to propose an initiative or to challenge someone else if their proposal was not in the best interest of children?

As outlined in the previous chapter, at its most basic level, *to advocate means to promote or support a particular idea.* This can take on many different forms depending on the context. It can also vary depending on who is advocating, for what purpose, the scope of the issue, and the resources needed for change. It can be through phone calls, in-person conversations, emails, written letters, or social media. A parent or guardian advocating for school counseling supports at their child's school may look different than a state-level school counseling association advocating for the right to practice comprehensive school counseling services in their state. While seemingly separate, the two are intertwined and can actually benefit and support each other.

For example, the caregiver who is advocating at the school level can reach out to the state-level school counselor association for support and resources to increase the counseling services in the school. Conversely, the state-level school counseling association that is advocating for a state statute to fully implement the American School Counselor Association Model, which includes increased access to school counseling services, can partner with the caregiver. The association can request that the caregiver tell their story to state legislators and other stakeholder groups to help paint the picture about what is really happening in the schools and how the students are being impacted. There are several other opportunities stemming from these advocacy activities for continued partnership between the caregiver and the state school counselor association. Additional advocacy might be necessary at the state regulation level or district level to support the implementation of greater access to school-based counseling services. In general, voices are stronger when carried by multiple people and/ or groups. Advocacy leaders are able to work with many people at once, and on many tasks at once. They think strategically about long- and short-term goals, are able to conduct broad social analyses, and keep their eye on their end goal (Anderson, 2009).

Fundamentally, in the education policy space, you may hear about two different types of advocates: lobbyists and content experts. *Lobbyists* are paid by a group to advance certain policy initiatives. *Content experts* are experts from the field who can inform on content to advance best practice policies. If you are a school-based mental health provider, your expertise will carry different, and often greater, weight than lobbyists. Educators who can advocate like lobbyists, but maintain the distinction as a content expert, will go far in achieving their identified policy initiatives. Other advocate groups such as parents, families, community groups, or associations can all provide valuable insight into mental health initiatives. Advocacy skills are critical; however, they are rarely taught in education, counseling, or psychology college courses, nor are they explicitly taught in schools of law or public health (Berman et al., 2019; Goodman et al., 2018).

Why become involved in policy advocacy? Most of us don't wake up one day and decide, "I'm going to become an advocate today". Day in and day out we advocate without even thinking about it: for our children, for our prep time, for our independence with instructional delivery. Most people who make the foray into policy advocacy have an urge that stems from an indistinguishable sense that something isn't fair. When their daily advocacy efforts fail and they realize that the core issue is something greater than they can solve alone, they begin seeking out change from those who can help unlock the answers.

- What experiences have you had that led you to want to advocate?
- Do you have any friends, family, or colleagues who are advocates?
- Who can you collaborate with as you start your advocacy journey?
- Looking back, have there been times you were advocating and might not have known that is what you were doing?

My entrance into the policy making space was not a slow dipping of the toe into a shallow pool of water. It was a double back flip off the high dive into the deep end – blindfolded. What prompted this drastic and complete emersion into policy advocacy? The answer is simple: I jumped off that high dive with a powerful conviction that the state reading policy was unjust. The enacted state reading policy was biased and detrimental to the short- and long-term wellness outcomes for students. Unpacking this issue was like peeling an onion. Once one aspect was pulled back and analyzed, it led to another layer, and another layer, and so on. It took three years but, in the end, we were successful in our efforts to remove mandatory retention and to increase health and wellness outcomes for students.

However, before embarking on this policy advocacy journey, I had to first see myself as an advocate who could make policy change on behalf of students.

Your Past Led You Here

It is easy to assume that advocates are born for debate and thrive in contentious situations. However, remember, at our core, advocates strive for equity and what is right for students. The media may portray advocates as loud, often obnoxious, individuals, but in my experience they are mild-mannered and strive to neutralize contentious situations with logic and compromise. Advocates are not crawling into boxing rings or court rooms for verbal and physical sparring. They are driving their children around to after-school activities and trying to figure out what to make for dinner.

- In the past, how would you define an advocate?
- Is this definition the same that you have today?
- What similarities exist; what are some differences?
- In what ways to do you see yourself as an advocate?

As a child, while willful, I was painfully shy and dreaded all situations where people would speak to me. It didn't matter if it was a neighbor, a friend of my parents, or even teachers; they were all potential provokers of my extreme anxiety, even with a polite, "How are you?" In most cases, I wished I could just disappear and avoid the awkwardness that followed this simple pleasantry. My mom was always great about interceding or providing a gentle prompt to lead me into a response. In cases when she wasn't around, a mumbled "fine" with my eyes on the ground would get me by. However, in both situations, I'd much prefer to have been able to teleport away from the horrific expectation of social interchange.

Social anxiety and shyness are not the most commonly thought of characteristics of a good advocate. As mentioned previously, advocates are usually confident and have no problem speaking with conviction, right? This is not necessarily true; anyone can be an advocate. It reminds me of the stories I've heard about the parent who can lift the car off the ground to give their child enough space to escape after a car accident. This is what advocacy is like. Caring so deeply about an issue that it doesn't matter what obstacles lie in the way. This depth of care, this depth of conviction, is what makes a good advocate.

To compensate for my shyness, I leaned on my little sister to be my voice. Two years younger than me, she was extroverted, articulate, and did not shy away from social situations. Not surprisingly, she eventually pursued theater and had a knack for the stage. In elementary school we were both involved with Campfire, a national youth development group focused on equity, advocacy, and leadership. We took part in various activities throughout the year, and for one of our fundraising activities, we sold Campfire Candy. My sister and I would load up our Red Flyer metal wagon with a variety of candy boxes and go door to door in our neighborhood selling the candy. My sister's job was to knock on the door, make our sales pitch, and handle all communications with the neighbor. My job was to deal with the money and to hand the purchased box(es) to the neighbor. This dynamic worked for us and played well to our strengths. While successful, this is not a very sustainable approach to life.

During this same time period I was so timid that I would not even ask my teacher if I could go to the bathroom during the school day. Heaven forbid I speak up for my own personal needs! Looking back, my lack of personal advocacy is shocking to me. Why on earth would I not ask for something as basic as a bathroom pass? This is something I eventually grew out of but still remember vividly to this day. Later, as a high schooler, my parents provided respite care for families with students with severe needs. I used to help out and would bring the students ice cream or just hang out and watch movies. My mom insists I was a good advocate for these students' needs and would speak out on their behalf. She framed it in a way that I hadn't even thought of. So, while there were times that I wouldn't speak out on my own behalf, I had no problem speaking out on behalf of others. On some level I think we can all relate to advocating for ourselves and/or others.

Regardless of whether we are talkative or shy, introverted or extroverted, loud or quiet, we've all personally experienced or witnessed injustice. This injustice may have been intentional or may have been an unintended consequence of some well-meaning initiative; but either way, injustice is injustice all the same. Your past led you here for a reason. In my case, familiarity with school psychology, a willful sense of right and wrong, and a need to speak up for others helped guide my path. Identifying what led you to want to advocate, or to learn more about the process, may stem from some deeper place or experience. As mentioned earlier, identifying how your past led you here and what your "why" is, will help make you a better advocate (Coggins, 2017).

- What injustices have you witnessed or experienced that influenced who you are today?
- What emotions from these experiences were invoked?
- Have these experiences informed your advocacy?
- What is your "why"?

Advocacy Is Personal

No two people will advocate the same way, and there is no "right" way to do it. Everyone forms relationships differently and may lean on others during certain times when other individuals would lean out. Identifying your "why" will help you as you pursue your advocacy efforts and when the days are challenging, your why will serve as a reminder and fortify you to keep doing what you do.

Nevada Superintendent of Public Instruction Jhone Ebert emphasizes the importance of having voice. She recommends starting small with your advocacy efforts as advocacy can become overwhelming quickly. Homing in on your message and your why can help to focus the purpose of your efforts. If your message is too broad, change will be difficult to achieve. However, the more specific you can be the more likely you are to achieve change. She recommends being very specific about the issue and the change you are hoping to see.

What life experiences might you have gone through that inform the basis of your why? Identifying your why and being specific about your message and the desired outcome you are seeking will maximize the effectiveness of your advocacy efforts.

Framing Experiences as Strengths

Now that you've thoughtfully contemplated the questions posed in this chapter, my hope is that you have begun to identify key experiences that have contributed to your why. For example, what experiences have you witnessed or lived that influence your perspective of right and wrong?

These injustices have shaped us, often unknowingly, just as they shape our children and the children we work with. This can often lead to implicit bias and is worth exploring further should there be any uncomfortable emotions or revelations that you uncover. *Implicit bias* is when we harbor attitudes, beliefs, or stereotypes about people or groups that we are not aware we hold (Gawronski et al., 2020). These implicit biases may even lead to unconscious untruths that we hold against ourselves. In my case, in reflection, I held an unconscious untruth against my ability to be in the policy and advocacy environment because I didn't know anyone who worked in this space. Do not fall into this trap! You belong in the advocacy world, and you are valued.

Re-examining our life experiences and perceived personality traits can be an asset to advocacy work. Having compassion and relating to others based on similar circumstances or perceptions will strengthen your ability to have an impact. Feelings of shyness or anxiety can be used as a mechanism to speak up for others who may be immobilized by even worse nervousness than your own. Be emboldened to serve as a voice for others; your past led you here for a reason.

Based on the key learning objectives, I can now:

- Identify what life experiences have impacted my pathway to advocacy.
- Understand how my past led me to where I am today.
- Frame my experiences as strengths to support my advocacy efforts.
- Recognize that advocacy is a personal journey and there is no "right" way to do it.
- See myself as an advocate.

References

Anderson, G. L. (2009). *Advocacy leadership: toward a post-reform agenda in education*. Routledge.

Berman, M. L., Tobin-Tyler, E., & Parmet, W. E. (2019). The role of advocacy in public health law. *The Journal of Law, Medicine & Ethics, 47*(2), 15–18. https://doi.org/10.1177/1073110519857308

Coggins, C. (2017). *How to be heard: 10 lessons teachers need to advocate for their students and profession*. Jossey-Bass.

Gawronski, B., Ledgerwood, A., & Eastwick, P. W. (2020). Implicit bias and antidiscrimination policy. *Policy Insights from the Behavioral and Brain Sciences, 7*(2), 99–106. https://doi.org/10.1177/2372732220939128

Goodman, L. A., Wilson, J. M., Helms, J. E., Greenstein, N., & Medzhitova, J. (2018). Becoming an advocate: Processes and outcomes of a relationship-centered advocacy training model. *The Counseling Psychologist, 46*(2), 122–153. https://doi.org/10.1177/0011000018757168

3

ADVOCACY IS UNCOMFORTABLE

Learning Concepts

In this chapter, readers will learn:

- What part(s) of the advocacy process makes them feel uncertain.
- How to take advocacy risks.
- Strategies for overcoming the uncomfortableness.
- The curiosity approach to advocacy.
- How to create a strategic plan to get started.

Chapter Keywords

- Uncomfortableness
- Advocacy plan
- Curiosity approach

There is no better way to say it: Advocacy is uncomfortable. For most of us, advocating does not come naturally, nor does convincing others to

DOI: 10.4324/9781003308515-4

come over to our way of thinking. If I find myself in a position where I am trying to bring you over to my side, then my way of thinking is probably not your way of thinking. Entire college courses and professional learning programs focus exclusively on debate, politics, advocacy, and negotiation. How can mere individuals or organizations without this expertise be successful at advocating?

The answer is simple: just get started. And yes, it will be uncomfortable.

Nevada state Senator Marilyn Dondero Loop is a retired educator and a fierce advocate for education. When asked about how others can become involved in the advocacy process, she recommends, "Don't be afraid, just do it. And when you step into that advocacy water and it's uncomfortable, it's okay. Anyone involved in children's lives can and should be involved. Every idea is valuable."

Take Risks

This notion to just start, to just do something, can be hard for many of us. It implies that action is required, perhaps without an extensive plan, accompanied by some degree of faith. It also implies that the action chosen is the correct path forward. If you are a sequential thinker, a planner, or a type A personality, this actionable leap of faith can be terrifying. Even debilitating. However, do not let your fear hold you back. If something needs to change, make that phone call, send that email, or attend that meeting to share your thoughts. Don't overthink it.

Over the past two decades I've heard many reasons for why people hesitate to become involved in advocacy. In no specific order, they are:

- It's not my personality
- I'm not persuasive enough
- I don't know how to do it
- I can't control the outcome
- I don't understand the process
- I don't want people to make fun of me
- I don't belong in the policy world

Do any of these reasons ring a bell? Do any of them sound like things you've told yourself? Just as we tell our students and children, you've got to at least try something to know if you like it or are any good at it. This is true for playing soccer, drawing, riding a horse, or being an advocate.

Part of the uncomfortableness is the sense of the unknown, the loss of control. For the planners out there, I will break it down for you now and save you the suspense: you cannot control every step of the advocacy process. You can influence, inform, guide, and persuade, but you cannot control every decision that gets made along the way. Hold fast to your why and your desired end-result, this will help you cope with any sense of chaos along the way. The most important thing is that you attain what you are advocating for, not that you micromanage every single step along the way.

That said, for larger reaching advocacy issues, such as statutory or regulatory change, a general advocacy plan can be very helpful. Identify your desired outcome, build coalition, and develop a flexible advocacy plan to carry you through the legislative session or workshop process. Advocacy considerations at a variety of levels are offered in the second half of this book along with a description of the overall advocacy process. Even when advocacy plans are developed and implemented, they very rarely go as intended. Constant revising, pivoting, and strategizing will be necessary. By the time you reach the end of your advocacy efforts you may feel like a contortionist, you've had to twist and turn and bend in ways that you never thought possible. So, again, even with a plan, you cannot control every step along the way.

Sometimes the advocacy process itself can be confusing (Coggins, 2017). This can lead to feelings of intimidation and a sense of not knowing what action to take, even when the willingness to do so is present. Unfortunately, inaction is an action and is not very helpful to promoting your desired outcome.

Feeling uncomfortable as you start your advocacy journey is not only okay, it is to be expected. This is especially true when you are advocating for supports and services relative to mental health. Mental health advocacy comes with its own challenges given the often personal nature of the topic. There is a certain level of vulnerability that goes along with it. Individuals may be hesitant to speak up and share personal stories about themselves or close family members as they engage in the advocacy work. While society has made great strides in recent years relative to the stigma of mental health, there is still more work to be done to overcome it.

There are several factors that bring about uncomfortable feelings: personal vulnerability, self and/or family relationship with mental health, social stigma, and general feelings of unease surrounding the advocacy process itself. None of these factors outweigh the others, and depending on the person, some may weigh in greater than others. As you endeavor on your advocacy journey, remember that taking risks is part of the process. Let go of fear, of strict control, and have faith that your why and your desired outcome matter. As Senator Dondero Loop said, every idea is valuable.

Grow as You Go

There is definitely a learning curve when advocating and you will begin to realize from experience what works. Additionally, you will learn that what works with certain groups will not work with other groups (Race et al., 2022). Through it all you will have successes and you will have learning experiences where you reflect, "it would have been better had I approached it this other way". Remember, this is all part of the advocacy process and is to be expected. Don't let these moments derail your overall objectives; they are all part of learning and growing. If it were comfortable, we wouldn't be growing or making a difference.

The most significant changes in society weren't made because everyone felt comfortable making them. Think back to the Women's Right to Vote or the Civil Rights Movement; hordes of people were uncomfortable giving women the right to vote or abolishing institutional racial segregation, disenfranchisement, and discrimination. Advocating for mental health supports is no different. On one hand, it poses unique challenges because mental health issues transcend all genders, races, ethnicities, and socio-economic categories. The scope of who is impacted can make it difficult to pinpoint a place to start your advocacy efforts. On the other hand, since its impact does transcend all genders, races, ethnicities, and socio-economic categories, you can pick almost any demographic group and they will be able to relate to the challenges, and need, for more mental health supports. The COVID-19 pandemic also created an additional challenge as a second pandemic of mental health issues is now impacting communities (Choi et al., 2020).

When I first started on my policy journey, I was mostly uncomfortable with the process of advocacy and speaking up in front of others. Fortunately, my willfulness outweighed my shyness. Over the years the shyness has melted away and now I feel more comfortable speaking to anyone about the need for more school-based mental health supports and providers. Throughout the years, I've learned that feelings of uncertainty can be resolved using one or several of the following strategies:

- Do what's needed
- Stick to the facts and ask questions
- Don't take yourself too seriously

Do What's Needed

Don't worry about having the right terminology, the right approach, or the right anything. Advocacy is like having a baby: no one is ever truly ready. You just do your best with what you've got and go from there.

As a parent and school leader I felt comfortable making informal recommendations about best practice, or in changes I would like to see for my children and students. For example, "Try this behavior modification technique" or "let's start asking students what topics they'd like for the counseling groups". Teachers and principals were usually receptive, and I felt pretty successful when speaking up. The audience was usually small, and I didn't need to prepare a speech, dress a certain way, or worry about my exact words or actions. Educators engage in this type of advocacy daily and it isn't usually something that we think twice about; we just do it.

Over the years I began hearing that other school psychologists were advocating on their campuses for a similar type of supports that I was advocating for on my campuses. This raised a red flag to me. If the issue is unique to my campus, it is most likely a site-specific issue that can be addressed at the school level. However, if multiple schools in my district are experiencing a similar issue, it might be a bigger problem that needs to be addressed at the district level. Taking this conversation to the next level, if multiple districts are experiencing a similar issue, the problem might need to be addressed at the state level.

As I grew in my career, I began taking on leadership roles beyond the school level and I helped revitalize the Nevada Association of School Psychologists (NVASP), becoming President-Elect. Through conversations with school psychologists statewide, we identified a difficulty with the annual evaluation framework for school psychologists. The problem was that school psychologists were being evaluated on the same criteria as teachers. To address the unique service delivery and work duties of our profession, we wanted our own evaluation framework. We were not alone. In having conversations with other Specialized Instructional Support Personnel (SISP), we quickly realized that all SISPs were advocating for their own evaluation frameworks that aligned with their national organizations and best practices.

We were told that NVASP should provide public comment at the state-level Teachers and Leaders Council (TLC) meeting and publicly state our desire for our own evaluation framework. The TLC was the group tasked with making recommendations to the state about the content of the evaluation frameworks. The recommendation to give public comment sounded like a good path forward. We drafted a two-minute speech and cleared our schedules to attend the meeting. We did not know what to expect and in this case, ignorance was certainly bliss. Without knowing what to expect, I didn't have time to engage my anxiety in days of pointless worrying and "what if" scenarios. For some reason, as the President-Elect, I was the one who ended up giving the two-minute speech. Walking into the room on the day of the meeting I began to get very nervous. There were important decision makers on the TLC who could make or break our future. The board consisted of principals, teachers, policy makers, and higher education leaders who were experts in their fields.

As I sat surveying this prestigious group, I thought to myself, "Thank goodness I was smart enough to dress the part!" While I highly respect my school colleagues and building administrators, advocating to them is a far cry from advocating in front of this TLC. I almost hyperventilated waiting for my two minutes of fame. My heart was racing, and my senses were at heightened levels. I had to keep reminding myself to breathe as my fight or flight instincts threatened to take over. Thankfully I did not run from the room and my name was eventually called. I walked up to the podium and microphone (microphone!) and almost blacked out due to lack of oxygen. Turns out I actually did forget to breathe, though I did not black out. I managed to squeak out my speech and hobble back to my seat without tripping over myself. This was a win! I didn't embarrass myself and I didn't fall over. Solid score. This moment of public comment is actually on YouTube (McIvor, 2015) and you can watch it there for yourself if you'd like to compare the internal experience with the external one.

I share this embarrassing story to highlight the fact that advocacy does not come easy to most of us. There are very few people I've spoken to who feel completely natural advocating in front of a group of decision makers, unless they've been doing it for years. Whether the audience is the school PTA, a non-profit you hope will sponsor an initiative, or a powerful governing body, advocacy can be nerve-wracking.

In these cases, I remind myself, *"Don't do what's comfortable, do what's needed"*. What was needed was for someone to speak up and advocate for an evaluation framework specific to school psychologists. It wasn't me speaking up on behalf of me; it was me giving voice to a group of professionals. This approach transcends any advocacy group or purpose and can help reframe feelings of unease.

In another example, as a caregiver, if my child's soccer team needed new uniforms and all the families wanted to find a sponsor to pay for the uniforms, I might be assigned to make phone calls and ask businesses for sponsorship. Is this the most comfortable thing I could think of doing? No. As a parent I'd prefer not to have to do that. However, I'd prefer even less for the team to not be able to afford new uniforms. Also, as part of the reframe, I can think to myself that I am advocating on behalf of the children. I am not calling around and asking for money for myself.

As advocates, we do what's uncomfortable because it's the action that is needed. We also learn coping strategies to make our next advocacy efforts more comfortable. Over time we gradually become accustomed to advocating and what used to make us uncomfortable will become less uncomfortable. Notice I did not say disappear. I'm not sure the unease will ever disappear, but we do get better at dealing with it. For me, while I'm waiting for my turn to speak, I've learned to take long, deep breaths. This helps prevent me from becoming lightheaded. When I am speaking, I've learned to start speaking very sloooowly. This prevents me from tripping over my words, losing my breath, and having to pause and gulp for air. I also have learned to tap my heel at the pace I want to speak as that helps me keep my speaking and breathing on track.

Stick to the Facts and Ask Questions

Sometimes advocacy is uncomfortable because we aren't sure what to expect from others. This is a legitimate fear and one way to combat the unknown is to prepare yourself with information and data. The best way to refute any naysayers and to keep your message from getting derailed is to stick to the facts. Fact: 20% of youth have a mental health condition and 80% of those students will receive mental health supports in schools (National Association of School Psychologists [NASP], 2021). If you provide evidence- or research-based facts in response to questions put before you, you can't go wrong.

I've watched hours upon hours of advocacy pitches in a variety of formats: public testimony, presentations, elevator speeches, formal and informal debates, and social media. I've participated in all of these, both as the advocate and as the receiving body. Those who can share their point of view respectfully and back it up with data tend to fare far better than those who simply state their opinion. If you can civilly state your case, back it up with data, and answer questions using facts you will be far more successful in your advocacy efforts than if you cannot do that.

Dr. Kari Oyen, Assistant Professor and Chair of the NASP Government and Professional Relations Committee recommends a curiosity approach to learning more about an issue. Always ask why. Frame your inquiry in such a way that you are curious to learn more about the issue at hand. For example, start with, "this is what I know about this issue, why is it this way?" In doing so, you will learn more about the issue from the other person's perspective and you might gain some unknown insight. This information can then help reshape your approach or reaffirm that you need to continue asking more questions to get to the bottom of the issue.

The *curiosity approach* is a great way to avoid coming at the issue from the angle of combativeness. It avoids putting people on the defensive and it gives you the advantage of appearing collaborative and possibly learning additional information. Asking questions can often lead to the other person realizing there might be flaws in their argument or that relevant information is missing. How a problem is understood or framed leads to how one goes about resolving it (Anderson, 2009).

One key piece of data that is often missing is a written policy. Time and time again we hear in education, "that's just the way we do it" or "we have to do it that way". Ask very calmly to see the policy in writing. Often the policy is not a policy at all but an unwritten practice that evolved over the years. Always ask questions; if it's not in writing, it's probably not a formalized policy and the practice can simply be changed.

Early on in my work as a bilingual school psychologist we were conducting assessments in a certain manner and writing consulting reports for the school district in a very prescriptive way. It was laborious and didn't feel like the most efficient use of our time, or that our reports provided any real benefit to the student or the school team. Our bilingual school psychology group wanted to streamline the process and offer greater value. We approached our supervisor and asked to change the process. She indicated that we could not change the process due to a federal Office for Civil Rights (OCR) policy which dictated how our process should be.

After about a year of being told no due to the OCR agreement we finally asked to see the policy. Our thinking was that if we could see the policy, perhaps we could find a way to streamline the process while still maintaining the OCR requirement. We were persistent in asking to see the policy and after a few months, after doing some digging, our supervisor realized that it did not exist. The current process we were following had been institutionalized over time and attached to some OCR requirement that was a myth. By persistently asking questions and requesting to see the policy, we were able to discover that there was not a policy in place at all, just a practice that could be changed. With this discovery we were eventually able to streamline our process and deliver a more valuable psycho-educational bilingual report to our schools. Had we not asked questions and not asked to see the policy, we would have kept doing the same thing and missed an opportunity to positively impact students.

Don't Take Yourself Too Seriously

For those of you who have a background in psychology or have done any research on the subject, I am reminded of the psychological state "imaginary audience". Imaginary audience is typically a young adolescent condition, though can be found in any age group. This is a state where the individual has an overdeveloped perception that others are watching them or are interested in everything they say or do. In our case with advocacy, it is easy to be overly self-critical in how we are engaging stakeholders to the point that it can debilitate our efforts. Do not let this fear or paranoia take hold! Take risk and kick that imaginary audience out the window. "They" (principals, superintendents, legislators, etc.) are not all going to laugh at you or talk about you behind your back. I say this with kind affection – get over it!

Think back to a situation where you said something to someone and you left the conversation thinking, "Did I say that right? Did I talk to much with my hands? Did the person notice that I spit a little when I got really excited?" You may have done all these things but there's no need to perseverate on them, they will only cause undue stress. The other person probably forgot about them as soon as they turned and walked away. We are all human and these things happen. The best thing you can do is have grace with yourself and get over it. Remember, you are valued, and your voice carries weight.

Think back to the earlier example about the TLC and advocating for an evaluation framework specific for school psychologists. What if I had let my fears hold me back from continued advocacy work? Someone else could have certainly stepped in, but I would have missed such incredible opportunities to advocate on behalf of students, families, and educators.

It has been my experience that people generally won't laugh at you if you speak up. What I've found to be far truer is the exact opposite. Your voice might be exactly what is needed in that moment to raise a point, idea, or solution that no one has thought of yet. In those moments, silence may actually follow as the group carefully weighs your suggestion.

It may take you 30 minutes to send a three-sentence email to a legislator. Or 20 minutes as you waffle back and forth about whether you should call the school principal and ask to meet about implementing a school-wide social-emotional learning program. Don't overthink things. If it's right for students, just get the ball rolling. The good news is that the more often you engage in this type of work, the less time you will spend perseverating on how to do it.

Moving Past the Discomfort

Taking the first steps of advocacy can feel uncomfortable, but don't let your fears take hold. There are several strategies you can use to help overcome the fear. See Table 3.1 to help get you started. First, ask yourself what is making you uncomfortable about taking a specific action. Naming your fears and understanding the root source can help you overcome them. If speaking in public gives you anxiety, type an email and send in public comment electronically. Aim for lower anxiety producing ways to advocate. Next, identify coping strategies you can use to get past the fear. It might be breathing techniques or kind words of encouragement repeated to yourself to just do something. Also, when you have questions about something, ask more about it. Gather more information until you feel comfortable with your path forward. Finally, formulate ideas for how you can get started and how to take that actionable leap of faith. You may join a group of advocates or invite others to join you on the journey. This strategic planning exercise can be used for every step of the advocacy process and at every level of advocacy.

Based on the key learning objectives, I can now:

- Describe what parts of the advocacy process makes me feel uncertain.
- Identify what advocacy risks I need to take.
- Identify strategies to help me overcome the uncomfortableness.
- Apply the curiosity approach to learn more about an issue.
- Use strategies to get started on my advocacy journey.

Table 3.1 Worksheet for advocacy planning and action; it can be used for any level of advocacy and at any point in the process

Strategic Plan to Taking Action

This is what makes me uncomfortable about taking action:
These are the coping strategies I can use:
These are the facts I know:
These are the questions I'd like to learn more about:
These are ideas for how I can get started on my advocacy journey:

References

Anderson, G. L. (2009). *Advocacy leadership: Toward a post-reform agenda in education.* Routledge.

Choi, K. R., Heilemann, M. V., Fauer, A., & Mead, M. (2020). A second pandemic: Mental health spillover from the Novel Coronavirus (COVID-19). *Journal of the American Psychiatric Nurses Association, 26*(4), 340–343. https://doi.org/10.1177/1078390320919803

Coggins, C. (2017) *How to be heard: 10 lessons teachers need to advocate for their students and profession.* Jossey Bass.

McIvor, T. (March 23, 2015). *Katie Dockweiler, President-Elect of NVASP, at TLC meeting regarding the NEPF* [Video]. YouTube. https://www.youtube.com/watch?v=NreLGpS7jCA

National Association of School Psychologists. (2021). *School psychologists: Qualified health professionals providing child and adolescent mental and behavioral health services* [White paper]. Author.

Race, R., Gill, D., Kaitell, E., Mahmud, A., Thorpe, A., & Wolfe, K. (2022). Proclamations and provocations: Decolonising curriculum in education research and professional practice. *Equity in Education & Society, 1*(1), 82–96. https://doi.org/10.1177/27526461211068833

4

ADVOCACY HAS A STRATEGIC SCOPE

Learning Concepts

In this chapter, readers will learn:

- How to identify the scope of their advocacy efforts.
- The shared characteristics of large- and small-scope advocacy.
- Strategic components to help plan their actions.
- The importance of agreement in principle.
- The importance of persistence.

Chapter Keywords

- Scope
- Advocacy mismatch
- Alignment
- Agreement in principle

DOI: 10.4324/9781003308515-5

When embarking on your advocacy efforts, how do you know where to begin? Who should you talk to? What things should you consider? This chapter helps you identify the scope of your advocacy efforts and the related strategic components. Whether your efforts are large or small in scope, there are common planning and action steps to help guide your efforts.

Scope of Advocacy Efforts

By nature, some advocacy requires large-scale efforts while other efforts require smaller scale advocacy efforts. *A general rule of thumb is that the closer the decision-making power lies to the student, the easier it is to change something.* For example, a child's seat assignment. If a child's seat assignment needs to be changed because the student sitting next to them makes fun of them all day, the teacher has the power to change the seats. At its most basic level, advocacy can be conceptualized as a continuum with a student or a classroom full of students at one end, and Congress at the other end. Between the two entities, many different advocacy levers exist. Moving out from the classroom is the school, then the school district and municipality, then the state Department of Education, the state Legislature, and then Congress. *The issue at hand will generally dictate the scale of your advocacy efforts.*

When planning where to start your advocacy efforts and the corresponding *scope* of what might be involved, you'll want to target your efforts at the level that can create the solution. Who or what group can make the solution happen? For example, Civil Rights issues permeate our entire society, and nothing less than Congress will bring the right level of advocacy required for national change. Some issues are more local and can be dealt with at the school or student level. This type of advocacy can usually be done with a lower level of advocacy and can be achieved through a conversation or email. For example, imagine if you were a teacher and there was a student, Little Katie, whom you thought would benefit from school-based mental health supports. The correct starting point would be contacting the school's school counselor, school psychologist, or school social worker (depending on the staffing and structure of your school). Emailing your congressional representative and advocating for Little Katie to receive small group counseling would be an ineffective path forward. This would be an *advocacy mismatch*. The more appropriate and effective path forward would be to start at the school level as this is the level in which the solution can be found.

When considering the level of advocacy, match the scope of your advocacy efforts to your particular issue. If your advocacy level does not match the level required to make the change you want, you are faced with an advocacy mismatch and probably won't get very far. Remember, you want to advocate at the level that has the people who can create the solution or grant what you are seeking.

Issues that typically are large in advocacy scope involve decision makers at the state or district level. School or classroom level issues generally require a smaller scope of advocacy. Large and small scopes are used in relation to the number of groups or individuals required to help make a change possible. The size of the scope does not necessarily describe the amount of work that will go into an advocacy effort.

This leads to the notion of *alignment*. Large-scope advocacy will typically align to a larger initiative and will have more policies and pieces involved. Small-scope advocacy may require less alignment. For example, if a principal makes a school level change, it will be important to make sure that the staff are following the new procedure and that implementation aligns with the new policy. Efforts will be needed to get buy-in from the staff to support and carry out the implementation. In another instance, if my high school does not have a standard referral process for student mental health concerns, small scale advocacy efforts are needed as they are constrained to the school. In speaking with the principal and school-based mental health staff, a referral process can be determined and put in place. After that, support for the staff can follow to make sure everyone on the campus is following the new process. Ongoing monitoring efforts will help to ensure that schoolwide actions are all in alignment with the new policy and procedure.

Table 4.1 Scope considerations

Large Scope	Small Scope
Many pieces to align	Few pieces to align
High levels of bureaucracy	Low levels of bureaucracy
Lengthy advocacy commitment	Short advocacy commitment
Large financial impact	Small financial impact

Small-Scope Advocacy

Advocacy efforts that are smaller in scope typically have fewer pieces to align and the initiative is more local and closer to the student(s). An instance of small-scope advocacy would include a school safety policy that needs to be changed that will only impact the students and staff at that one school. In such cases, there will be fewer actions required than efforts that would impact many schools and at higher bureaucratic levels. In another example, if my children attend a school where the morning drop-off procedures feel unsafe, I can reach out to the school principal to share my concerns. It would also behoove me to not only state the problem, but to also propose a solution. This is a core communication strategy that will significantly increase the likelihood of your request being successful.

Advocacy efforts that are smaller in scope tend to have the follow characteristics:

- Few pieces to align
- Low levels of bureaucracy
- Short time frame
- Small financial commitment

The following strategic components apply to advocacy efforts that are smaller in scope. They can often be streamlined and tend to be more informal than advocacy efforts that are larger in scope.

- A Champion
- A solution
- Data to support the position
- Diverse stakeholders in support
- Financial impact and/or solutions
- Outcome comparison
- Persistence

Let's expand on the example about school drop-off procedures. If you are concerned about your school's morning drop-off procedures, you can be the champion. You can reach out to the school principal to share your concerns and then offer a solution. If you have data to support your concern and solution, share that. Also, if you've spoken with different stakeholders such as families, crossing guards, or school police, share their perspective and support for your proposal. If a school safety coalition has been formed, ask representatives from the group to speak up with you. If there are any financial components required with your proposal, identify them, and to prevent them from being a barrier, offer a solution to the financial cost. Finally, summarize why your proposal is the best solution by comparing the current reality with the potential reality. For example, you could state, "this year we have had 10 safety infractions during morning drop off times, but with my proposal, we can reduce or completely eliminate that number". Other outcomes could also be discussed depending on the number of proposals you put forward or the different variations that could exist. If your idea is not well received or acted upon immediately, don't give up. Be prepared to persist and keep bringing solutions forward until something sticks.

Large-Scope Advocacy

Advocacy efforts that are large in scope generally have more pieces to align than efforts that are smaller in scope. If a state policy needs to be changed that will impact many stakeholder groups, more time and effort will go into bringing the different groups on board. These stakeholder groups may include school districts, educators, law enforcement, and students; many efforts will be needed to ensure that all these stakeholder groups are in support and can align their implementation efforts. For example, if I live in a state without mandatory schoolwide suicide prevention efforts, I might want to propose that a statewide suicide prevention policy be put in place. This is an initiative that requires a large scope of advocacy as there are many players to align. The pool of stakeholders that may need to be brought on board is very big. If I tried to get traction for this initiative at the school level, I wouldn't get very far because the principal or school-based mental health providers on campus do not have the authority to mandate this change statewide. They cannot grant the solution to this issue. There may be some components of this prevention effort they could be put in place without a formal state policy, but it wouldn't be the statewide solution I am looking for. *Advocacy efforts with a large scope generally require the alignment and support of a large stakeholder base.*

Large-scope advocacy efforts tend to have the follow characteristics:

- Many pieces to align
- High levels of bureaucracy
- Lengthy time frame
- Large financial impact

In addition to the mentioned characteristics, efforts with a large scope will also typically have the following strategic components, similar to small-scope efforts:

- A champion
- A solution
- Data to support the position
- Diverse stakeholders in support
- Financial impact and/or solutions
- Outcome comparison
- Persistence

These four characteristics and seven strategic components are general considerations that may impact or define the scope of your advocacy efforts. Depending on your context, it may look different for each initiative proposed. Let's take a look at Nevada Assembly Bill 289 (2019). This bill was drafted to revise the state's Read by Grade 3 law. Read by Grade 3 is a statewide reading law that outlines student expectations relative to literacy. There are many nuances within this law, but the general intent behind the law is that by the end of 3rd grade, all 3rd grade students would be proficient in reading. While an admirable goal, the reality is that students are not widgets; they all learn at different rates, and they all have unique learning conditions. Under the then existing Read by Grade 3 law, if a student was not proficient, they would be retained and made to repeat 3rd grade.

Ms. Melody Thompson, a school psychologist in Las Vegas, took a step back and reframed the law from a mental health standpoint. There is an abundance of data available to indicate negative impacts to grade retention on students. Such negative impacts include decreased rates of graduation, earlier experimentation with drugs and alcohol, increased sexual activity, decreased economic opportunities, increased likelihood of mental health conditions, and an increase of students who enter the school to prison pipeline (Naglieri et al., 2010; Belfield et al., 2015; Mallett, 2015; Bal et al., 2017). These are all undesired outcomes that have the potential to significantly impact the overall health and wellness of students.

Ms. Thompson was concerned for the students in her school district and across the state. She wanted to change the law to prevent generations of students from being penalized under the current version of the law. Since this law was put into statute by the state legislature, this is where her level of advocacy needed to begin. If she tried to advocate at the school level the principal would not have been able to make the necessary changes. The principal's hands would be tied in this case as they are required to follow the state law, whether or not they philosophically agreed with it. Similarly, if the school psychologist had taken this issue to the school district, they would have had a similar reaction; the district's hands would be tied because the law is required by state statute.

In the case with laws such as Read by Grade 3, advocacy efforts of a large scope were needed given the level of advocacy required and the number of stakeholder groups who were necessary to get on board. The goal was not to remove the law, but to strengthen the good parts focused on literacy intervention and remove the penalizing retention component that stood to negatively impact students' well-being.

Many stakeholder groups were brought in to support the efforts. The Nevada Association of School Psychologists were champions of the effort and were asked by the sponsor of the bill, Assemblyman Thompson (no relation to Ms. Thompson), to lead the stakeholder work groups. Stakeholder groups who were part of the eventual change included entities such as employee unions, school districts, professional state associations, non-profit community groups, and parent groups.

It took three years and two legislative sessions to get the law changed. The changes were necessary to improve the short- and long-term outcomes for students and were worth the efforts and time required to make the change happen. Eventually the updated law passed with the prevention and intervention parts strengthened and the mandatory retention component removed. Retention is still an option available to principals, parents, and school teams; it is just not mandatory. More importantly, generations of students are not faced with the detrimental health and wellness consequences that research has shown impacts students who are retained.

Agreement in Principle

Advocacy efforts are most successful when the key stakeholder groups are all on board. When the key stakeholder groups are supportive of an initiative, it is more likely that the policy will pass and be implemented as intended. Not everyone has to be in agreement with all components of what is proposed. However, at the very least, they will need to agree in principle. *Agreement in principle* means that you agree with the general intent of a proposed initiative. You may disagree with the means in which to achieve it or all the tiny details along the way, but you agree that "it" is needed. Dr. Sondra Cosgrove, Professor and Vice Chair of the Nevada Advisory Committee to the U.S. Commission on Civil Rights, explains it this way:

> We all want to go to the beach. The beach is 200 miles away. Some of us might drive, some of us might take the bus, some might take the train, or some may fly. There is no right or wrong way to get there. As long as we all agree that the beach is where we are going and we get there somehow, that is the important part.

In this example, everyone agrees in principle that going to the beach is important. The means of getting there may be different for each person or group, but everyone still agrees that the trip to the beach is necessary and that is where they are all headed.

Advocacy is MTSS

The Multi-Tiered Systems of Support (MTSS) Advocacy Model is a conceptual way to envision levels of advocacy support, similar to how we conceptualize instructional support for students. MTSS is an equitable framework to ensure each student, or group of students, receives the type of support they need in order to be successful (Clark & Dockweiler, 2020, 2019). Tier 1 is advocacy efforts that are closest to the students, typically at the school level. Tier 1 includes staff, students, administration, and families. Tier 2 is advocacy efforts that are somewhat removed from the student and originate at a level such as the school district, school board, local union, or municipal government. Tier 3 is advocacy efforts that are furthest away from the student and originate at the state legislature, state department of education, state school board, or Congress.

Eventually, school-based mental health supports will trickle down from their level of origination to the students. Any advocacy effort that is large in scale, such as those at the Tier 3 or state level, will also require the support and implementation alignment of stakeholder groups in the previous tiers: district or Tier 2 and school level or Tier 1. Similarly, Tier 2 or district level will also require the support and implementation of school level or Tier 1 school groups. Finally, for efforts that originate at the Tier 1 school level, they probably will not require advocacy at higher tiers because the decision-making power is contained within Tier 1.

Wellness Data

Advocating for mental health supports can be a challenge because mental health is a fairly abstract concept to most people. There is no one "test" to give students in which they can earn a grade equivalent or developmental score of overall mental wellness. Assessments can categorize various mental health factors, but they can't take into account all the nuances of the individual, the adverse childhood experiences they may have experienced, or the innate resilience of the person. With other domains in education, such as English Language Arts, Mathematics, Science, or Social Studies, there are a variety of assessments that can be given to determine what students have learned and if they are on track to mastery. There are even exit tests or tests of competency for students to provide evidence that they've achieved the desired level of proficiency.

With mental wellness, there is no exit score. Wellness is not a static variable; it constantly changes. Daily interactions or variables can cause overall wellness to fluctuate. In lieu of wellness assessment scores, other data is typically presented to indicate if students are struggling with their mental health and may require additional supports. Data might be school-wide and relative to groups of students, or data might be person-specific. It may be collected via a screener or by observation. Schoolwide data may include the total number of major behavior incidences on a campus, the total number of expulsions, or the overall number of suicide attempts. On a more individual level, the data may include observational information such as a student who has become withdrawn, a student who is not caring for their personal hygiene, or whose schoolwork appears to be suffering.

The problem with all the above data is that it is reactionary; we are counting the frequency of occurrences after the fact. But what if, instead, we prevented these numbers from occurring in the first place? How wonderful would it be if we didn't have these numbers to report at all? This would be a great problem to have and would suggest that the preventative supports we are providing to students are working. Herein lies the crux of the difficulty with mental health data: how do you know your mental health supports are working? *The answer lies not in the abundance of incidences, but in the absence of incidences.*

The goal with implementing mental health supports and services is to decrease the number of negative internalized or externalized behaviors that students manifest, and to increase the positive ones. Seeing a decrease in the number of undesired behaviors is one way to validate the impact of your mental health supports. We may never be able to concretely identify how many suicide completions we prevented or how many students we prevented from being bullied. However, not having incidence data to report, or having less incidences to report, is how we know we are making a difference.

Data used will look different depending on the scope of your advocacy efforts. It may be qualitative, quantitative, or both and may be in the form of research studies, evidence-based practices, or observations.

For example, a parent or caregiver who wants to advocate for a stronger anti-bullying policy in their district might appeal to the local school board. They may state the reason they are seeking this stronger policy is because their high school daughter is being sexually harassed. The parent might share anecdotal data as well as statistical data to support their cause. They might share at a district school board meeting that their daughter, and other female students, are being subject to obscene remarks, jokes of a sexual nature, or unwanted sexual advances by male peers. The parent might also share districtwide data stating nearly 80% of female students report similar unwanted advances. As a result of the harassment, the parent's child is now experiencing signs of somatization, social withdrawal, and stress. The parent may also support their request for a stronger anti-bullying by stating that 83% of students in grades 8–11 have experienced sexual harassment as documented in a study by the American Association of University Women (K–12 Academics, 2002). The parent could argue that statistic is similar to what their own district is experiencing and that something must be done.

The Nammer

The scope of advocacy efforts can feel both empowering and frustrating. Some days you may feel that the small incremental steps you are taking aren't having much of an impact in the broader scope of your efforts. But, other days, you may feel that you are making great progress. It all depends on the scope of your efforts, how many steps are needed, and how you perceive the challenges along the way.

One day my nine-year-old son and I were on our way home from his fencing practice. He had had a particularly difficult session and he didn't end up with as many touches (points) as normal. He began to cry and wanted to quit fencing altogether because it was just too hard. At this point, he had only been fencing for about four months and most of the other students in the class had been fencing for over a year. Wanting to validate his feelings, while encouraging him to keep trying, I had to think on my feet. I said to him, "It's okay, this is all part of the process. Some days you're the hammer, and some days you're the nail."

We talked about how some days you feel like you are the nail: nothing is going right, and you feel like you are constantly taking beatings. But then, some days you may feel like the hammer: in charge, moving with confidence, and building beautiful things. He immediately identified his fencing practice as feeling like the nail, but he did acknowledge that some days he also felt like the hammer. Then he surprised me with the following insight, "Some days I'm the nail, and some days I'm the hammer. But most days I'm just a nammer." This same scenario is true for advocacy. Some days we feel like we are moving mountains with our efforts, while other days we feel like nothing is going right. However, most days we are just the nammer, plugging along doing the best we can, and that is okay!

Based on the key learning objectives, I can now:

- Identify the scope of an advocacy effort.
- Describe the shared characteristics of large- and small-scope advocacy.
- Outline the strategic components to help me plan my actions.
- Recognize why it is important for individuals and groups to agree in principle.
- See the value in being persistent when advocating.

References

Bal, A., Betters-Bubon, J., & Fish, R. E. (2017). A multilevel analysis of statewide disproportionality in exclusionary discipline and the identification of emotional disturbance. *Education and Urban Society, 51*(2), 247–268. https://doi.org/10.1177/0013124517716260

Belfield, C., Bowden, B., Klapp, A., Levin, H., Shand, R., & Zander, S. (2015). *The economic value of social and emotional learning.* Center for Benefit-Cost Studies in Education.

Clark, A. G., & Dockweiler, K. A. (2019) *Multi-tiered systems of support in secondary schools: The definitive guide to effective implementation and quality control.* Routledge.

Clark, A. G., & Dockweiler, K. A. (2020) *Multi-tiered systems of support in elementary schools: The definitive guide to effective implementation and quality control.* Routledge.

K–12 Academics. (2002). Statistics of Sexual Harassment. https://www.k12academics.com/education-issues/sexual-harassment/statistics

Mallett, C. (2015). The incarceration of seriously traumatised adolescents in the USA: Limited progress and significant harm. *Criminal Behavior and Mental Health, 25*, 1–9.

Naglieri, J. A., Goldstein, S, & LeBuffe, P. (2010). Resilience and impairment: An exploratory study of resilience factors and situational impairment. *Journal of Psychoeducational Assessment, 28*(4), 349–356.

5

ADVOCACY IS RELATIONSHIP BUILDING

Learning Concepts

In this chapter, readers will learn:

- How to amplify their message.
- The power of grassroots advocacy.
- Why individual and collective advocacy are both important.
- How to build coalition and advocate together.
- The importance of relationships and effective communication.

Chapter Keywords

- Grassroots advocacy
- Coalition
- Quiet influencer
- Mentor appointment

DOI: 10.4324/9781003308515-6

Relationships make the world go around, and societies have long engaged in relationship building. Whether the relationships were with trusted traders along the Silk Road, with members of modern sports teams, or with family members and their shared love, relationships are an inescapable part of life. The timeless and critical nature of relationships is also true for advocacy and mental health. Relationships are important to advocacy efforts through the connections we build with stakeholders, the community, and key decision makers. Ensuring positive regard for your efforts will make it more likely that you will succeed. If you, your message, or your cause are not respected or regarded in a positive light, your overall efforts will be more challenging.

Relationships are also important for mental health consultation and services (Waalkes et al., 2019). We have long known that connections with caring adults are critical for our students to succeed in school and in life. Relationships with others can help students feel supported, encouraged, and can offer them a sounding board for feedback and problem-solving. Engaging in mental health supports with students relies on relationships and trust as the backbone to that work. Without trusting relationships, students will not meaningfully connect with the adults in their lives and will be less receptive to support.

The same is true for advocacy work. Without trusting relationships, advocates will not meaningfully connect with stakeholders and groups will be less receptive to supporting initiatives. As we navigate and work our way through the advocacy process, relationships can help support, encourage, and help us to amplify our voice and trouble-shoot any potential barriers.

Grassroots Advocacy

Advocacy efforts that start locally are typically considered grassroots (National Association of School Psychologists [NASP], 2018). Ideas that are planted by a seed of opportunity or injustice, and nurtured overtime to bloom into a fully thought-out initiative, are oftentimes homegrown. Whether one person or a group of caring persons planted the idea and helped cultivate its growth, these ideas can lead to very impactful advocacy efforts.

Anyone can contribute to grassroots advocacy. Are you a parent, teacher, school counselor, school psychologist, community member, association leader, or policy maker? Odds are you wear at least one of these hats. These many hats suggest that there are many perspectives to contribute to the dialogue. Depending on the audience, there might be more power in wearing your parent hat, your educator hat, or your community member hat.

Powerful advocacy rests with being able to examine a situation from multiple perspectives. Examining multiple perspectives and then presenting an idea that considers each of these lenses can be very powerful. Especially if you are able to present an issue, tailor your narrative to a particular stakeholder group, discuss the ways students are impacted, and share solutions based on how that particular stakeholder group can contribute.

Grassroots advocacy can take many forms. It may start as individual advocacy with the voice of one person. That one person may join a group of other individuals who are collectively part of a union, professional association, or parent–teacher group to amplify their individual voice. This group may then join other groups, through a process called coalition building, to more broadly amplify their shared voices and advocate with a much larger group toward a shared goal.

Individual Advocacy

There are several ways that individuals can advocate. While you might advocate as part of a group, it is important to remember that you still have an individual voice that can be used to deliver a message. Depending on the hat you are wearing, you can amplify a message from the perspective of a parent, caregiver, educator, community member, or professional. For example, if the local Parent–Teacher Association (PTA) is advocating for more mental health supports in a school district, you can contribute to efforts individually and collectively. You can share the PTA message with key stakeholders and decision makers in a collective manner. You can also reach out to these people or groups of people with your own personal message of support. Share your "why" behind the position you hold on the issue and offer any personal insight that you may have. Personal stories matter to decision makers, and it helps them put a face to an issue. Maybe not your face exactly, but by inserting real people into the narrative it takes the issue from the abstract to the concrete. Whatever the issue is, it demonstrates that it is impacting actual people, and these are the concrete ways it is happening.

Collective Advocacy

How can I become engaged? This is a question I hear a lot. Educators, parents, and community members want to increase mental health supports in schools, but they don't know where to begin. In addition to identifying the scope of the advocacy efforts, you can also identify individuals or groups to advocate with.

Some issues can be promoted or resolved with individual advocacy, and some may require the voice of a larger group. As a school psychologist, it was difficult at first to accept that others might actually want to hear what I had to say. However, I've learned that it is my duty – that's right, duty – to speak up.

As we learned in the previous chapter, some initiatives require a large scope of advocacy efforts while others require a smaller scope of efforts. Regardless of the scope, individual and collective voice is a beneficial advocacy tool (NASP, 2019). Both are necessary to achieve more mental health supports for students. At first, individual advocacy may feel uncomfortable because it is a foreign pursuit. However, it gets easier and you'll feel more comfortable the more you do it.

Part of the uncomfortableness may be that your advocacy feels self-serving. An example might be a school psychologist advocating for more school psychologists. If there are not enough school psychologists in your district and you are feeling stressed, overworked, and not compensated for your extra duties, it can feel like admitting defeat to advocate for more school psychologist professionals, or for more pay. In some small corner of your mind, it's like admitting: I can't do it all. Well, you know what, given the needs of our schools and students, no one person *can* do it all! Nor should you be expected to. And if the demands are being put on you to do it all, then you should be compensated for the extra time and expertise you are contributing.

If you are a teacher or school-based mental health provider, advocating for your role and your profession is not self-serving. It is vital in serving students, and it is a necessity in order for your profession to thrive, not just survive. If you notice that you are advocating alone and someone else from another school or district is advocating for the same thing, join up. Your collective voice will be amplified. If multiple people are speaking up and advocating for the same thing, odds are the issue is greater than what can or should be tackled at the school level. If the issue is widespread, a higher level of advocacy is probably needed. It might require Tier 2 advocacy at the district level, or Tier 3 level advocacy at the state level.

Educators, caregivers, and community members may all be experiencing shared feelings. Educators may know they are overworked and that there aren't enough school-based mental health providers to support the mental and behavioral health needs of students. Caregivers may know their children are stressed, anxious, fearful, depressed and don't know what resources are available at school or in the community. Community members may read about the rise in mental health needs of students and want to live in a community with children who grow into healthy adults, not children who are scared or who perpetuate violence.

Each of these stakeholder groups can become engaged by joining with other stakeholders who are asking the same questions. Dr. Zac Robbins, high school principal, shares that advocates and influencers must be intentional about their intent to disrupt. It's not enough to talk about disruption and making change. It requires intentional actions and motivation to advocate over time. For example, disrupting the school-to-prison pipeline is not a new idea, but it does take time, and people tend to give up due to a lack of mental energy and the large scale of effort that is needed.

Dr. Robbins suggests joining with other people and policy makers who not only share similar beliefs as yourself, but also with those who tend to think differently. Echo chambers emerge when homogenous ideas are siloed together. Building relationships with people who think differently than you is important so that policy making spaces don't become echo chambers. While this can be uncomfortable, being around others who think differently than you ensure that multiple and diverse voices are heard.

Build Coalition

Building coalition is important, especially when many groups are advocating around a particular topic or issue (NASP, 2018). A *coalition* is a group of parties coming together to advocate for a unified cause. Similar to collective advocacy, coalitions represent multiple voices. Where collective advocacy and coalitions differ is in the number of groups who represent these voices. Collective advocacy is typically one group where a coalition represents more than one group. There are several benefits to advocating as part of a coalition:

- *Large-scope efforts typically require many voices.* Coalitions are a great way to have impact at a larger level and may have resources not available to individuals or a single group.
- *Many more ears to the ground.* It is impossible to be in multiple places at once and to hear all the discussions surrounding an issue. The larger the coalition, the larger the base of individuals who can keep an ear out for additional opportunities to advocate.
- *Increased advocacy capital.* Each advocacy group will have relationships with different decision makers and access to different spaces. Coalitions comprised of respected, well-reputed groups are more likely to have their messages heard and taken seriously. This is true at the national level as well as the local level.

When joining a coalition, it is helpful to make sure there is some sort of formalized goal or mission. This may be issue specific or broader in scope. An example of issue specific may be to advocate for a particular mental health bill that is introduced in the state legislature. An example of a broad mission may be to advocate for more mental health supports in schools that align with national recommendations. Being clear about what the mission and goals are, and are not, is a good way to identify whether or not joining the coalition make sense for you.

States often have local chapters of their national organizations, for example, the New York Association of School Psychologists (NYASP) or the Washington School Counselor Association (WSCA). There are also state and local chapters of community groups or associations such as the Parent–Teacher Association. Joining these organizations and advocating as part of a group is an excellent way to increase the strength of your voice for a shared cause. Even better is when these groups join together with other groups to amplify their shared voice.

In Nevada, the three school-based mental health state associations joined together to advocate for adopting state practice standards that aligned with national best practice standards. Senate Bill 319 (2019) emerged as that bill and directly aligned the best practice models of the National Association of School Psychologists, the American School Counselor Association, and the School Social Work Association of America for each profession, respectively. The collective advocacy of the three groups made the bill stronger as it worked its way through the legislative process. The sponsor of the bill was Senator Dondero Loop who is a strong advocate for educators and mental health services in schools. She graciously sponsored the bill and carried it successfully through both houses of the legislature, and signature by the Governor.

Kristin Barnson, school counselor and President of the Nevada School Counselor Association during the time of Senate Bill 319 (2019,) offers sage advice for advocates to consider. She recommends building relationships with policy makers and other advocates. As professionals, "we can advocate, but if we don't have the right people to advocate to, our words go unheard". She also suggests getting involved in the state chapters of national professional associations. Advocating with the voice of a state association carries tremendous weight. Its voice can speak to what members and the profession need. Joining a coalition of other like-minded professional associations further amplifies its voice and what the groups can accomplish.

Joining a coalition may be formal or informal, depending on the scope or issue. In the above example, the state's school-based mental health associations represent a coalition that may take formal action together on specific initiatives, or not. They may also take action as individual associations. There is nothing to say that a coalition needs to formally act together on everything. If there is an initiative that only impacts one group, that group has the freedom to act on that initiative alone, representing the collective voice of its members. Whether actions are taken individually, by a group, or by a coalition, it is important to state in what capacity the action is being taken.

For initiatives that will be formally acted upon together, it can be helpful to create a document with the joint logos of the groups represented in the letterhead to demonstrate a shared position. This document can detail the shared perspective of the groups including their specific ask of the decision maker(s). The document can be emailed and shared on social media as the position of the coalition.

Associations are in a unique position in that decision makers form relationships with the association as a whole or with the roles of individuals within an association, such as the role of president. One recommendation for associations is to have positions such as president create an association email such as president@yourassociation.org that can be passed down to the next president. This is a great way for an incoming president to have historic knowledge of an association's communications and relationships with key decision makers and other community leaders. While communications and relationships with an individual aren't transferable, communications and relationships with a position can be.

Quiet Influencers

One of the most fascinating things I've observed doing advocacy work is the role of the quiet influencer. This quiet influencer may also be known as a connector. This person works behind the scenes, advocating for a certain initiative(s), with many invested parties. They may or may not speak up publicly and they are rarely the spokesperson of an initiative. However, they seem to know everyone and are often a connector, introducing like-minded groups or individuals to each other. They also know how to influence decision makers by delivering the message in an advantageous way. In doing so, they attain buy-in and support for the initiative. Quite often, decision makers actually leave these conversations thinking that the idea for the initiative was theirs all along.

The quiet influencer is focused on change, not on power. Ironically, in being able to influence change, they have tremendous power. If you can identify who the quiet influencer is for mental health, education, and/or workforce development, it would be a great idea to have coffee with that person. They can help you devise an advocacy plan or point you in the right direction regarding who to talk to, and how. In doing so, they can help alleviate feelings of discomfort, chaos, and uncertainty. After hearing what you are hoping to accomplish, if they support the initiative, they may also end up being a quiet influencer for your efforts.

Identify Mentors

When I first started my advocacy journey, I encountered advocates that inspired me. Advocates by nature like to share and they are very open to others approaching them. One day I decided to be bold and asked one of these inspiring advocates if they would have coffee with me. There was an issue that we were both advocating about, and I didn't have a clear understanding of the policy making process. I asked if I could pick their brain on the issue. She said absolutely! This was the beginning of many informal *mentor appointments*, and it is still a thing I do to this day. There is no way we can all know everything. Learning from others is a great strategy and can help build trusting relationships.

Mentors may be issue specific or process specific. They may be formally appointed or informally appointed. Some of the best learning I've had is when I've talked stories with other advocates after meetings or gatherings. Learning what they have been up to and how they are navigating their own advocacy can trigger new thoughts and approaches to the work. It might spark an idea that was niggling in the back of my mind or frame an issue in a way that I hadn't thought of before. The primary goal of appointing mentors is to learn from others. Whether in person or virtual, there is always room to learn and grow with others.

Effective Communication

Good advocacy and policy making both rely on effective communication. Effective communication helps ensure that the intended message is heard by the listener. And heard in a way that is productive to moving your initiative forward. There is nothing to be gained by being overtly argumentative or offensive. It will be detrimental to the relationships that you are trying to build. There are polite ways to offer a counter consideration or to identify alternative paths forward. Always use a professional, factual approach to your communication. Whether the communication be verbal, nonverbal, or written, make sure your message is delivered effectively and professionally. Your message is your action. It leaves a professional imprint in the minds of others, and you want this imprint to be positive (Di Giusto, 2014).

There is no one right way to go about anything. When I was small, I thought adults had all the answers. Now that I am an adult I realize that adults rarely have "all" the answers. Adults make decisions based on available information, and the quality of that information impacts the decisions made. Policy makers rely on advocates, educators, and content experts to provide them with accurate information with which to make good decisions. Be that voice and provide that information so good decisions can get made. Effective communication can help develop lasting, meaningful relationships that contribute to the policy making process.

Based on the key learning objectives, I can now:

- Identify how to amplify a message.
- Explain why grassroots advocacy is so important.
- Describe benefits to both individual and collective advocacy.
- Recognize what a coalition is and the power of advocating together.
- Explain the need for effective communication and its role in relationship building.

References

Di Giusto, S. (2014). *The image of leadership*. Executive Image Consulting.

National Association of School Psychologists. (2018). *ADVOCACY: The role of grassroots advocacy in policy solutions*. GW/NASP Public Policy Institute, Georgetown, District of Columbia.

National Association of School Psychologists. (2019). *NASP policy playbook*. https://www.nasponline.org/research-and-policy/advocacy

Senate Bill 319, Nevada 2019.

Waalkes, P. L., DeCino, D. A., Haugen, J. S., & Dalbey, A. (2019). The relationship between job roles and gender on principal-school counselor relationship quality. *Professional School Counseling, 22*(1). https://doi.org/10.1177/2156759X19861105

SECTION II

THE POLICY MAKING PROCESS

6

BOOMERANG POLICY MAKING MODEL

Learning Concepts

In this chapter, readers will learn:

- The overarching tenets of the Boomerang Policy Making Model.
- The advocacy opportunities available within the model.
- What the different policy levers are.
- What the three phases of advocacy are.
- Why decision makers and advocates have a shared responsibility in the policy making process.

Chapter Keywords

- Boomerang Policy Making Model
- Lever
- Agendize
- Advocacy action phases

DOI: 10.4324/9781003308515-8

- Intra-lever boomeranging
- Inter-lever boomeranging

Policy making can take on many different forms. The process will look different depending on the scope and the state you live in. Policy making in Tallahassee, Florida will look different than policy making in La Crosse, Wisconsin or Omak, Washington. Regardless of the state or the scope of your efforts, there are still a few common denominators that will be true universally. This chapter will cover these commonalities and offer suggestions for effective policy making. Your individual context will look different, and may shift with each issue, but there are some universal processes, levers, and actions that will remain constant.

Boomerang Policy Making Process

Good policy making should be like a Boomerang. It should travel broadly, collect information on its journey, and bring that information back to where it started. Making a full circuit, it allows for policy making that is multi-directional. Boomerang policy making is the opposite of Frisbee policy making. Frisbee policy making only goes in one direction and does not collect information or the perspectives of others.

First and foremost, good policy making should be a shared responsibility between decision makers and advocates. As a multi-directional model, Boomerang Policy Making relies on a shared responsibility of both decision makers and advocates to engage in the process. This not only prevents a Frisbee model of policy making, but it also creates opportunities for multiple voices to be heard. These perspectives can then be incorporated into a policy draft and optimal policies can be moved forward.

This model is presented for its capacity to explain policy formation, much as the renowned multiple streams model put forth by Kingdon to do the same (Rawat & Morris, 2016; Zahariadis, 2007; Kingdon, 1984). While Kingdon emphasized the role of policy windows, the Boomerang Policy Making Model emphasizes the role of advocates in opening these windows. Further, the advocacy-coalition and punctuated-equilibrium theories help us to understand that a window may have opened, and policy change occurred, due to actions over time; it did not happen overnight (Schlager, 2007). For additional information about these theories and how they may influence the Boomerang Policy Making Model, readers are encouraged to conduct a deeper investigation beyond the scope of this practical how-to guide.

There is a functional need for practice to impact policy. *Policy should not always dictate practice.* There are exceptional practices happening in our schools that can help inform and strengthen statewide policies (Coggins, 2017). There are also realities happening in our communities that decision makers may not be aware of. They may also not know how those realities are impacting students in the school setting. Good statewide policies are important because they can protect best practices, support educators, and positively impact students. Advocacy leaders can help support this process by seeking solutions to root causes, not just the symptoms (Anderson, 2009)

One guardrail for good policy making is that it should include the perspective of those most impacted. In the school setting, this principally includes the voice of educators and students, but should also include the voice of families and the community. Another critical rule of thumb should be, *does the policy align with the intent of the law?* This is important to ensure alignment of policies at every layer, reducing ambiguities and strengthening implementation. What type of policy making have you experienced? Boomerang or Frisbee?

Before embarking on a policy making journey, it is helpful to first understand the process by which policies get made. Advocacy requires levers and action, and these are two different perspectives to think about within the policy making process. The lever process and the action process are both needed and are important to understand as you advocate for change.

From the lever perspective, what layer of government or bureaucracy is the right place to begin your efforts? Are there existing policies in place at these various levels that impact the thing you are advocating for? Depending on your advocacy lever there may also be certain deadlines to be aware of, legal ramifications to consider, and guardrails to uphold.

From the action perspective, how can advocates actively move their initiative successfully through the policy process lever by lever? What actionable steps can advocates take to communicate effectively and to have their initiative implemented?

Boomerang Levers

A *lever* is the level of government or bureaucracy needed to advance a specific initiative. Examples of levers include the federal level, state legislature (statutory), state board (regulatory), state department, higher education, municipal, district, or school. The lever is basically the entity that has the authority to make the change you are hoping to see. Within the Boomerang Policy Making Model, these levers are the outer circles. Within each lever there may be sub-levers to target that you will identify as you begin your work.

At the federal level, the classic Schoolhouse Rock! cartoon video of "I'm Just a Bill" (1976) comes to mind and shows an animated figure as it sings its way through the bill making process on Capitol Hill. This video depicts the pathway that a bill takes as it moves from bill drafting to being signed into law. If you haven't seen it, I highly recommend the few minutes it takes to watch.

At a level closer to home, similar components of policy making also exist. For example, policies will start with an idea, and creating change at the district or school level will follow a pre-established pathway. There may be existing policies in place that influence the change you seek and there are certain deadlines that must be upheld in order to agendize an item for the local school board to hear. *Agendize* means to schedule an item onto the established meeting agenda. There will also be certain established processes in place for how an item works its way through the policy making process after the item is heard by the board. Each state and district will have its own processes and understanding the procedural side of policy making can be very advantageous. I encourage you to start learning about the various processes as you begin advocating. This will help you identify what lever to engage so you don't waste valuable time barking up the wrong tree. It will also help you manage expectations, timelines, and efforts.

Boomerang Actions

From the action perspective, all the steps *leading up to, between,* and *after* the lever aspects of the policy making process are critical. Identifying what it is you want to advocate for, and speaking up about it, is the first step.

As voiced by the various education leaders interviewed for this book, just do it.

Within the Boomerang Policy Making Model, the action process is the rotating inner circle within the outer figures. There are three phases that comprise the *advocacy action phases* of policy making, and they rest at the center of all efforts. The three phases are referred to as the Message, the Puzzle, and Puzzle Management. The various levers of bureaucracy that revolve around these three phases are the legal processes of policy making. They circle the periphery and as each new level is engaged, it must re-engage with the advocacy core. It doesn't matter if you are advocating at the school level or the congressional level, some variation of these three phases will need to be considered.

Boomerang Policy Making Model

Boomerang policy making weaves in and out of a central advocacy action hub with levers that act as spokes (see Figure 6.1). These levers represent the different layers of policy making from the classroom to the federal level. They are each connected by a central, established advocacy action model that remains constant regardless of which spoke, or lever, is being focused on. The three phases of the central advocacy model remain constant but may be operationalized slightly different for each lever.

Boomerang policy making can happen one of two ways. It can happen intra-lever or inter-lever. *Intra-lever level boomeranging* occurs when more information or additional advocacy is needed within a specific lever, for example, when additional action is needed within one lever such as the district. As additional action is needed, the three core phases of advocacy are engaged. Efforts to promote your initiative are re-evaluated, expanded, or refined to make your message more clear, robust, or compelling. The action planning may be formal or informal, and the more you do it, the more you will find your brain starts to shift and engage in these actions reflexively.

It is quite common within a specific policy making lever to repeat the action phases. There are many reasons for this. The item may appear on a board's agenda multiple times, and each time it appears, you will want to advocate for your initiative. You will want to revise your message so that it remains relevant and compelling. While the central theme of your

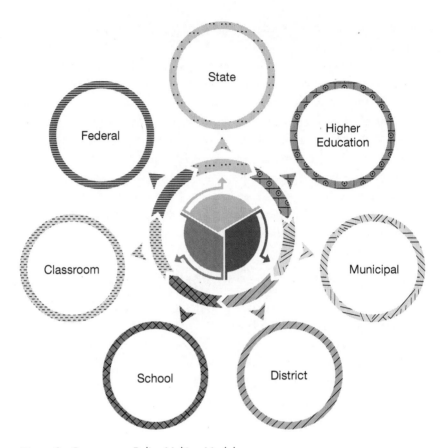

Figure 6.1 Boomerang Policy Making Model

message will remain constant, you can customize and update it with any new information learned since the last time the board heard the item. With each new hearing, your advocacy efforts may need to boomerang back to the central action hub to regroup before heading back out to the lever in question.

Inter-lever boomeranging happens when a policy passes from one lever on to the next. If a policy passes in one lever and needs to move on to the next, it must first boomerang through the three core advocacy phases. For example, if a policy passes in the state legislature and is signed into law by the governor, it may need to move on to the state board or state department of education. As it moves on, new action planning will need to take place. From an advocacy perspective, the policy will boomerang from its current lever, the state legislature, into the central advocacy hub, and then out to the next lever, the state board or state department of education. While traveling into the central hub, the advocate can enact all three advocacy phases. Similar to intra-lever boomeranging, specific aspects to consider may include strategizing, messaging, and action. Depending on how complex an issue is, you may need to be actively advocating in one lever while laying the groundwork for future action in subsequent levers.

Outer Figure: Levers

The outer circles of the Boomerang Policy Making Model represent the various levers of government or bureaucracy that policies may move through. Each will require separate considerations depending on where your initiative starts and how many levers may be impacted. The following are broad examples of governing entities that may fall under each lever and who might have a governing right to education and school-based mental health policies. There may also be sub-levers to explore. Each state will have their own specific terms for the entities, and you are encouraged to seek out what they are in your state.

Congressional delegation

- Senate
- House of Representatives

Federal departments

- U.S. Department of Education
- U.S. Department of Health and Human Services

State government

- Legislature
- State Board of Education
- Mental Health Board
- Health and Human Services Board

State departments

- Department of Education
- Department of Health and Human Services

Higher education

- Higher Education Board
- Department of Higher Education

Municipal

- City Government
- County Government

District

- School Board
- District Leadership Cabinet

School

- Student Leadership Groups
- Principal
- Organizational and Mental Health Teams
- Parent–Teacher Associations

Classroom

- Teacher
- School Leadership

Inner Figure: Advocacy Action Phases

There are three action phases to Boomerang Policy Making. All three phases have unique functions and moving between the phases can be fluid depending on where in the process the initiative is. Each of the three phases requires strategizing and planning. They also allow you to revise your advocacy actions, depending on what new developments have been learned. Depending on the scale and scope of your initiative, this may be simple planning or extensive political strategizing and researching. Remember, the closer the decision-making power is to the student, the easier the change may be. In these cases, all three phases may not be necessary. However, in advocacy efforts that are larger in scope, they will be.

Phase 1: The Message

The first phase is to construct and deliver your message. This includes the preparation, drafting, and action under a framework described as the 3 As (Dockweiler, 2021; Franks-Thomas et al., 2020; Clark & Dockweiler, 2019, 2020). This framework is described in depth in Chapter 7. The broad process includes the following steps:

- Awareness
- Access
- Action

Phase 2: The Puzzle

The second phase is to assemble all the parts and pieces of your initiative and move them around until they fit. The ending picture may not be what you initially thought it would look like, but as long as it addresses the issue at hand, it's a win. The Puzzle solving phase is described in Chapter 8 and includes the following components:

- No is never no
- Build coalition
- Monitor progress
- Expand messaging
- Strategize ahead

Phase 3: Puzzle Management

The third phase is Puzzle Management. This includes following your initiative through to implementation, including any additional layer or lever that it must pass through. The goal is to keep all your puzzle pieces; you don't want to lose any once you get them all lined up and your picture becomes clear. Depending on how many levers your initiative includes, you may need to engage in this process simultaneously for each one. More about Puzzle Management is discussed in Chapter 9.

- Monitor levers
- Track implementation
- Continue messaging
- Repeat phases

Iterative Revision and Feedback Loops

Boomerang Policy Making allows for many opportunities for advocates to share their voice and perspective. It also allows for iterative revision and layered implementation of the policy. Iterative revision is critical for continuous improvement. Each time the Boomerang gets tossed, whether by public hearing or by being an agendized item, new feedback will be picked up that can inform the initiative. The policy maker and their team will need to consider the information and decide what parts to include. This iterative revision cycle is also critical for transparency and collective buy-in. As policies work their way through the different advocacy levers, they will become more refined and targeted as to what that policy will actually look like when enacted in a classroom or a school.

Boomerang Policy Making works best when the public is actively engaged in the process. It is a policy making model uniquely constructed to include an advocate's perspective. Each time a policy moves through a new lever in the policy process, it should go through the central hub of the advocacy phases. If there are no advocates actively engaged in providing feedback or strategizing their messaging, there is no feedback or message for policy makers to hear. This is why policy making should be a shared responsibility of both advocates and policy makers.

This shared responsibility is present regardless of an effort's scope. The decision maker may be the principal and the advocates may be the students and families. A principal who seeks feedback on a proposed school-wide initiative is attempting to engage in Boomerang Policy Making. Likewise, the students and families who provide feedback are also participating in Boomerang Policy Making. In a reverse example, the families could reach out to the principal with a proposed initiative. The principal might meet with the parents and/or guardians, provide feedback, and then implement what was agreed upon. Advocacy efforts that are smaller in scope and require fewer levers of bureaucracy are easier to reach consensus and move forward.

On a broader scope, I have sat though many public meetings where the policy makers have created a forum for community feedback, genuinely wanting public input, but there was no one in the audience to provide any. At no fault to the policy makers, a Boomerang tossed that does not collect information on its return trip might as well be a Frisbee; the form it started in is the same form it ended in. If advocates do not participate, Frisbee policy making may take place, setting a dangerous precedent. We can ensure Boomerang Policy Making takes place by taking action, submitting public feedback, and advocating for what we'd like to see change.

Active engagement can help avoid any feelings of ill will down the road. It can also help avoid accusations, finger pointing and shaming or blaming. If policy makers create conditions for Boomerang Policy Making and the public does not engage, that tells one kind of story. Similarly, if advocates actively engage in Boomerang Policy Making and the policy makers do not create conditions to hear their feedback, this tells a different kind of story. Having healthy conditions conducive to supporting both policy makers and advocates is critical for Boomerang Policy Making to be successful.

Layered advocacy and policy implementation is a key feature of Boomerang Policy Making. As previously mentioned, boomeranging will happen many times both intra- and inter-levers. This process will perhaps be separated by gaps in time as policies move through the various bureaucratic structures. As part of this layered implementation approach, multiple feedback loops are needed. Feedback may be in the form of single loop or double loop (Hanson, 2001; Argyris, 1999). Single feedback loops occur in the short term and influence decisions in the immediate lever. Double feedback loops occur over time as processes and policies are re-examined and revised across levers. Within Boomerang Policy Making, the intra-lever trips into the core three phases of advocacy are the single feedback loops. The inter-lever trips into the core are the double feedback loops. Both are important for long-term policy success.

Conclusion

You should now have a high-level view of the Boomerang Policy Making Model and the nuances at each phase and lever. Depending on the scope of your issue, the policy lever to engage, and the context of your state or local community, your action steps may look different. However, there are a few common denominators that will transcend the varying contexts and can be used to guide your advocacy efforts. First, there is a shared responsibility for decision makers and advocates to engage in the process. There are also common processes, levers, and actions to consider when formulating your message and identifying where to start your advocacy efforts.

Based on the key learning objectives, I can now:

- Explain the overarching structure of the Boomerang Policy Making Model.
- Describe how there are many advocacy opportunities within the model.
- Identify the different policy making levers.
- Describe why action phases are important to policy making.
- Understand why policy making is a shared responsibility held by decision makers and advocates.

References

Anderson, G. L. (2009). *Advocacy leadership: Toward a post-reform agenda in education.* Routledge.

Argyris, C. (1999). *On organizational learning* (2nd ed.). Blackwell.

Clark, A. G., & Dockweiler, K. A. (2019). *Multi-tiered systems of support in secondary schools: The definitive guide to effective implementation and quality control.* Routledge.

Clark, A. G., & Dockweiler, K. A. (2020). *Multi-tiered systems of support in elementary schools: The definitive guide to effective implementation and quality control.* Routledge.

Coggins, C. (2017). *How to be heard: 10 lessons teachers need to advocate for their students and profession.* Jossey-Bass.

Dockweiler, K. A. (2021). EUREKA! The five-year rehabilitation of school psychology in the Silver State. *Communiqué, 49*(6), 23–25.

Franks-Thomas, A., Comizio, R., Saint, J., & Dockweiler, K. A. (2020). Communication as advocacy. *Communiqué, 49*(2), 1, 19–22.

Frishberg, D. (1976). I'm just a bill. *Schoolhouse Rock!* [Video]. YouTube. https://www.youtube.com/watch?v=ax6PDAjjbgs

Hanson, M. (2001). Institutional theory and educational change. *Educational Administration Quarterly, 37*(5), 637–661.

Kingdon, J. W. (1984). *Agendas, alternatives, and public policies.* Longman.

Rawat, P., & Morris, J. C. (2016). Kingdon's "streams" model at thirty: Still relevant in the 21st century? *Politics & Policy, 44*(4), 608–638.

Schlager, E. (2007). *Theories of the policy process* (2nd ed., P. Sabatier, Ed.). Westview Press.

Zahariadis, N. (2007). *Theories of the policy process* (2nd ed., P. Sabatier, Ed.). Westview Press.

7

ADVOCACY ACTION PHASE 1
The Message

Learning Concepts

In this chapter, readers will learn:

- What the 3 As of advocacy are and how they work together.
- Several ways to be aware of advocacy and messaging opportunities.
- The components of "the ask".
- What an elevator pitch is and how to deliver it.
- How to create messages using the Message Development Framework.

Chapter Keywords

- 3 As
- Awareness
- Access
- Action
- Key message

DOI: 10.4324/9781003308515-9

- The ask
- Elevator pitch

Have you ever heard the expressions "bring your own chair to the table" or "if you are not at the table, you are on the menu"? These suggestions are correct and suggest an underlying nuance. Conceptually, how can you know to grab a chair or that you will be on the menu? Prior to a chair being grabbed or a menu being read, there are things happening behind the scenes. These behind-the-scenes processes can help influence your initiative. I call these things the 3 As: awareness, access, and action.

As we learned in the previous chapter, optimal policy making takes place through a Boomerang Policy Making Model. Advocacy can occur at multiple levers and will follow several established phases. Phase 1 of the advocacy action process is The Message and includes the 3 As. Each A will be discussed by its unique characteristics and purposes.

The 3 As of Messaging

The Message is the first of the advocacy phases and includes the 3 *As*: awareness, access, and action (see Figure 7.1). First is awareness. Awareness is having knowledge about what is currently going on surrounding an issue. It includes the general sense, or appetite, that the public has for the issue. Next is access. Access is having digital, in-person, or public access to key decision makers. Last is action. Action is the decided upon action that you take to move your issue forward. This is the point where you reach out to make your ask using your predetermined message.

Advocacy is multi-factional and can encompass many different components as seen in the Advocacy Action Phases. Depending on the initiative, your level of comfort advocating for the issue, and your relationship with key decision makers will influence whether you move through the advocacy process easily or jarringly. When I first started advocating, I thought that the advocacy action itself was the first step in promoting an issue. However, as the years went by, I grew in my skills. I started coaching others on how to navigate the advocacy process, and it became very clear to me that the action itself is actually the last step in the first phase. Before you ever get to the actual action, there are other foundational strategies to put in place to help you successfully implement the action.

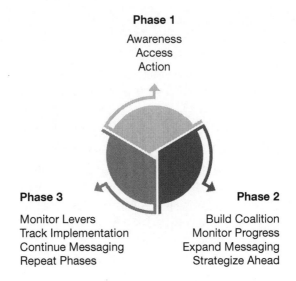

Phase 1

Awareness
Access
Action

Phase 3

Monitor Levers
Track Implementation
Continue Messaging
Repeat Phases

Phase 2

Build Coalition
Monitor Progress
Expand Messaging
Strategize Ahead

Figure 7.1 Advocacy Action Phases

Awareness

The first step of Phase 1 is *awareness*. Before any sort of advocacy can happen, there must be some awareness of what is happening relative to your particular initiative of interest. Is your initiative of interest a critical need? Are others sharing interest in the idea too? Are there groups or people out there who are opposed to your area of interest? What meetings are happening where this issue is being discussed?

Having your radar tuned in to what is happening locally, within the state, or nationally can be very advantageous for many reasons. First, it can help you identify where to start your advocacy, or which lever is the appropriate entry point. Second, it can help you identify allies and potential barriers to your efforts. Third, you can begin learning what the key talking points are so you can begin devising your message. Fourth, you can learn how far along others are in their advocacy efforts and support or fill in areas that may have been overlooked.

The more awareness there is surrounding a particular issue, the better chance you have for getting traction and support. Doing an environmental scan and observing what is happening surrounding the issue broadly is important. If there is limited or no awareness around a particular issue, and there needs to be, then this is a perfect opportunity to begin waving the awareness flag.

Knowledge of key decision makers is one form of awareness. Be vulnerable and don't be afraid to introduce yourself to key decision makers. I've approached and introduced myself to members of Congress and local elected officials in airports, carnivals, and sporting events. Most times, I made no specific ask or requested any action be taken. I was simply introducing or re-introducing myself and making them aware of me, our state school psychology association, and our cause to improve mental health supports for students.

None of this was comfortable for me, but I did it because building relationships with key decision makers is necessary for successful advocacy. The first step in building these relationships and communicating your message is to be *aware* of who these decision makers are in the first place. Policy makers look like everyone else, and it is easy to think they are just another community member attending an event or going someplace. One of the benefits of social media is that policy makers at all levels usually have a media presence. At the very least, if you search their name online you can typically find numerous images of what they look like. Pay attention to the formal photos, but also seek out photos in a more natural setting so that you can recognize them across diverse environments.

Another form of awareness is knowing when meetings, hearings, and public forums are taking place. Knowing when meetings are happening is another foundational step to making your message heard. If you don't know that a meeting is happening, then how will you know when to share your message? There are usually several options for learning about meetings:

- *Sign up for your state and local governmental listservs.* Locate these sign-up forms on the government entity website. If they are not readily located, email or call the contact person listed and request to be added. There may be filters where you can sign up for all meeting announcements, or just meeting announcements relative to your specific area(s) of interests, such as education and/or mental health.
- *Target the specific governing bodies, or levers, that are key for your issue.* Go to their website and locate their meeting schedule. Many established

governing bodies will have their meeting schedule posted for the next several months or an entire year. They may also meet on a regular rotation, such as the first Wednesday of each month, and you can plug these meetings into your calendar.

- *Follow the governing bodies on social media.* They will often post meeting announcements the day before, or the day of, their meetings. They will also post updates, meeting changes, or key activities. Staying abreast of their happenings will help you keep your message relevant and timely.

Depending on your particular state or governing body of interest, one or more of these options might be helpful. Often it is helpful to engage all three methods as a way to cross-reference and ensure that no meetings get overlooked. If you are working as part of a group or coalition, you can delegate these awareness activities to specific individuals or groups who can then report back.

Many public meetings follow open meeting law. In such cases, there will be an agenda posted a week prior to the meeting. You or someone from your group can keep an eye out for the agenda and read through it to see if there is anything on the agenda relative to your area of interest. If there isn't, you can do one of two things. You can disregard the meeting and focus your efforts elsewhere. Or, you can use the meeting as a place to build public interest. You can give public comment and talk about your area of interest and request that the governing body put your item on a future agenda. There is often a public comment period where members of the public can speak to any item that is not on the agenda. This would be the time to formally request that your issue be agendized and discussed. At the very least, you've raised awareness. Someone from the governing body might even reach out to you and ask for more information about the issue.

Access

The second step of Phase 1 is access. Once you are aware of a meeting or event, how do you ensure that you have *access* to it? If the meeting or event is public, you are always welcome to attend. If the meeting or event is by invitation only, it will be harder, but not impossible, to gain access.

Let's start with public meetings. Public meetings are just that, meetings that are open to the public. They are a cornerstone of our democracy and impactful to public and political decision making (Schumaker, 2008; Stone, 2002). As part of the Boomerang Policy Making Model, it is imperative that advocates attend these meetings to voice their concerns or make their requests. If no one is at these public meetings to provide feedback to the key decision makers, Frisbee policy making takes place which is not optimal for good policy making.

In the past, public meetings were largely held in-person inside buildings. This created barriers for people who could not physically be present at the meeting. Common barriers include having to work during the meeting time, not having transportation to get to the meeting, or having childcare demands. A frustration of mine is when families are made to feel that if they need to bring their children to the meeting, they are not welcome. Children are the very reason that we are advocating and should not be a barrier for participation! If the children are old enough, policy makers can actually ask their perspective on a policy and get feedback from the students who would be most impacted by the issue being discussed.

The increased reliance and normalized use of technology has leveled the playing field in terms of access to meetings. As a result of the COVID-19 pandemic and more generalized familiarity with technology, more and more public meetings are being held online or will have a virtual component. The entire meeting may be viewable online, there may be ways to submit public comment electronically, or there may be methods for calling in and providing public comment verbally. If these options are not available, they might be a good thing to advocate for. The rising use of technology has decreased barriers to access and participate in public meetings.

If you have identified an event that you'd like to attend but don't have access to it, there are a few steps to take. These events are great opportunities to meet with many stakeholder and policy makers across several levers of decision making. If you can gain access to these meetings, I highly recommend it. First, I would recommend emailing the host or organizer directly and asking if you can attend. If you don't ask, it will be guaranteed that you can't attend. If you reach out and ask, there might be a possibility. If you know someone who is attending, it might be possible for them to bring a guest. In this case, ask your friend to request the possibility of bringing a plus-one. If your group has financial reserves and access can be granted by making a donation or buying a table, it might be money well spent. Finally, if access cannot be gained in any of these ways, the next best thing is to follow the event on social media. Engage with those who are posting and make comments or respond to their posts. In this sense you are still able to engage virtually if not in-person.

If appropriate and of interest, it is helpful to have members of your advocacy group actually participate or serve on key decision-making boards. This way you will always be aware when key meetings are taking place and someone from your group will always have access. Depending on a board's governance model, they may even have specific positions carved out, such as a parent or educator, to serve.

Action

The third step in Phase 1 is *action*. Once you are aware of a meeting space or format and have access to it, what do you do? You will want to have several key messages ready to deliver depending on the circumstances. You will want to practice delivering them in a variety of ways depending on your audience and the purpose. There are also several components that you will want to include in the construction of your message.

When thinking about what to communicate there are a few different things to consider. For every audience you will need to modify your message even if it is only slightly. Each entity you advocate to will play a specific role in the policy making process. It is helpful to have a core message that you can easily adjust. There is no need to reinvent the wheel when you've already got a wheel framed out. The reason for adjusting your message is simple: every audience will have their own "why" or points of interest. You will want to target their why and demonstrate to them how your request supports and helps to further their own interests.

The first type of communication is called the key message. Key messages are just that – critical messages that succinctly convey a key point. They will coincide with the key theme of your initiative. The second type of communication is "the ask". Once you've identified your key message, the ask is how you convey the problem and solution to decision makers. The third type of communication is the elevator pitch, or a message that can be succinctly delivered in a brief amount of time. Each of the three are discussed in greater detail below.

Key Message

Always have your key message ready to deploy (National Association of School Psychologists [NASP], 2019). Key messages are high-level sound bites that convey a specific message. They also align with the initiative that you are trying to move forward. For example, if students in my school district are having increasing rates of mental health issues, but there aren't enough professionals to address the students' needs, my initiative might center around increasing the number professionals in the field. My key message might be the following: all students benefit from access to school-based mental health providers.

You may have different key messages depending on how big your group is or how large your efforts are. If you are part of a large association, you may have several talking points or key messages that your group is looking to advance. If you are advocating as an individual or part of a small group, one key message may be all that you need. For each key message you will want to construct an ask. Depending on how broad your key message is, you may have several asks.

The Ask

In your key message you will want to outline what you perceive the current problem to be, the action you want the decision maker to take, and the benefit of taking the requested action (NASP, 2016). When possible, you will also want to offer potential solutions to any associated costs. This type of message is considered "the ask". It is beneficial to practice saying this message out loud a few times to make sure you are delivering it in a succinct and clear manner.

Components of your ask:

- Problem – state what the current problem is and the negative impact it is having on students. Use data to support your narrative. Keep your message factual and accurate. Use social math to convert data into how many students are impacted in your school, district, or state.

- *Ask* – The ask is a specific request made from one individual or group to another. In this case, you've already stated the problem, now tell them what the solution is. The solution is what you are asking for.
- *Benefit* – Outline what the benefits are to your solution. Who will benefit and to what degree? Use data again, if available, to demonstrate the significant impact your identified solution will have.
- *Cost* – If there is a financial cost to what you are asking for, be very open about it. State what the associated cost is and propose a solution to acquiring the funding. Don't worry about having the funding already secured to propose it as an option. By offering possible funding solutions you're demonstrating a high level of strategy and commitment that the decision maker will appreciate.

If the format that you are delivering the message is via public comment in a meeting, you will typically have 2–3 minutes to deliver your message. Write it out and practice reading it to ensure that you stay within your time window. When drafting a communication, regardless of the format, never tell a decision maker, "You need to do this because . . .". Frame the ask using language such as, "Students would greatly benefit from a suicide prevention policy that proactively supports their mental health, such as . . .".

If you are constructing an email, you are not constrained by time. However, you will probably want to consider shortening your message to ensure the recipient reads the whole email. You will want to catch the reader's attention quickly, get your point across, and then close the email before they lose interest. If possible, draft your message to fit within one frame of what can be read on a smartphone. People will read the first frame of an email, but they may not scroll down. If you don't get to the actual message of your email until the very end, the reader may never actually get to it.

The National Association of School Psychologists (2016, pp. 2–3) offers the additional tips to effectively communicate your message. These tips are relevant for all advocates whether you are a school psychologist, parent or guardian, educator, or community member.

Be clear and concise:

- Identify your main point
- State it at the very beginning

- Repeat it
- Conclude with it
- Back it up with 2–3 facts (most people will only remember 2–3 points)
- Provide concrete actions/suggestions
- Use audience-appropriate language, and avoid acronyms or technical language
- Use active tense and bullet points when possible
- Ask a colleague to review/proof your work
- Briefly describe your role/relevant skills

Resonate with your audience:

- Connect with you audience's concerns/priorities
- Appeal to emotion as well as intellect
- Use "social math", not just statistics
- Put a "face" on the issue
- Tell stories, not just facts
- Be a good listener
- Need a clear "call to action"
- Don't expect your target audience to guess what you want

Elevator Pitch

Another type of message you will want to have at the ready is your elevator pitch (NASP, 2018). The thinking behind the Elevator Pitch is just that: you find yourself in an elevator with a key decision maker or stakeholder. This is an unexpected and opportune time to convey your message. If you are prepared for such moments, you will easily be able to share your key message in 30 seconds or less. If you are not prepared, you will have missed out on a wonderful opportunity to deliver your message.

These messages can't convey everything, but they can open a door to a longer conversation. They are an abbreviated ask message and include the problem, ask, benefit, and cost. Always offer to follow up, share resources, or answer any questions. Demonstrate value. Keep the door open. Make sure you do as you say and follow up in a timely manner with the resources promised or with answers to the questions that were posed.

If you are able to hook your audience's attention, your message will be more likely to be heard. Hook the audience, deliver the message, and follow up on the proposed actions. Ask for the person's contact information or business card. Another critical way to have your message acted upon is to link your message to your audience's "why". Just as you have your why, other people or groups will have theirs. Conveying to the audience how your message connects to and supports their why, is much more likely to result in sparking their interest. Finally, keep the door open for future engagement. Let the decision maker know that you will follow up in the future as new information becomes available or if events are scheduled that might be of interest to them. Always have your elevator pitch ready!

Messaging Takes Practice

Below is an example of how an advocate can take the core issue that they are advocating for and translate it into a key ask to decision makers using the Message Development Framework. An abbreviated message is included at the end for that 30-second opportunity that might arise unexpectedly. This type of framing can also be expanded into larger messaging such as a letter or presentation.

- *Overarching issue*: students in my school district are having increasing rates of mental health issues, but there aren't enough school-based mental health professionals to address the students' needs.
- *Initiative*: to increase the number of school-based mental health professionals.
- *Target audience*: district leadership, including superintendent, members of leadership team, and local school board.
- *Key Message*: with adequate staffing, school-based mental health providers can help decrease the frequency and intensity of mental health issues in students.
- *Problem*: there are not enough school-based mental health professionals in our district. To meet nationally recommended ratios, we are short eight school counselors, four school psychologists, and five school social workers. With our current numbers, 50% of students do not have access to school-based mental health providers and the

comprehensive services they offer. If these 17 positions were filled, all students would have adequate access.

- *Ask*: the request is to create a partnership with the local university or state training program and have the district offer incentivize graduates to come work in the school district with signing bonuses.
- *Benefit*: more graduates will come to work in the district and the students will have greater access to providers.
- *Cost*: if each of the 17 graduates were given a $10,000 signing bonus for coming to work in the district, the total cost would be $170,000. These funds could be allocated from Medicaid reimbursements, grant funds, fundraising, or the general fund budget. They could also be paid out of braided federal, state, and local funding sources.
- *The Elevator Pitch*: students are in dire need of more school-based mental health services, but we don't have enough professionals to deliver the support. Our district is short 17 professionals. Perhaps we can create a partnership with our local training programs and offer incentives for their graduates to come to our district by offering them a $10,000 signing bonus. This way, instead of 50% of our students having access to school-based mental health providers, 100% of our students would. The money to pay for these bonuses could come from Medicaid, grants, the community, the general fund, or braided funding sources. I'd love an opportunity to share more information. Do you have a card so I can reach out with more info?

Time to practice! Here is a framework to help you begin homing in on your messaging. Try this with a variety of initiatives to get a feel for how the messaging process remains similar, and how it changes with each new issue or decision-making group.

Based on the key learning objectives, I can now:

- Describe the 3 As and why all three are necessary.
- Identify awareness opportunities for my own initiative.
- Develop my own "ask" using the four core components.
- Draft an elevator pitch and feel comfortable delivering it.
- Use the Message Development Framework to create messaging for a variety of initiatives.

Table 7.1 Application of the framework components can assist when translating core issues into key asks for decision makers

Message Development Framework
Overarching Issue:
Initiative:
Target Audience:
Key Message:
Problem:
Ask:
Benefit:
Cost:
The Elevator Pitch:

References

National Association of School Psychologists. (2016). *Effective communication: Tips for school psychologists.* https://www.nasponline.org/research-and-policy/advocacy/communications-strategies-and-resources/effective-communications-strategies

National Association of School Psychologists. (2018). *ADVOCACY: The role of grassroots advocacy in policy solutions.* GW/NASP Public Policy Institute, Georgetown, District of Columbia.

National Association of School Psychologists. (2019). *NASP policy playbook.* https://www.nasponline.org/research-and-policy/advocacy

Schumaker, P. (2008). *From ideologies to public philosophies: An introduction to political theory.* Blackwell Publishing.

Stone, D. (2002). *Policy paradox: The art of political decision making* (3rd ed.). Norton & Company.

8

ADVOCACY ACTION PHASE 2
The Puzzle

Learning Concepts

In this chapter, readers will learn:

- That no is rarely no.
- The role of coalition building in the advocacy process.
- How the Phase 2 advocacy action components work together.
- How to repackage an "ask".
- The role of financial costs in policy making.

Chapter Keywords

- The Puzzle
- No
- Coalition building
- Monitor progress
- Expand messaging
- Strategize ahead

DOI: 10.4324/9781003308515-10

Now that you've got your key message and you've shared it with the relevant decision makers, what do you do? There are three general reactions you can anticipate after you deliver your ask or message: silence, contact, or "no". Keep in mind that none of these responses are inherently good or bad; they are just the next step in the policy making dance.

The first reaction you can anticipate is a no response. Frequently you will hear nothing, especially the first time you deploy your message. It might take a while for your message to gain traction. During this time of silence, you can expand your message and continue reaching out. You may eventually hear from other stakeholder groups who are interested in learning more about your message. This is a great opportunity to build coalition with these other groups.

The second reaction you can anticipate is contact from the decision makers. This is a huge step in moving your initiative forward and should be celebrated. The decision maker may reach out from a curiosity perspective and have questions. This is a great time to offer data, additional information, and to be a resource. Avoid being overly persuasive or pushy as this might put the decision maker off. The goal is to keep them on your side and moving your initiative forward.

The third reaction you can anticipate is a flat-out "no". Be most prepared for this and do not get discouraged. No does not truly mean no. It just means not at this time, not in this form, or not with these people. No matter which of the three responses you get, you should constantly be monitoring the progress of your message and strategizing ahead. Always remember that no never truly means no. When advocating for systems level change or change on behalf of groups of people, "no" will be a common response. However, these are core elements of social justice advocacy and are worth pursuing (Grapin & Shriberg, 2020).

With Boomerang Policy Making you will find yourself revisiting these reactions regularly. Each conversation, each new revelation, and each new piece of data become a *puzzle piece* in your advocacy efforts. Your intended end-goal might start out looking like one picture but may end up looking like a different picture.

Every time you make an ask or the policy shifts from one lever to the next, new messaging and strategizing will be required (see Figure 8.1.). Understanding how to adjust all the puzzle pieces to create a recognizable picture is critical. The picture might ultimately look different than you

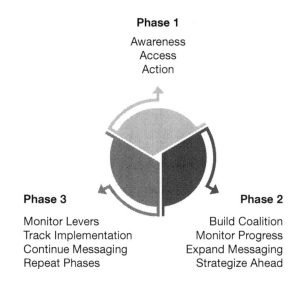

Phase 1

Awareness
Access
Action

Phase 3

Monitor Levers
Track Implementation
Continue Messaging
Repeat Phases

Phase 2

Build Coalition
Monitor Progress
Expand Messaging
Strategize Ahead

Figure 8.1 Advocacy Action Phases

had originally intended, but if the end result aligns with your intended goal, your efforts are on the right track.

Build Coalition

The first component of Phase 2 is *coalition building*. Once you begin putting your message out and sharing your desired initiative with others, there is a good chance that other individuals or groups will want to join your efforts. Building a coalition around a specific issue can be a powerful way to amplify your message (Coalition for Community Schools & National Association of School Psychologists, 2016). Partnering with other individuals or groups also gives you access to their stakeholder communication networks (Dockweiler, 2018). These networks increase the access you have to others. For example, if your contact list contains 100 emails, you will only reach 100 people. However, if the two stakeholder groups you are partnering with each have a network of 100 people, your access or message reach expands immediately to 300 email contacts.

You may encounter groups who are opposed to your message. In these cases, you probably won't build a coalition with them. *Your strategy with these groups is to mitigate opposition.* If you can get a stakeholder group who is opposed to your initiative to take a neutral stance versus an opposed stance, you can count this as a major success.

If reasonable dialogue does not lead to neutralizing an opposed position, complete opposition may still happen. However, it is important to try and find some common ground if at all possible. It is likely that there are only certain parts of your initiative that the other stakeholder group will be opposed to, not the whole thing. Bringing their opposition to a neutral stance on these few points will significantly increase the likelihood of your initiative gaining traction. For example, if you are advocating for a restorative practices program at your child's school and another group is actively advocating in opposition to it, it will be much more difficult to get what you want. However, if you can speak with the other group, answer their questions, and neutralize their opposition, you are more likely to get the restorative practices program. In this case, as you are advocating for the program, instead of public opposition from the group, there is silence. This silence can be used in your favor and will keep your efforts on track.

Monitor Progress

The second component of Phase 2 is to *monitor the progress* of your message. After deploying your message, it will be important to see what kind of reception it gets. Did you receive silence, contact, or "no"? Silence means you need to keep trying. Revise your message, share it with a larger audience, or use some other approach. Perhaps it is the medium. Did you send an email? If so, next time show up to the meeting and deliver your message in person. If you did deliver your message in person, follow up with an email. Reinforce your original message, provide additional information, or just offer to be a resource should the decision maker have any questions.

If you received contact from your desired audience, continue the conversation with the decision maker and make sure your points are clearly heard. Sometimes misunderstandings occur and what you thought the decision maker heard was not the message you were actually trying to convey. Clarity of message is critical. If you heard "no", there are several strategies you can use to turn that no into a yes.

Regardless of the reception you received, you will need to monitor it. Policy making is not static and what was a yes today might be a no tomorrow. Monitoring the progress of your issue is the only way to keep the message on track. There may be other stakeholder groups who show up and begin offering information. This has the potential to derail your efforts, or it can split the track and take the initiative in a different direction. You will need to follow up with decision makers immediately about why your pathway forward is still the best choice. Otherwise, even if the other group's ask may be close to what you were advocating for, it won't be your ideal situation. Or it might be the complete opposite of what you want. Staying on top of the messaging and its progression is the only way to ensure your desired success. No one is going to stay on top of your message except for you or a member of your team.

Expand Messaging

The third component of Phase 2 is to *expand your messaging*. As you monitor the progression of your message, you may notice that additional information is needed, or that your message needs to be modified. This is normal, message expansion and revision are a must. Remember, there is no one audience and you will need to adjust your message for each new group you target. Constant examination of your message, its reception, and new information learned will all inform your messaging. There may be an election that will influence how your messaging gets deployed, in what form, and with what frequency. You will also need to change your messaging depending on the political audience. Democrats may need the message expanded to include the benefits of the initiative for the social good. Republicans may need the message expanded to include the fiscal savings of the initiative over time. Know you audience and expand your key message accordingly.

Strategize Ahead

The fourth component of Phase 2 is to *strategize ahead*. Solution navigation is an essential part of the advocacy process. Many different contingencies must be brainstormed, and potential solutions should be devised in response to a variety of eventualities. Strategizing ahead reduces roadblocks or barriers to your efforts. Projecting where potential barriers may be and proactively taking them down will keep your initiative moving forward smoothly. This way, if your initiative eventually encounters one of the projected roadblocks, it won't be a big deal. It would be the difference between encountering a speed bump versus a brick wall. A speed bump might be annoying and briefly slow your effort down. However, a brick wall has the potential to be an insurmountable obstacle that halts your efforts. Solution navigation and strategizing ahead are necessary to minimize any roadblocks encountered.

No Is Never No

Rarely does "no" actually mean "no". No can mean a lot of things depending on the audience. Imagine a petulant child in an ice cream shop screaming at the top of their lungs for a double scoop of chocolate ice cream in a waffle cone. The parent adamantly says "no" and offers the child one scoop of chocolate ice cream in a regular sugar cone. The child persists in their negotiation for the double scoop in a waffle cone and the parent, exacerbated and embarrassed, comes back with, "fine, one scoop of chocolate ice cream in a waffle cone". The child finally calms down, smiles, and accepts the compromise.

On the flip side, the parent could have held strong and offered an ultimatum of no ice cream if the child kept up their screaming demands for a double scoop of chocolate in a waffle cone. The child then could have come back with a compromise or settled for nothing. In all situations, both parties came to the ice cream shop ready to discuss ice cream. Rarely does one party get all they want and the other gets nothing. Usually, it is some form of compromise where ideally, both parties walk away feeling like they benefited in some way.

The advocacy process follows this ice cream example in much the same way. Be prepared to navigate obstinate behavior, patience, passion, and compromise originating from yourself and others. Presence, persistence, and long-term vision are necessary to see your efforts ultimately succeed (DeLeon, 2006). These characteristics are all hallmarks of what you can expect as you head down this advocacy path. If the policy making world were an ice cream shop, both policy makers and advocates come to the shop wanting ice cream. Compromising on the size, flavor, and toppings are where things can get messy.

However, as mentioned in previous chapters, good advocacy work doesn't have to feel contentious; it can feel like a coming together of like minds for a united purpose. We each hold different pieces of a puzzle and finding the right pieces, in the right orientation, is the key to solving the puzzle. It requires patience, passion, and compromise as we work diligently to get the puzzle right.

It is rare when embarking on advocacy endeavors to only hear "yes". *Resilience in policy making is essential as many barriers will be encountered.* These barriers are merely puzzle pieces to subsume or neutralize as you build your puzzle.

With advocacy, "no" never truly means no. When you hear no, it just means not at this time, not in this form, or not with these people. Understanding what each of these actually means and how to create work arounds for them is critical. If you receive a "no", ask yourself which of these three categories the no falls into. Understanding what the underlying barrier truly is will help you repackage your ask and come at the initiative again from a stronger advocacy angle.

Not at This Time

If the no you hear is in reference to bad timing, there are a few different options to pursue. The first is the path of least resistance – just wait. Once the next legislative session comes around or the next principal is hired, you can try your ask again and see what the response is. For advocates, this passive approach doesn't tend to sit well. While bad timing can be a legitimate reason for not moving on an initiative, it doesn't mean you have to wait around doing nothing. While you are waiting you can be growing coalition, finding new angles to direct your messaging, and remaining persistent. Let's reflect on Chapter 3 and the example given about the Office for Civil Rights policy. We were told that there was a policy in place that dictated the procedures for our bilingual psycho-education evaluation reports. Through biding our time and persistently bringing the issue up, we were able to finally identify that the procedure was actually just an informal practice, not a real policy.

Schools unfortunately tend to be very reactive environments. They are often more likely to put mental health supports in place only *after* an unfortunate situation has occurred. For example, anti-bullying or suicide prevention programs are frequently put in place only after students have been bullied or there has been a student who has taken their own life. Communicating the need for these programs *before* something bad happens is critical. If the answer you get is "no, it is bad timing for this", you may have to wait until the unfortunate has happened to get your initiative to be taken seriously or implemented. This can be frustrating and detrimental to student well-being. However, if this is the case in your context, and you are forced to wait until a tragedy occurs, it will be imperative to advocate for mental health supports without politicizing the tragedy that has just happened.

Not in This Form

"Not in this form" is one of my favorite ways to hear "no". Not in this form basically means yes, we just need to tweak a few things. Learning what the hesitancies are and offering to work with the decision maker to land on a version that is acceptable might be all that is needed. Being collaborative, offering value, and finding consensus are the main strategies with this "no". As presented earlier, flexibility with policy making is key as you cannot control every single aspect or decision that gets made along the way. If you cannot be flexible or are too rigid in your approach, you run the risk of alienating decision makers and stakeholder groups. In doing so, you create opponents where you could have had allies. If there is room for flexibility, and you are able to creatively tweak your ask while still getting what you are hoping for, this is a win.

There may be times when the tweaks are not really tweaks. If the form that is being offered is a complete 180-degree shift away from what you are aiming for, don't be afraid to say no thank you. While consensus is the goal, if you discover that it is just not possible, it is okay to politely walk away from an issue. In this case you can either choose to be neutral on the issue, or if it is an initiative that is harmful or a disservice to students, you can be opposed. Remember, the advocacy phases are cyclical, and you might just have to drop back a step to ultimately move forward.

Not With These People

Sometimes you identify your lever and present your message to the corresponding group of decision makers. If you present your ask and discover that the answer is "no", it might be that they were not the right group of people who can grant your request. If this is the case, simply adjust and re-examine the lever and your strategy. Perhaps there is a different lever or group that is better suited to hear your message. Or there might be an individual or group that you can speak with who can connect you to the right group of people. "Not with these people" is typically a no that can be circumvented. It just means that the audience you targeted is not the correct audience. They mostly likely are not opposed to your ask; they are just not the correct group to grant the solution to your ask.

Repackage Your Ask

When you encounter a "no" that is not at this time, not in this form, or not with these people, the first thing you should do is take some time to regroup. Remember, no is never no. Take the information that you learned and use it to your advantage. How can you use time to strengthen your message? Can you build coalition or amplify your message in some way for it to gain traction sooner? How can you find consensus and tweak the form of your message to turn the no into a yes? What groups might be a more appropriate audience for hearing your message? Perhaps there are preliminary layers of people who need to hear your message first before the targeted audience will be in a position to hear and act on your ask? Creative problem solving and repackaging your ask will significantly increase the likelihood that your message will be received. It will also increase the likelihood that you will hear a "yes" in response to your ask.

Find Financial Solutions

The big elephant in the room, as with many things related to education, is cost. When approaching a principal, legislator, or district leader for any support or service, one of the first things they will probably ask is, "How much does it cost?"

Cost could be the one thing that makes or breaks your initiative. If you are using effective advocacy strategies and the messaging technique of problem, action, benefit, and cost, the cost could be a defining aspect. You may have the most beautifully researched and articulated problem, a reasonable action that you'd like the decision maker to take, and a very compelling benefit to students. However, if the funding source for the desired action is unknown or exorbitantly expensive, it mostly likely will not happen.

Asks that are low on costs and high on benefit are most likely to be granted.

One day I was having a conversation with a state legislator about the lack of school-based mental health professionals in his state. I was explaining the problem, outlining what action I think needed to happen, and how the action would benefit students. The legislator kept nodding politely and I could tell that he had heard this message before. However, I didn't stop there. I went on to explain that funds could be taken from this specific federal bucket of funds, from this specific state bucket of funds, and from this specific local bucket of funds. I said, "we can braid them together and structurally come up with a long-term solution to fund our initiative!"

The legislator stopped nodding his head and just stared at me. I began to get very nervous and thought one of two things: 1) I overstepped and shouldn't have told the legislator how to fund the action, or 2) I completely misunderstood how the funding streams worked. The legislator started laughing and said, "You don't know how rare this is! You've identified a problem, found a solution, and then found a way to pay for it!"

I took this comment to heart and added it to my advocacy toolbox. Now, with every initiative I advocate for, I include a financial solution. This reduces financial problem solving on the decision maker's part, or at least gives them a starting point from which to work from. If there is no cost associated, I make sure to explicitly mention that, too.

Grants are a great way to pay for school-based mental health initiatives. The primary drawback to grant funds is that they are time bound and are only available for a specific amount of time. However, if you can use the funds as seed money to establish your initiative and begin to grow it, more stable funds may be provided after the grant timeline expires.

Most of the instances of "no" I've come across over the years have not been "no" because they weren't good ideas. Usually there was a cost associated with it that was insurmountable. Or I was ahead of my time and had to wait a year or two to get all the necessary stakeholders on board. Or something about the idea needed to be tweaked to be more palatable to decision makers or community groups. Or I was barking up the wrong tree. If you hear no, identify why it was a no and strategize forward using this information.

Controlling the Advocacy Narrative

Sometimes, it is not enough to simply stay on top of an issue, sometimes you have to get ahead of it. During the advocacy process you will get curve balls thrown at you where you think to yourself, "where in the world is this coming from?!?" Someone will post a message on Twitter signaling to the world that something other than what you are advocating for is the way to go. The problem with curveballs is that they can derail the carefully cultivated message you have created surrounding your issue.

One way to keep your message on track is to control the narrative and strategize ahead. Curveballs or not, controlling the public messaging surrounding an issue can help build support while keeping your initiative moving forward. This signals two things: one, you've done your research and have data to support your ask; and two, you are a consistent and accurate voice on the subject. If your messaging waffles and you seem to switch back and forth on an issue, you lose credibility. Period. There are certainly times when flexibility is needed and refining or building on messaging is needed. This is a normal part of the policy making process. However, you should never do a complete 180-degree turn in your messaging. This signals that you were unsure to begin with, and you will lose trust with policy makers, key decision makers, and the public.

If you do receive a curveball there are several approaches to take. One is to simply ignore it. If the message is not credible it won't get any traction. A second approach is to find out more why the message was made. Understanding the context will help with solution navigation and joint understanding. This is a good way to turn a potential opponent into an ally. A third approach is to reach out to your allies and find out their stance on the curveball. A joint response made by like organizations in response to the curveball can carry greater weight than one voice alone might. A last option is to publicly refute the position of the curveball. This should be exercised with caution as it can backfire and end up making you or your association look like you are the ones in the wrong.

Be prepared for the various responses you may hear from decision makers after you deploy your message. Whether you hear silence, contact from a decision maker, or "no", these are all typical responses and are part of the policy making process. Rarely does no ever truly mean no. Identify the why behind the no and problem solve ahead. There are always creative ways to keep an initiative moving forward.

Based on the key learning objectives, I can now:

- Explain how to turn a no into a yes.
- Understand how coalitions can help amplify an initiative's cause.
- Describe the four advocacy action components of Phase 2.
- Repackage an "ask" to keep it viable and move it forward.
- Understand why potential costs must be considered with any initiative.

References

Coalition for Community Schools & National Association of School Psychologists. (2016). *Nine elements of effective school community partnerships to address student mental health, physical health, and overall wellness* [White paper]. Authors.

DeLeon, P. H., Loftis, C. W., Ball, V., & Sullivan, M. J. (2006). Navigating politics, policy, and procedure: A firsthand perspective of advocacy on behalf of the profession. *Professional Psychology: Research and Practice, 37*(2), 146–153. https://doi.org/10.1037/0735-7028.37.2.146

Dockweiler, K. A. (2018). Responding to tragedy through stakeholder communication networks. *Communiqué, 46*(7), 26.

Grapin, S. L., & Shriberg, D. (2020). International perspectives on social justice: Introduction to the special issue. *School Psychology International, 41*(1), 3–12. https://doi.org/10.1177/0143034319897359

9

ADVOCACY ACTION PHASE 3
Puzzle Management

Learning Concepts

In this chapter, readers will learn:

- Why levers must be managed.
- How to track a policy's implementation.
- The importance on ongoing messaging.
- That the phases will often repeat.
- How to align specific issues with the different levers.

Chapter Keywords

- Puzzle Management
- Feedback loop
- Practice advocacy

Now that you've got all the puzzle pieces assembled together and a picture is beginning to emerge, what do you do? Managing the various pieces to keep the picture looking like you want will be critical.

DOI: 10.4324/9781003308515-11

Puzzle Management is Phase 3 of the advocacy action plan. Monitoring levers, tracking implementation, continuing messaging, and repeating these advocacy phases are the key features of this phase. Implementation of this phase will look different depending on your context and state. Given the great variation that exists across states and their respective levers, there is no magical formula that says, if X is true, do Y. Advocating for more mental health supports in schools would be far easier if this were the case.

In reality, however, advocacy is much more complex and nuanced. Instead, if X is true, consider exploring Y while also looking into A, B, C, and D. At the same time, speak with L, M, and N about H, I, and J. The Boomerang Policy Making Model can help organize your efforts by providing considerations for each lever and phase. Being nimble, having strong relationships, and thinking forward will go a long way as you work through these phases.

The realities of advocacy work are not meant to discourage those wanting to make change. I find the ambiguities liberating as it encourages creative problem solving and multiple pathways for solution making; hence the belief that "no is never no". Having some guidance or structure to follow as you engage in the advocacy process is beneficial. The Advocacy Action Phases help provide that structure (see Figure 9.1).

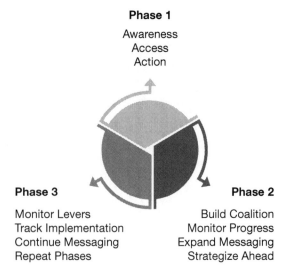

Figure 9.1 Advocacy Action Phases

As advocates we must be comfortable living in the gray spaces as very few situations are ever black and white. We must re-evaluate and repackage information to shape it into "yes" solutions. And then repeat and revise as we shift to the next lever in the process.

Monitor Levers

The first component of Phase 3 is to monitor the levers. Each lever will have its own set of conditions that will need to be considered whether it be a state lever or the school lever. Another way to conceptualize this step is to think of it as lever management. I liken this to a household full of busy people. For example, if there are several people in the household, there will be multiple schedules to coordinate any given week. School times, work commitments, after-school activities, social obligations, pets' needs, family duties, the list goes on. Managing these commitments will help you anticipate what might be coming up next and what you might need to plan for.

Managing bureaucratic levers is no different for an advocate. Coordinating timeframes, meetings, and action plans will help keep your advocacy efforts on track. Communicating with representatives from the different levers ahead of time will help lay the groundwork for when your initiative transitions into that lever.

Track Implementation

The second component of Phase 3 is to track implementation. One piece of the advocacy puzzle that often gets forgotten is the implementation piece. If your initiative passes out of one lever and into the next, there is often some implementation component that needs to happen. If there is no one monitoring that action, it may not happen. As an advocate you are not responsible for the implementation of an initiative. However, you can track its implementation to help make sure it actually happens. Monitoring and evaluating policies are critical, especially as new innovations are implemented (Gault, 2020). There is nothing worse than finally getting your initiative to pass only to find out that it was not actually implemented!

Once a policy goes through the entire policy making process and is being successfully implemented with students or at the classroom level, implementation fidelity must be considered and monitored. If the initiative is not being implemented as intended or not being implemented with fidelity, a *feedback looping* process must be in place. If there are not adequate resources, training, or tools to successfully implement the initiative, these things must be identified and provided. Or, if implementation is derailed months or years after initially starting, then efforts must be made to get implementation back on track. Policy advocacy might not be needed at this point, but practice advocacy would be. *Practice advocacy is needed when there is a policy in place, but it is not being implemented through practice.* Practice advocacy typically occurs close to the students at the district, school, or classroom level. Identify the lever that is breaking down and target practice advocacy efforts there.

It could be that these closer levers are unaware that they should be implementing the policy. If you bring it to their attention, that might be all that is needed. They will then put the structures and procedures in place for the policy to be implemented. However, if you do this and the policy is still not being translated into practice, consider reaching out for help. You may want to contact representatives from the governing body who passed the policy and let them know. They can direct you to possible next steps or to the contact person who can help reinforce the need for implementation.

When reaching out to any lever, I would refrain from overtly accusing the district, school, or classroom of not implementing the policy. Instead, I would ask what the plan is for implementing the policy and what the anticipated time frame might be for it to start. I would also suggest offering to be a resource or to answer any questions they may have as you helped support the initiative from the beginning and are familiar with the conditions in which it was passed.

Continue Messaging

The third component of Phase 3 is to continue messaging. Continuing to build and expand your messaging goes hand in hand with monitoring an initiative's progress. Depending on what you identify with your monitoring efforts, new messaging efforts may be needed. During Phase 3 you are hopefully at the end of your advocacy efforts within one lever and are preparing for your initiative to pass on to the next. You may need to do forward messaging with the next lever, or just continue to reinforce your message in the current lever.

If you are at the last lever of your journey, begin messaging about implementation steps. Once a policy is put in place it needs to translate into practice to ultimately reach the students. Offer to help with the implementation in any way that makes sense. Raising awareness on social media can also be a good way to heighten the need for practice to follow the policy.

Repeat Phases

The fourth component of Phase 3 is to repeat the phases. Your advocacy efforts may need to be repeated within a lever, or they may begin again in a subsequent lever. Whether the boomeranging is intra-lever or inter-lever, repeat the advocacy action steps of Phases 1, 2, and 3. Odds are you will not need to actively construct each component from the ground up. The components merely serve as considerations until you get familiar with what actions need to happen. After you've been through the advocacy action planning process a few times, you will probably instinctively know how to construct your key message and how to strategize ahead.

What Lever to Engage and When?

Lever management and implementation tracking can create new questions. Arising from these questions are new considerations and answers that must be determined before moving forward. Before heading down an advocacy path, two key questions must be considered:

- What lever is being impacted?
- What lever will help solve the issue?

There may be multiple levers being impacted and multiple levers may need to be engaged. This is often the case, and each large component must be broken down into its smaller components. By analyzing the disaggregated parts, we can better determine how the various levers are impacted. You can also determine how many levers to engage and how to approach stakeholders with your ask. This will help facilitate and expedite the determined solution. Below are some guiding questions to ask as part of the lever analysis:

Is the issue created by a policy or by a practice? This is a common issue that can impact how mental health services are delivered. The solution will differ depending on if the issue was created by policy or by practice. If the difficulty lies with a poorly crafted policy, the policy will most likely need to be targeted for change. If the difficulty lies with a poorly implemented policy, the implementation practice would need to change. Poorly drafted policies are often difficult to implement or just don't get implemented at all. If you've identified that the policy needs to be revised, this would be a good place to start your advocacy efforts. Poorly drafted policies are rarely implemented well as they were flawed to begin with. Issues with implementation fidelity, ambiguity of responsibilities, and accountability all arise from poorly written policies.

If the issue is a policy issue, who made the policy? Answers to this question might include state legislatures, state regulatory boards, local school boards, or school leaders. Once this answer is determined, you have found your lever in which to target your advocacy efforts. The closer the lever is to students, the easier and faster it will be to change the policy. For example, if the policy issue resides at the school level it can be a much quicker change to make than if the policy issue resides at the state legislative level.

If the issue is a practice issue, who controls implementation of the policy? In most cases there is a general hierarchy of policy making to refer to. If policies are made at the state level, most school districts are in charge of the implementation, especially if they are local control states. In these states, the policy is set at the state level (statutory or regulatory) and implementation is controlled by the school districts and/or local school boards. The district superintendent or school board will determine how a particular policy will be implemented, or what procedures will need to be put in place to support the policy. In this case, if the issue identified is a practice issue, then appealing to the district superintendent and/or school board can bring about change.

If the issue were to be brought to the attention of a decision maker at a higher lever, such as the state superintendent or state school board, they would most likely tell you that they do not have purview over your identified practice issue. They would then direct you to your district superintendent and/or local school board. Sometimes it is easy to back-map who controls implementation of a particular policy. In cases where it is not clear, always feel free to reach out to the decision makers who passed the policy, and they can help navigate the policy-to-practice implementation web.

If the issue is a state policy issue, is it statutory or regulatory? States have statutory governing bodies, such as state legislatures, and regulatory governing bodies, such as state boards of education. The exact terminology of these two entities may vary slightly, but the duties and authorities are fairly consistent across states. Bills are passed through state legislatures into laws called state statutes. Additional details of laws are often delegated to state boards of education for regulatory considerations. States generally have two code books or sets of laws, one for statutes and one for regulations. For example, in Nevada there is the Nevada Revised Statutes (for statutes) and the Nevada Administrative Code (for regulations). If you don't know how your state level laws are coded, I encourage you to find out where your statutes and regulations are located online and how to search within them.

For example, in 2019 Senate Bill 89 was passed in Nevada as part of a school safety omnibus bill. One provision of the bill was that "nonbinding ratios be set for all SISP categories by the State Board of Education". This was codified into the Nevada Revised Statutes (NRS 388.890) and sent to the Nevada State Board of Education for the ratios to be determined by regulation. In 2020 nonbinding SISP ratios were passed in alignment with national best practice recommendations and entered into the Nevada Administrative Code.

If concerns arise and a change to the ratios is wanted, a request to change these ratios does not need to be brought to the state legislature. The Nevada State Board of Education has the authority to change the ratios themselves so the request to change ratios would be a regulatory issue. If issues arise with the part of the law concerning the need to establish ratios, this would be a statutory issue and would need to be changed through the state legislature.

Conversely, Kentucky has a statute that requires goal ratios for school counselors. Under the School Safety and Resiliency Act (Senate Bill 1, 2019), schools are required at minimum to hire "at least one school counselor in each school with the goal of having one school counselor for every 250 students". While it does later include school psychologists and school social workers under a defining category of school-based mental health service providers, it does not explicitly require ratios for these professions. The intent to establish ratios for these professions may have been present when the bill passed, but they were not included. Now, if advocates want to have ratios for school psychologists and school social workers provided for by law, they will have to find a bill sponsor to make a statutory change.

Is the issue a higher education issue? Across the United States the most common issue I hear surrounding school-based mental health providers is that there just aren't enough of them. This is predominately a result of having too few higher education training programs. This is true for school psychologist programs, school counseling programs, and school social worker programs. Underlying all higher education issues are typically funding constraints, which lead to difficulty staffing and expanding programs. For example, in Oregon, school psychology programs are being reduced, with programs being eliminated altogether. This leads to a domino effect of issues that must be tackled comprehensively. Within the higher education lever, subsequent questions must be asked relative to who controls the funding decisions, what role does the state legislature play, and what role do higher education regulatory boards have? Is it an institutional challenge with issues that lie at the president, provost, or dean level? Once these questions have been answered additional explorations within the levers can transpire.

Is the issue a municipal issue? In some cases there may be a municipal policy that needs to be addressed as it is impacts how services are delivered to students in the schools. This may include how wrap-around services are coordinated within the community or how they are funded. Oftentimes, municipalities are not the *source* of any particular issue, but can be a *solution* to an issue. For example, there may be grant funds available to local communities for mental health and wellness prevention. If the school district or an individual school can apply for, and receive, the funds it may alleviate existing issues. Memorandums of understanding (MOUs) or memorandums of agreement (MOAs) are another way to maximize resources and bring in additional supports to students. This may be in the form of school-based clinics or coordination of Medicaid billing. States such as South Carolina are leveraging their local and state partnerships. Approximately 60% of South Carolina's schools have mental health clinicians from the Department of Mental Health (Franke et el., 2021). Many opportunities at the school-municipal level can be brainstormed as this is frequently no-man's-land. If no partnerships, agreements, policies, or practices exist at this level it doesn't mean that there shouldn't be any. It just means that the door is wide open for new ideas, and it is the perfect opportunity to explore what possibilities could exist.

Is the issue a district or school issue? The key hallmark of this issue is who is the decision maker? If the principal has the authority to select the mental health supports it wants in its school, start with the principal. However, if the district is selecting and determining the mental health supports for all its schools, the principal may not have much voice in what gets selected. In both cases it is wise to start the conversation with the principal. They will know whether or not the thing you are proposing falls within their jurisdiction, or if it will need to be approved or selected from a higher level. If the decision-making power rests at the district level, the principal could be a key ally for your proposed initiative. They can propose your idea to the district's key decision makers who can determine if it is a viable option. While the principal may not be an actual decision maker in this case, they can be part of the solution-seeking process.

Is the issue a classroom issue? Teachers can have incredible discretion relative to instruction and activities within their own classroom. When mental health initiatives are passed at the state level and the district puts procedures in place to outline implementation parameters, it is still the classroom teacher who delivers the support. Or, in the case with mental health supports, it could be the school counselor, school psychologist, or school social worker; or a combination of the teaching staff and the school-based mental health staff. Either way, there is usually some flexibility in delivery of the support and translating the outlined procedure into practice. While delivering a support consistently across a school is important, so is understanding the unique context of classrooms. Mental health supports might be provided in each classroom, but some classrooms may require additional or more intensive supports. Understanding these tiers of support is important for adequately addressing students' unique mental health needs.

Based on the key learning objectives, I can now:

- Identify what happens when levers aren't managed.
- Understand how policies do not get implemented.
- Describe why ongoing messaging is important.
- Explain why phase repetition is important.
- Align issues to their corresponding lever.

References

Franke, K. B., Paton, M., & Weist, M. (2021). Building policy support for school mental health in South Carolina. *School Psychology Review*, 50(1), 110–121. doi:10.1080/2372966X.2020.1819756

Gault, F. (2020). *Measuring innovation everywhere: The challenge of better policy, learning, evaluation and monitoring.* Edward Elgar Publishing.

Senate Bill 1, Kentucky 2019.

Senate Bill 89, Nevada 2019.

SECTION III

LEVELS IN ACTION

10

ONE STATE'S POLICY JOURNEY

Expanding Access to School-Based Mental Health Providers From the Federal Level to the Classroom

Learning Concepts

In this chapter, readers will learn:

- How large-scale efforts might align at multiple levers of policy making.
- That each lever of the policy making process plays a critical role in implementing a policy.
- How advocates can work with the state and local education agencies to support policy making.
- That districts and schools have authority to devise implementation solutions that align with an initiative.
- The conceptual impact of multiple policies supporting each other.

Chapter Keywords

- ARTERY Pipeline Framework
- Psychological services assistant

DOI: 10.4324/9781003308515-13

- Specialized instructional support personnel
- Ratio improvement plans

Intentional alignment of policies at all levers is critical for effective implementation of large-scale initiatives such as workforce development pipelines and programs. The following narrative outlines how one state prioritized their school-based mental health workforce and began making policy changes to support their initiative. The overall initiative aligns with the ARTERY Pipeline Framework (Dockweiler, 2019) and supports implementation at several levels.

At each lever, the policies look different; however, they still maintain alignment to the overall intent of the initiative. As you read through the subsequent chapters, please feel free to refer back to this example to get a sense for how policies at one lever impact policy and practice in another. Reflecting on the policy in context will lend deeper understanding and application to your own policy situation. You may also notice that some of these recommendations appear in subsequent chapters. This allows for a deeper dive into the policy recommendations presented here and offers opportunity for greater reflection and discussion.

Boomerang Policy Making was used to achieve the following policies and practices. The advocacy action phases were used repeatedly to develop key messages, present asks, and follow up every step of the way. These basic processes will serve you well as you engage in the process yourself. Build relationships, determine the scope of efforts, and boomerang away!

Federal

Most policies are not initiated at the federal level, most are created at the state and local levels. However, while policy making follows an established pattern at each lever, there is great value in revisiting previous levers. For instance, while the following policy examples were initiated at the state legislative level with subsequent regulatory and local policies put in place, federal funds were sought to support their implementation *after* the policies had passed. Specifically, the federal School-Based Mental

Health Services grant (Office of Elementary and Secondary Education, 2020) was awarded to the Nevada Department of Education (2020a) and helped support local education agency implementation and efforts on behalf of institutes of higher education, including the *ARTERY Pipeline Framework*. A coalition of state professional associations, professionals, higher education professionals, and local education agency leaders came together and helped the state education agency with a comprehensive plan and application.

State Statutes

At the statutory level, having policies that address the following key topics will set a solid foundation for your SBMH workforce efforts. If your state does not have these in policy yet, a bill sponsor could build them into one bill focused on school-based mental health providers. If some of these policies already exist, the missing components could be added to an existing law. Sometimes it is easier to add to, or modify, an existing law than to create a new one.

- Establish ratios
- Implement ratio improvement plans
- Outline required components of a ratio improvement plan
- Create accountability reporting and metrics for the ratio improvement plans
- Define professional roles, licensing, and continuing education for the three SBMH professions in accordance with their respective national practice models
- Establish paid internships
- Allocate state funds to financially incentivize national certification

These seven components are all in place in Nevada and are spread across four different laws and two different legislative sessions. For each legislative session, there has also been an appropriations bill that includes funding for a 5% salary increase for educators who are nationally certified. Each session, school-based mental health providers have been successful in being included in those appropriations.

Nevada State Senate Bill 89 (2019, enacted). This was a large school safety and wellness omnibus bill with many different sections. Physical safety and student wellness initiatives were both included in the bill. Section 7 outlines language relative to the ARTERY, expanding access to school-based mental health providers, and workforce development. This language was codified into NRS 388.890 and also required regulatory changes.

> Sec. 7. 1. The State Board shall develop nonbinding recommendations for the ratio of pupils to specialized instructional support personnel in this State for kindergarten and grades 1 to 12, inclusive. The board of trustees of each school district shall develop a 15-year strategic plan to achieve the ratio of pupils to specialized instructional support personnel in the district.
>
> 2. The recommendations developed by the State Board must:
>
> (a) Prescribe a suggested ratio of pupils per each type of specialized instructional support personnel in kindergarten and grades 1 to 12, inclusive;
>
> (b) Be based on evidence-based national standards; and
>
> (c) Take into account the unique needs of certain pupils, including, without limitation, pupils who are English learners.

Nevada State Senate Bill 319 (2019, enacted). The following language details the intent of the entire bill. There are eight different sections that provide specifics relative to each profession. This language was codified into NRS 391.293–391.296.

> AN ACT relating to education; defining "school counselor," "school psychologist" and "school social worker" for certain purposes; establishing the duties of a school counselor, psychologist and social worker; and providing other matters properly relating thereto.

Nevada State Senate Bill 151 (2021, enacted). This bill expanded on SB89 (2019) and the requirement for local school boards to develop *ratio improvement plans.* Accountability domains, reporting requirements, and progress toward meeting ratios are all included. There was also a section about continuing education requirements for SBMH professions. This language was codified into NRS 388.892 and also required regulatory changes.

> AN ACT relating to education; requiring the boards of trustees of certain school districts to develop a plan to improve certain pupil to personnel ratios; requiring the boards of trustees of certain school districts to submit an annual report on the plan to the Department of Education; requiring the Department to compile and submit the reports to certain governmental entities; requiring school counselors, school psychologists and school social workers to complete certain continuing education; requiring the Commission on Professional Standards in Education and the Board of Examiners for Social Workers to adopt certain regulations; and providing other matters properly relating thereto.

Nevada State Senate Bill 352 (2021, enacted). This bill was proposed to support paraprofessionals during their student teaching. If your state or local districts employ *Psychological Services Assistants* (PSA), this bill language could work for you. If your state or local district does not currently have a PSA position, this model language could be used as an advocacy tool to institutionalize the position into law as well as to grow your pipeline. From Section 1, subsection 1(m); this language was codified into NRS 391.019.

> Authorizing a person who is employed by a public school to provide support or other services relating to school psychology, if the person does not hold a license or endorsement as a school psychologist but is enrolled in a program that would allow the person to obtain such a license or endorsement, to complete a program of internship in school psychology while remaining employed in such a position.

State Regulations

Following these model policies for school-based mental health providers we arrive at the regulatory level. Senate Bills 89 (2019) and 151 (2021) had regulatory components that had to be developed once the bills were passed and signed into law by the Governor.

2019 Regulation

Recall from the bill language (SB89, 2019) above:

> Sec. 7. 1. The State Board of Education shall develop non-binding recommendations for the ratio of pupils to specialized instructional support personnel in this State for kindergarten and grades 1 to 12, inclusive . . .
> 2. The recommendations developed by the State Board must:
> (a) Prescribe a suggested ratio of pupils per each type of specialized instructional support personnel in kindergarten and grades 1 to 12, inclusive;
> (b) Be based on evidence-based national standards; and
> (c) Take into account the unique needs of certain pupils, including, without limitation, pupils who are English learners.

To support the State Board of Education to determine what these ratios might be, the Nevada Department of Education (2020) gave a presentation outlining who specialized instructional support personnel where, what their current ratios were, and what national best practice recommends.

From the Nevada Revised Statutes (NRS 388.890): "*Specialized instructional support personnel* includes persons employed by each school to provide necessary services such as assessment, diagnosis, counseling, educational services, therapeutic services and related services, as defined in 20 U.S.C. § 1401(26), to pupils."

Current ratios were shared along with national best practice ratios. In April 2020 the State Board of Education adopted national best practice ratios for the following professional domains:

- School psychologists at the 1:500 ratio
- School counselors at the 1:250 ratio
- School social workers at the 1:250 ratio
- School nurses at the 1:750 ratio

The establishment of these ratios boomeranged to the next phase of the policy implementation process. The State Department of Education began working on a guidance document for local education agencies surrounding the relevant statutes, regulations, and suggested action steps.

2021 Regulation

Recall from the bill language (SB151, 2021) above that the Commission on Professional Standards in Education and the Board of Examiners for Social Workers will adopt continuing education requirements for school psychologists, school counselors, and school social workers. Specifically, from Chapter 2 of the bill:

> Each school counselor and school psychologist shall complete continuing education as determined by the Commission. . . . Each school social worker shall complete continuing education as determined by the Board of Examiners for Social Workers.
>
> To support the Commission on Professional Standards in Education to determine what these continuing education criteria might be, the Nevada Department of Education (2022) gave a presentation with suggested regulation language to consider. The suggested language shared information about each professions' national standards and how the standards aligned with the Nevada Educator Performance Framework for each profession.

This bill is an example of how two different divisions can support school-based mental health services. In this case, continuing education requirements for school psychologists and school counselors were to be determined through a regulatory board of education. Similarly, continuing education requirements for school social workers were to be determined through the Nevada Board of Examiners for Social Workers.

State Education Agency

Each of the four statutes that passed into law, and the two corresponding regulations, required action on behalf of the Department of Education.

The first immediate action was to begin aligning statewide efforts, policies, and procedures to the newly passed statutes. Additional actions included preparation of presentation materials, guidance documents, and ongoing monitoring.

Ratio Improvement Actions

Relative to the ratios and ratio improvement plans statutory laws (SB89, 2019; SB151, 2021), the Department of Education began collecting data in preparation for a presentation to the State Board of Education. They also accessed existing stakeholder networks, such as the Nevada School Counselor Association, the Nevada Association of School Psychologists, the Nevada School Social Worker Association, and the Nevada School Nurse Association for their input regarding national best practice ratios for their respective professions. Once the presentation was made and the ratios were passed into regulation, the department went to work on a guidance document for the local education agencies. They again collaborated with the four state associations and other stakeholder groups to produce a comprehensive version of a guide as well as a short reference document.

The thinking behind the guidance document was that implementation could happen with greater efficacy if there was a suggested outline for districts to follow. Additionally, improving ratios in the districts also had to involve the higher education institutes, not just the school districts. With fewer higher education institutes than school districts, the school districts would have to communicate and collaborate with these institutes to increase the number of training programs to produce the number of graduates to begin inching closer to the established ratios.

Continuing Education Actions

Relative to continuing education requirements (SB151, 2021), the department began collecting data in preparation for a presentation to the Commission on Professional Standards in Education. In collaboration with the Nevada School Counselor Association and the Nevada Association of School Psychologists, recommendations were created that align with national best practice domains and state licensing requirements.

Licensing Actions

Relative to licensing and paid internships for support professionals (SB151, 2021; SB352, 2021), the department was contacted by stakeholder groups to support regulatory work required by the statutes. Representatives from Nevada State College, the Clark County School District, and the Nevada Association of School Psychologists reached out to the department, specifically the licensing division, to share ideas about proposed regulation. The department was receptive to these proposed regulation changes as they supported the foundation work begun with SB151 (2019) and SB352 (2021). Proposed regulatory changes relative to the licensing of school psychology support professionals (Psychological Services Assistants) and school psychology students completing their internship were presented by the Department of Education (2022) to the Commission on Professional Standards in Education and are currently waiting official regulatory adoption.

The department continues to support and monitor the statewide implementation efforts of these statutes and regulations from their role as the state education agency. Transitioning from the foundational policies put in place to support expanding access to school-based mental health providers, institutes of higher education and local education agencies take over as the boots-on-the-ground implementors of the laws.

Institutes of Higher Education

The combined policy work surrounding ratio improvement and workforce development triggered a massive campaign to create more higher education training programs in the state. With the true need of school-based mental health professionals identified, it was a huge shock to the education community to realize how significant the shortages were.

One institute adopted the ARTERY Pipeline Framework and began creating career pathways for school-based mental health professionals with funding from the U.S. Department of Education's School-Based Mental Health Services grant program. Additional grant funding opportunities are currently pending. Elected officials, including members of Nevada's Congressional delegation and state legislature, have publicly voiced support for expanding access to career pathways for school-based mental health careers. Their public support further amplifies the need for these professions and increases likelihood for program expansion, funding, and related solutions to address the shortages.

Local Education Agencies

Local education agencies in Nevada, or school districts, are now required by law to align their local policies and practices with these four statutes and two regulations. In some cases new policies were created, and in other cases old polices were revised.

Relative to their workforce, districts must strive for hiring ratios that align with the recommendations passed by the State Board of Education. In school districts with a population of 100,000 or more, they are also required to implement a ratio improvement plan. They must demonstrate progress toward these ratios in an annual report to the Department of Education who then prepares a report for the Governor. In odd years, the department will also submit a report to the Director of the Legislative Counsel Bureau to share with the Senate and Assembly Standing Committees on Education. In even years, the department also prepares a report that is submitted to the Legislative Committee on Education and the State Board.

Specifics of what must be included are provided for within SB151 (2021). These specific accountability domains and reporting mechanisms are critical for monitoring progress and transparency of efforts. It also helps identify challenges toward implementation and opportunities for additional support. For example, they help to identify whether support from institutes of higher education is needed or additional state level policies.

In order to meet the recommended ratios, districts can change their hiring and position allocation processes. They can create policies that fund school psychology positions at a 1:500 ratio, and school counselor and school social work positions at a 1:250 ratio. This will most likely change their overall budgeting numbers and will need to be accounted for over time. In most districts, positions are allocated at a much higher number of students. For example, instead of allocating one school psychology position for every 500 students, districts often allocate one position for every 1,800 students. Reducing this number will increase the amount of money that needs to be set aside for school-based mental health provider positions.

Creating or expanding the psychological services support position is a cost-effective way for districts to work toward ratios, increase access for students, and support a pipeline of school-based mental health professionals. Institutionalizing through policy the creation or allocation of this Psychological Services Assistant (PSA) position is another policy change districts can make.

Also, in alignment with PSA support is to offer paid internships. This includes PSAs who are in the pipeline and training to be school psychologists. Districts can offer paid internships to these individuals under SB352 (2021) to retain their pay and benefits while they undergo their internship in school psychology. This is a highly attractive retention and recruitment strategy because most internships are unpaid. If a PSA can work full-time for a district with benefits while earning into the retirement system, they can continue at this level of pay and benefits during their internships. This prevents students from taking out excessive student loans, not completing their internship, or experiencing financial hardship. It also entices them to stay in the state as they are already engaged in the state retirement system.

In addition to the 5% annual salary increase provided for in the legislature's appropriation's bill, districts can choose to offer an additional percent increase and a retention bonus for employees who remain in the district. This further supports retention and recruitment of these hard to fill positions. Creating district level policy to reflect these financial benefits is another recommendation.

Finally, assigning mentors to early career practitioners and compensating supervisions who are assigned practicum and internship students is another great policy to practice recommendation. Districts can come up with any number of creative strategies to meet initiative requirements.

School

At the school level, teams are impacted by the four statutes and two regulations passed. Awareness of state and district policy, and what expectations are at the school level is critical for building leaders. For example, in the case of PSAs being eligible for paid internships at their current salary and benefits rate, awareness is key. While the funds for this may, or may not, come out of their budget, remaining aware of the possibilities can make a significant difference in a professional's life.

If your school has complete hiring and funding discretion, it can create and fund the PSA position itself. It can also choose to pay school-based mental health professionals annual salary increases or bonuses. Foster relationships with higher education training programs and offer to take their practicum and internship students onto your campus. Allow school-based mental health providers to practice within the comprehensive scope of their professional practice model. Do not pigeonhole them into doing recess duty or discipline. Utilize all facets of their training, specifically the full range of mental health supports and services.

If possible, hire providers at your school in alignment with the state adopted ratios. This work might need to start small with the goal of one school counselor, one school psychologist, and one school social worker each working full-time on a campus five days a week. This can then work to be increased to hiring at the recommended ratios. For example, if your children attend a middle school with 1,000 students, the goal would be to have the following full-time staff: two school psychologists, four school counselors, and four school social workers.

Having recommended ratios in practice improves the overall school and classroom environment. In the classroom, students and teachers feel supported. Teachers can teach, and students can learn. Fewer students exhibit externalized and internalized behaviors, and those who do can get the help they need. This help can be provided by a team of school-based mental health providers who can provide the targeted and/or intense supports that the student, and possibly the family, may need.

With adequate school-based mental health ratios, teachers are not trying to provide these well-being supports on their own. Additionally, instructional delivery does not risk being compromised due to the severe mental health needs of a few students.

Conclusion

Many policies can be created at the building level. However, many large-scale initiatives require multiple levels of policy making. These policies must support each other and align with the intent of the initiative. As state policies trickle down to local policies, districts and schools can have strong influence over the policies that get made. Advocates are encouraged to work at all levels to assist with alignment and implementation of best practices.

Based on the key learning objectives, I can now:

- Explain how large-scale efforts might align and how pitfalls may occur at the various levers of policy making.
- Describe how each lever may contribute to implementation of a large-scale initiative.
- Identify advocacy opportunities at the state and local levels to support policy making.
- Describe how districts and schools might create their own policies to support a large-scale initiative.
- Conceptualize how formalizing initiatives through policy can create an interconnected foundation for best practices to thrive.

References

Dockweiler, K. A. (2019). *School psychologist pipeline framework ARTERY: Active Recruitment, Training, and Educator Retention to serve our Youth.* Nevada Department of Education [Virtual].

Nevada Department of Education. (October 13, 2020a). *Nevada Department of Education receives federal grant to support student mental health* [Press release]. https://doe.nv.gov/News__Media/Press_Releases/2020/Nevada_Department_of_Education_Receives_Federal_Grant_to_Support_Student_Mental_Health/

Nevada Department of Education. (2020b). *Non-binding recommended ratios for specialized instructional support personnel (SISP).* State Board of Education Meeting, Las Vegas, Nevada. https://doe.nv.gov/uploaded Files/ndedoenvgov/content/Boards_Commissions_Councils/

State_Board_of_Education/2020/April/Follow-upSISPRatiosper SB%2089.pdf

Nevada Department of Education. (2022). *Commission on Professional Standards workshop materials.* Commission on Professional Standards in Education Meeting, Las Vegas, Nevada. https://doe.nv.gov/upload edFiles/ndedoenvgov/content/Boards_Commissions_Councils/ Commission_on_Professional_Standards/2022/May/NAC%20391. 319%20Psychology%20NAC%20391.xxx%20Psychology%20 Assistant.pdf

Nevada Revised Statutes 388.890, 2019.

Office of Elementary and Secondary Education. (2020). *School-Based Mental Health Services Grant Program. U.S. Department of Education.* https:// oese.ed.gov/offices/office-of-formula-grants/safe-supportive-schools/ school-based-mental-health-services-grant-program/awards/

Senate Bill 89, Nevada 2019.

Senate Bill 319, Nevada 2019.

Senate Bill 151, Nevada 2021.

Senate Bill 352, Nevada 2021.

11

FEDERAL ENGAGEMENT

Learning Concepts

In this chapter, readers will learn:

- How the federal government influences mental health professionals and supports in schools.
- The roles different federal entities play in the policy making process.
- Different approaches to fund school-based mental health initiatives.
- Ways to engage their congressional delegation.
- To think big about advocacy and the asks that are possible at the federal level.

Chapter Keywords

- Act
- Federal grant
- Sub-awardee
- Earmark

DOI: 10.4324/9781003308515-14

What is the Federal Role in Education?

Oftentimes it is difficult to identify how exactly the federal government influences mental health services in schools. They don't train professionals or directly implement mental health supports in schools, so what exactly is their role? How can we advocate at the federal level to best support students?

Broadly speaking, when we are talking about the federal role in education, we are talking about the role of Congress and the role of the U.S. Department of Education. Just like your state legislature passes laws that your state department of education is responsible for carrying out, Congress passes laws that the U.S. Department of Education is responsible for carrying out. Advocacy can occur at the congressional level with your state delegation, and it can happen at the department level with representatives from the U.S. Department of Education.

Bills that must go through the House and the Senate are generally referred to as "Acts". Once an Act is passed and the President signs it, the bill becomes a law. Have you heard the expression "it will take an Act of Congress"? The often lengthy process of getting a bill to pass is where that expression comes from. With this expression, "*act*" refers to a noun, a law, not a verb, to do.

To better understand the congressional process, here is an excerpt from the U.S. House of Representatives (2021) website:

> Laws begin as ideas. First, a representative sponsors a bill. The bill is then assigned to a committee for study. If released by the committee, the bill is put on a calendar to be voted on, debated or amended. If the bill passes by simple majority (218 of 435), the bill moves to the Senate. In the Senate, the bill is assigned to another committee and, if released, debated and voted on. Again, a simple majority (51 of 100) passes the bill. Finally, a conference committee made of House and Senate members works out any differences between the House and Senate versions of the bill. The resulting bill returns to the House and Senate for final approval. The Government Printing Office prints the revised bill in a process called enrolling. The President has 10 days to sign or veto the enrolled bill.

The federal role may be enacting policies themselves, such as the Individuals with Disabilities Education Act or the Every Student Succeeds

Act. They may also be fiscal in nature and provide funds to states for specific purposes, such as school-based mental health services. If you are advocating for a particular issue, have a new idea, or require funding to support an initiative, never hesitate to reach out to your state's congressional delegation or the U.S. Department of Education as they may be able to lend support at the federal level.

Tips for Funding

There are several ways that the federal government can offer fiscal support for school-based mental health supports and providers. Funds will typically come from the U.S. Department of Education or the U.S. Department of Health and Human Services. Within the U.S. Department of Education funding sources may include the Every Student Succeeds Act or grant programs. Within the U.S. Department of Health and Human Services, funding sources may include Centers for Medicare and Medicaid Services, Substance Abuse and Mental Health Services Administration Grants, or Centers for Disease Control and Prevention Grants (Rafa et al., 2021).

It is perfectly fine to broadly advocate for more funding for education or school-based mental health. However, if you have a specific purpose in which you envision the money could be used to benefit students and communities, pursue that. When planning your advocacy efforts to include federal funding, think big. Federal funding opportunities can help fund entire programs and produce large-scale results. If you are looking for more social-emotional learning support in your child's school, federal advocacy and funding may not be your direct solution. However, if you wanted to support the creation of an entire social-emotional learning department within your school district in partnership with a local higher education institute, federal advocacy and funding could be a great fit.

Education funds may be allocated directly to states or local agencies depending on how the law is written and how the funds are intended to be used. In addition to direct allocation, funds can also be offered to agencies through a competitive grant process. The three funding sources offered below are high-level, and more specific information for each can be found from the awarding agency. Additional information is also available when the call for applications is released, and applications are being accepted. Broadly speaking, there are grants that are available directly from the U.S. Department of Education, grants from funds delegated for the state to release, and earmarked community funds for specific projects.

Grants from U.S. Department of Education

The U.S. Department of Education offers a plethora of grant opportunities, including discretionary grants, student loans or grants, and formula grants. Discretionary grants are the ones most closely align with school-based mental health services and providers and are offered on a competitive basis. Applicants must make sure they are qualifying entities and meet the application requirements. Typically, recipients include organizations such as, but not limited to, higher education institutes, local education agencies, or non-profits. There are six different offices within the U.S. Department of Education that the grants may originate from:

1. Institute of Education Sciences
2. Office of Elementary and Secondary Education
3. Office of Post-Secondary Education
4. Office of Special Education and Rehabilitative Services
5. Office of Career, Technical, and Adult Education
6. Office of English Language Acquisition

Additional information can be found at the U.S. Department of Education's funding opportunities website: https://www2.ed.gov/fund/grant/find/edlite-forecast.html.

Grants from State-Delegated Funds

The federal government will also delegate funds to states to offer as grants to sub-awardees in their states. They may also offer grants directly to local education agencies. Specific to school-based mental health workforce development is the Mental Health Service Professional Demonstration grant program (Office of Elementary and Secondary Education, 2019) eligible to local districts. There is also the School-Based Mental Health

Services grant program (Office of Elementary and Secondary Education, 2022). Under this grant, the eligible recipient is state education agencies. The grant specified that the state agency was able to maintain 10% of the funds to execute duties at the state level, and 90% of the funds were offered as grants to local education agencies and institutes of higher education to support increasing the number of school-based mental health providers in their state. In 2020 six states received this grant: Nevada, Rhode Island, Wisconsin, Ohio, Virginia, and New Mexico. Efforts can be small in scale or larger in scale depending on the size and needs of the sub-applicant. For more information about each of these six states' efforts, I encourage you to read their application abstracts on the Office of Elementary and Secondary Education's (2020) web page.

Community Funding Projects

Formerly known and commonly referred to as "earmark" funds, these are monies that are set aside for certain projects that fall within priority categories. These congressionally directed priorities circumvent competitive grant processes and are written into the bill or report language itself. Basically, it is money set aside for a specific purpose. These community funding projects may serve to strategically establish a program or support what can be self-sustaining after the one-time funds expire. They must demonstrate a benefit to the greater good of the community. Non-profit entities such as institutes of higher education, local education agencies, or municipalities are all examples of qualifying applicants. This is not an exhaustive list, and you'll want to verify that your organization is able to apply before going too far down this funding path.

Federal earmarked funds were banned by Congress in February 2011 and were brought back in 2021 (Hernandez, 2011; Shutt, 2021). This certainly is not a reliable funding source, but if available and you have an idea that the funds can help support get off the ground, this could be a good option to consider. Each member of Congress can submit up to ten earmark requests. These requests are not automatically considered funded; they must first demonstrate evidence of community support and be approved by the Appropriations Committee. All earmark requests must be posted on the delegate's website. I encourage you to investigate what projects were approved in your state to get an idea for the type of projects that might be considered favorable. During fiscal year 2022, some examples of mental health projects that were funded by these earmarks include: expansion of mental health facilities, improvement of mental health care and access for children, administration of mental health trainings, and expansion of mobile crisis response teams (U.S. Appropriations Committee, 2022).

Tips for Workforce Development

Partner with local education agencies, institutes of higher education, unions, and community organizations to:

- Apply for federal grants to support SBMH workforce development using a model such as the ARTERY Pipeline Framework (Dockweiler, 2019)
- Develop or expand training programs for school psychologists, school counselors, and school social workers
- Create recruitment strategies to attract school-based mental health providers using incentivization such as tuition reimbursement or forgiveness
- Promote retention initiatives to prevent qualified professionals from leaving their professions

Tips for Mental Health Services

Build coalition with your state to request federal funds to support statewide school-based mental health programming. The federal government can play a role in the wide sweeping type of supports that are implemented at the local level, such as reading, math, or special education. However, it does not typically specify how to deliver the support, what curriculum to implement, or what program to use. It sets the guardrail by designating the type of support and leaves it up to the state or district to select the best tool or implementation method. Relative to school-based mental health, these guardrails may include the following:

- Multi-tiered systems of support
- Suicide prevention
- Anonymous tip line for students who exhibit alarming behaviors

The federal government may allocate monies to fund specifically designated supports and guardrails that can assist with implementation efforts.

Advocacy Opportunities

As mentioned earlier, advocacy opportunities exist with members of Congress and with representatives from the U.S. Department of Education. Advocacy can happen in different ways depending on the issue and your role when engaging. You may engage as an individual constituent who seeks to advocate as a member of your state community. You may engage as a content expert such as a school-based mental health professional, teacher, or principal. Or you may advocate as a representative of a group or organization, such a state school psychology association.

It is important to build relationships with representatives from your congressional delegate's office. Depending on the state you live in and the number of representatives your state has, it may make sense to create relationships with all members of the state delegation or with just your unique delegates. All states have two Senate delegates, but the number of House delegates will vary state by state. For example, New Mexico has three House of Representative delegates and two Senate delegates. Comparatively, New York has 27 House of Representative delegates and two Senate delegates. In New Mexico, it would be feasible to build relationships with all your congressional delegates, whereas in New York, that might be a more challenging task.

If possible, build relationships with delegates themselves. While this would be best case scenario, it is not always the norm. One tip I would strongly offer is this: build a relationship with someone in the delegate's inner circle. This may be the Chief of Staff or the Communications Manager. Regardless of their title, it needs to be someone in the delegate's inner circle who can be your point of contact and provide you with access to the delegate. These staffers play a critical role of gatekeeper and can provide you with access to the delegate where access may otherwise be difficult to obtain.

Delegates always want to hear from their constituents; that is their job. Gatekeeping is simply a necessary evil in that the delegate can't be everywhere at once or attend to every constituent at the same time. If there are specific issues that are happening in your state and you have a very specific ask of the delegate, you have a better chance getting an audience with the delegate if you already have a relationship with them or with one of their key staffers.

Oftentimes if you have a leadership role within an organization and the delegate has an existing relationship with the organization, you have a better chance of getting an audience. For example, if you are the new PTA president of your state's PTA, and the delegate has an existing relationship with your PTA group and the past president, you are much more likely to get an audience in a timely manner. In this case the relationship is with the role or the organization, not with you as a constituent.

Depending on what you are advocating for, it may make sense to advocate as part of a larger group representing a larger voice. This is where state associations can hold great power and may have access where individuals would not. For example, advocating to your state's congressional delegation on behalf of your state school counselor, school social worker, or school psychology association would be more powerful than advocating as an individual content expert. Each form of advocacy is needed and impactful. As part of your planning during the Advocacy Action Phases, determine how to best formulate your message, how to deliver it, and how to build coalition to best advance your initiative.

To support student well-being and school safety, the National Association of School Psychologists (2019, p. 59) recommends federal advocacy center around the following points:

- Increase investments in Title I of ESSA to help mitigate the negative impact of poverty and support neglected and migrant youth in our nation's schools.
- Live up to its original promise from when IDEA was enacted of providing 40% of the excess cost of educating students with disabilities.

- Continue to invest in existing professional development opportunities for teachers, specialized instructional support personnel and other school staff by supporting increases in Title I, Title II, Title IV of ESSA, and IDEA.
- Fully fund Title IV-A of ESSA to allow for increased access to a well-rounded curriculum; support safe and healthy students; and increase the effective use of technology.
- Maintain and expand programs that support a positive school climate, access to comprehensive school mental health services, and the availability of comprehensive learning supports.
- Continue to fund federal research and technical assistance centers to equip schools and educators with the evidence-based tools they need to support the learning of all students.

Based on the key learning objectives, I can now:

- Identify how the federal government contributes to the development of mental health professionals and supports in schools.
- Explain the role the federal entities play in the policy making process.
- Identify several approaches to fund school-based mental health initiatives.
- Plan an approach to engage my congressional delegation.
- Conceptualize how various types of federal funding supports can impact initiatives proposed locally.

References

Dockweiler, K. A. (2019). *School psychologist pipeline framework ARTERY: Active Recruitment, Training, and Educator Retention to serve our Youth.* Nevada Department of Education (virtual).

Hernandez, R. (February 4, 2011). *District liked its earmarks, then elected someone who didn't.* The New York Times. https://www.nytimes.com/2011/02/05/nyregion/05earmarks.html

Office of Elementary and Secondary Education. (2019). *Mental health service professional demonstration grant program.* https://oese.ed.gov/offices/office-of-formula-grants/safe-supportive-schools/mental-health-service-professional-demonstration-grant-program/

Office of Elementary and Secondary Education. (2020). *FY 2020: School-based mental health services grant program abstracts.* https://oese. ed.gov/files/2022/02/SBMHS_CFDA-84.184H_FY2020_abstra cts_2.4.2022–1.pdf

Office of Elementary and Secondary Education. (2022). *School-based mental health services grant program. U.S. Department of Education.* https:// oese.ed.gov/offices/office-of-formula-grants/safe-supportive-schools/ school-based-mental-health-services-grant-program/awards/

Rafa, A., McCann, M., Francies, C., & Evans, A. (2021). *State funding for student mental health* [Policy brief]. Education Commission of the States.

Shutt, J. (February 26, 2021). *House appropriators officially bring back earmarks, ending ban.* Roll Call. https://rollcall.com/2021/02/26/house-appropriators-to-cap-earmarks-at-1-percent-of-topline/

U.S. Appropriations Committee. (2022). Congressionally directed spending items. https://www.appropriations.senate.gov/imo/media/doc/ LHHS_CDS2.pdf.

U.S. House of Representatives. (2021). *The legislative process.* https://www. house.gov/the- house-explained/the-legislative-process

12

STATE STATUTES

Learning Concepts

In this chapter, readers will learn:

- What statutes are.
- Who makes statutes.
- How to begin advocacy at the statutory level.
- The importance of public record.
- Statutory tips for SBMH workforce development and mental health services in schools.

Chapter Keywords

- State statutes
- State legislature
- Public support

States carry incredible power when it comes to supporting mental health efforts in schools. This chapter outlines how to gain the support

DOI: 10.4324/9781003308515-15

of elected officials to effectively advocate for legislative policy change. Actionable ideas for policy change are shared and strategies to engage key decision makers are discussed. Policy examples to increase access to mental health providers and services in schools are offered.

What Are State Statutes?

State level change can take on different forms. The two main types of policy change at the state level are statutory and regulatory. *State statutes* are passed by state legislatures while regulations are passed by state governing bodies such as boards of education. In general, a state statute is the overarching law, and regulations are the rules that support implementation of the law. These rules help eliminate ambiguities and provide guidance as to what structure must be put in place to carry out that law. The National Conference of State Legislatures succinctly explains the process this way, "Elementary and secondary education policy is defined broadly by state constitutions, specified by state statutes and implemented by state agencies, school boards and local school districts" (2022, section 2).

When I first began my doctoral research, I knew I wanted to study policy. How do policies impact students? How do they impact educators? Why do bad policies get enacted? How can we make sure to only enact good policies? My dissertation focused on language of instruction policies across the United States and how better policy frameworks were needed to analyze the potential impact of a policy. While designing my own policy framework I came across a language of instruction policy from Colorado that I was very excited about. I shared the law with my dissertation chair, and she asked me what should have been an easy question to answer: "Is that policy a statute or a regulation?" At that moment I realized how very little I knew about policy making.

Looking back, I can easily say now that that particular policy was a statute. At the time I thought that all state level laws were the same. I now know the difference between a statute and a regulation, and who the governing entity is for each. Whether a law is a statute or a regulation also impacts how difficult or easy it is to change that law. More information surrounding state regulations is detailed in Chapter 13.

For example, a state might pass a statute requiring all school districts to develop and implement programming relative to suicide prevention following guidelines established by the state board of education. The statute is not dictating the details of what the suicide prevention programming needs to look like; it is simply setting the bar at a certain level and leaving the guidelines to the state board to determine. Corresponding regulation that the state board of education could pass as guidelines might include annual suicide prevention training for school staff. Again, the state board of education is not dictating the how; they are providing guidance to the school districts for components that must be included in their prevention activities.

- State Statute passed by the legislature: *develop and implement programming relative to suicide prevention following guidelines established by the State Board of Education*
- State Regulation passed by State Board of Education: *School districts must train school staff at least annually on suicide prevention programming and procedures that at a minimum must include . . ..*

Mental health supports in schools often only happen because state statute requires it. This has been a trend in recent years as states are increasing the number of statutes relative to mental health supports in response to the significant needs of students and schools. According to policy analysts at the Education Commission of the States (ECS), a non-partisan education policy research organization, from 2019 to 2021 more than 30 state legislatures passed 72 laws relative to student mental and behavioral health (McCann et al., 2021). Their findings indicate that these laws fall into the following six domains (p. 2):

- Mental health and wellness curricula
- Suicide prevention programs and services
- Staff training and professional development
- Mental health screening
- Mental health professional staffing ratios
- School-based mental health programs and services

Who Creates Statutes?

Statutes are created by members of a *State Legislature* or General Assembly. Less common title variations of these entities include General Court or

Legislative Assembly. All these governing bodies pass laws called statutes that apply to all jurisdictions within a state as they are statewide policies. Every state except Nebraska has a bicameral legislature meaning there are two bodies that comprise the overarching legislative body. For example, the bicameral bodies may be the House and the Senate, or the Assembly and the Senate.

If you are unsure what the overarching statutory body is called in your state, or its two bicameral bodies, I encourage you to start doing some research to learn more about your state's governing structure. This information will help you as you engage in the advocacy and policy making process.

How to Begin the Statutory Process

No one policy will solve all student and mental-behavioral health issues. Each state will have an existing set of statutes on the books that either help or hinder student mental health services in the school setting. While many laws are well intended, they may have unintended consequences that need to be examined and possibly problem solved. The good thing about state laws is that they can be changed. Similarly, if a law does not exist but needs to, this too can change. One of my favorite things is creating positive change. If a policy needs to be drafted to improve outcomes for students, let's do it!

Sometimes an organization may have a state policy agenda that they continuously advocate for and revise. These groups tend to know what the existing laws are relative to their particular issue(s) and seem to know innately what needs to happen and who they need to talk to. From an outsider's perspective, they seem to run like well-oiled machines and have the social capital to make change happen.

Advocates who are individuals or small volunteer organizations may not operate as well-oiled machines and may be more grassroots in nature. These types of advocates are driven by a personal sense that "something isn't right" and a belief that state level change is needed to correct this inequity. In these cases, one of the first things that can be done is to review existing state statutes and determine where the breakdown is. It may be that there actually is a law about your particular issue and the breakdown isn't the law itself, but the implementation of the law. This would be a practice issue and could be addressed at a lower lever, such as the district or school.

Or it really might be the law itself. Laws are often on the books for years and while the current law may have been relevant and sufficient when it was first passed, it may no longer meet the needs of those it is meant to serve. In this case, the law might need to be amended to capture the present reality.

Whether a new bill is needed, or an existing law needs to be changed, a bill sponsor is needed. A bill sponsor is a legislator who can propose and carry a bill through the legislative session. Using effective communication and relationship building, the individual or group must seek out a bill sponsor to file a bill draft request. Each state will have different timelines and requirements for these bill draft requests, so check with your legislative counsel bureau for your state's unique requirements.

Senator Dondero Loop suggests reaching out to legislators by email, or even Twitter. It could be your elected legislator or one with a particular interest, such as in education or homelessness. Emails are a great place to start a conversation, especially if you aren't able to attend events or be at other gatherings where legislators and other decision makers may be. Email is a safe space and easy to access. In your email, she recommends sharing what you are experiencing at your school. From there, the legislator can reach out to other individuals, groups, and experts to see how widespread the issue is and what solutions might be possible. She strongly encourages educators and families to reach out to their legislators and ask questions if something is not working in their schools.

Generally, it will behoove you or your group to join advocacy forces with other likeminded groups. Prior to seeking out a bill sponsor, build a coalition (phases 2 and 3 of the Advocacy Action Process), and determine what you collectively hope to see enacted. Every bill draft request has an intent behind it. Remember that state statutes are specifically vague, so the intent does not need to be lengthy and detailed. The actual bill language will be determined by a group of policy makers. However, depending on how your state operates and the relationship you have with your bill sponsor, you may have an opportunity to help draft the actual language of the bill.

When approaching a bill sponsor, have your data ready. This is where details are not only helpful, but necessary. Recall the various phases of advocacy action planning within the Boomerang Policy Making Model. Phase 1 is awareness, access, and action. Through the action step of the first phase, you will have already constructed your ask, and you are prepared to deliver your message. Remember to use social math and real-life examples.

Talk stories about cases or instances where students have been negatively impacted. Explain that if this proposed law had been in place at that time, the negative outcome would never have happened. Use social math and present the data in terms of numbers of students impacted. If speaking to a legislative committee of ten people, you can use those ten committee members as the basis for your example. If using the statistic that one in five school-aged students require some type of mental health support (National Association of School Psychologists [NASP], 2021a), repeat that statistic using a different lens. You could state that if this committee were a group of students, two out of the ten committee members sitting at the dais today would require a mental health support. Another way to reframe it the message using social math is that 20% of students, or one in five, require mental health supports, which equates to nearly 100,000 students in your state (determine your state's actual number).

Trust the guidance your bill sponsor provides. They will be politically savvy and will have the ability to strategize and navigate the legislative process. They are acutely aware of the personalities and motivations of their fellow legislators. If they offer specific advice about what data to collect, who to share it with, or what manner it should be presented in, follow it. Likewise, if they make suggestions about what NOT to do, follow that advice as well.

Public Support

Perhaps you or your group is not looking to have a new bill proposed or to have an existing law amended. You may just be looking to support mental health laws in general or to prevent laws from being enacted that may be harmful to students. In these situations, it is helpful to offer support or opposition for the particular bill as it becomes available.

Support or opposition can be offered privately or off the record. However, remember that there is power in numbers and if your voice isn't part of the public record, its impact may not be amplified. Additionally, policy makers can build a stronger case for or against a bill when there are multiple voices in support or in opposition of a proposed law. What if everyone advocated privately? There would be no justification for passing or blocking a law and you may not achieve your desired outcome.

There are several ways you can offer support or opposition for a bill. The most common is public comment in the form of an email, a call-in, or an in-person testimony. National organizations such as the National Association for School Psychologists have templates that are available to professionals and community members. They also offer a State Association Resource Guide (NASP, 2021) and Policy Playbook (NASP, 2019) to help educators and state organizations increase the efficacy of their advocacy.

Tips for Workforce Development at the Statutory Level

The following are policy recommendations to help you begin building a statutory foundation for your SBMH workforce. These pipeline efforts will help ensure that your state has enough SBMH providers to deliver the much-needed mental health services that are needed in schools.

Depending on the structure of your state, some of these recommendations may fall under a different agency or policy lever. You will notice as you read through the policy examples in subsequent chapters that some of the policy recommendations fall under multiple levers. They are listed in multiple places because multiple levers may be needed to fully enact the policy. Also, involving multiple levers helps support alignment of the pipeline.

Some of these recommendations may be more applicable than others, and to varying degrees. I encourage you to begin conceptualizing how these recommendations build on current efforts already in motion in your context. Also, what policies are not yet in place that need to be?

- Establish statewide ratio targets for all school-based mental health professions
- Require ratio improvement plans involving all relevant stakeholders and policy levers
- Define the scope, practice, and licensing for the three school-based mental health professions (this can also be used to support the establishment of ratios and Medicaid billing)

- Establish accountability mechanisms for the ratio improvement plans that are reinforced through regulation
- Create paid internships, offer provisional licenses to interns, pay psychological services assistants at their support staff salary and benefits, allow re-specialization of teachers and permit them to maintain their salary and benefits during internships
- Offer state tuition scholarships to incentivize school-based mental health careers with memorandums of agreement to ensure graduates remain in state
- Allow dual-credit opportunities to all institutes of higher education, not just two-year colleges
- Encourage districts to reinvest Medicaid dollars in school-based mental health provider pipelines
- Formalize career paths for school-base mental health providers using a model such as the ARTERY Pipeline Framework

Tips for Mental Health Supports and Services at the Statutory Level

Supports and services at the statutory level may be vast and identifying where to target policy efforts can often feel overwhelming. When considering what type of mental health supports to put into policy, review the following seven high-level domains to help guide your thinking (ECS, 2022):

- Curriculum requirements
- Data and reporting requirements
- Fiscal support
- Pilot programs
- Program infrastructure requirements
- School-based health professional ratio requirements
- Staff training and professional development

Conversely, you may be ready to advocate for specific mental health policies. While not an exhaustive list, specific mental health bills might target the following supports and services:

- Establish a multi-tiered system of support (MTSS) framework for mental health service delivery
- Include a school-based mental health professional on education regulatory boards
- Establish a Safe Voice, or Safe2Tell, anonymous call line
- Require suicide prevention programming
- Align health standards to include social, emotional, and behavioral well-being
- Require trauma informed practices
- Establish restorative practices and proactive disciplinary procedures
- Establish universal screening and intervention supports
- Provide training for educators on social-emotional competencies, signs of distress, and ways to support students

Model Policy Examples

The following are policy examples from across the country demonstrating how they are addressing mental health services in schools. Please note that this is not an exhaustive list of available school mental health policy options. Research the topics that seem relevant in your context and investigate how the corresponding state drafted policy is a solution. Often the policy can be modified and used as draft language in your state. States often borrow conceptual language from each other and then customize it to meet the needs of their unique contexts.

- *Allow student mental health days.* Since the COVID-19 pandemic and the exacerbated mental health issues of students, states have been looking for ways to support, not penalize, students who may just need to take a day off from school to regroup or recharge. Legislation has been passed in several states to allow students excusable absences for mental health days. Examples include Utah's House Bill 234 (2018) and House Bill 81 (2021), Nevada's Senate Bill 249 (2021), Colorado's Senate Bill 20–2014 (2020), and Arizona's Senate Bill 1097 (2021) (Rivera, 2022).
- *Grants for school-based health services.* Oregon passed House Bill 2591 (2021) providing for the deployment of ten grants dedicated to

the planning of school-based health services. After the planning phase additional grant funds are available to fund pilot projects and mobile school-linked health centers targeting increased access to mental and behavioral health services through telehealth (ECS, 2022).

- *Establish ratios and ratio improvement plans.* Establishing desired ratios for school-based mental health professionals and the reporting mechanisms to reach these ratios through legislation was passed in Maryland with House Bill 844 (2019) (Whinnery, 2019) and in Nevada with Senate Bills 89 (2019) and 151 (2021).

- *Adopt trauma-informed practices.* Kentucky passed Senate Bill 1 (2019) requiring schools to adopt a trauma-informed approach to education. The law directs the department of education to develop a toolkit to assist schools including strategies, interventions, practices, or techniques. The law also has a provision to hire school counselors at a desired ratio of 1:250 to assist with implementation (Whinnery, 2019).

- *Establish suicide prevention programs.* Several states have enacted laws regarding suicide prevention programs, services, resources, and funding opportunities. Such states include Utah (House Bill 336, 2021), Oregon (Senate Bill 52, 2019), Wisconsin (Assembly Bill 528, 2020), and Arizona (Senate Bill 1446, 2020) (McCann et al., 2021).

- *Adverse childhood experiences training.* In New York, Senate Bill 4990 requires childcare providers to receive training on adverse childhood experiences with an emphasis on understanding trauma and fostering resiliency (ECS, 2020).

- *Connections between physical and mental health.* Maine (S.P. 303 [L.D. 1024], 2019) and Virginia (House Bill 1604 and Senate Bill 953, 2019) passed laws requiring that school curricular standards must identify and address the relationship between physical and mental health for optimal overall wellness (Whinnery, 2019).

- *Funds for safety screenings and services.* Pennsylvania passed Senate Bill 1142 (2018) establishing the School Safety and Security Fund. Funds can be accessed and used for trauma-informed approaches to education, evidence-based screenings for adverse childhood experiences, and counseling services (ECS, 2020).

- *Educator trainings on social-emotional well-being.* Increasing teacher and staff awareness of what social-emotional well-being is and how to support students is often overlooked. The following states have implemented laws regarding this type of training and how to recognize signs of distress: Virginia (House Bill 74, Senate Bill 619; 2020) and Washington (Senate Bill 5082, 2019) (McCann et al., 2021).

Based on the key learning objectives, I can now:

- Describe the role of statutes in the policy making process.
- Identify my state's overarching governance body and bicameral bodies.
- Explain how to start advocacy at the statutory level.
- Describe the benefits of publicly supporting or opposing a proposed bill.
- Identify policies to begin enhancing SBMH workforce policies and policies for mental health services in my state.

References

Education Commission of the States. (2020). *Education policy approaches to trauma-informed practices.* Author.

Education Commission of the States. (2022). *Elements of student health supports* [Policy outline]. https://www.ecs.org/elements-of-student-health-support/

McCann, M., Fulton, M., & McDole, T. (May, 2021). *State approaches to addressing student mental health* [Policy brief]. Education Commission of the States.

National Association of School Psychologists. (2019). *NASP policy playbook.* https://www.nasponline.org/research-and-policy/advocacy

National Association of School Psychologists. (2021a). *Comprehensive school-based mental and behavioral health services and school psychologists* [Handout]. Author.

National Association of School Psychologists. (2021b). *State association NSPW resource guide.* https://www.nasponline.org/research-and-policy/advocacy/national-school-psychology-week-(nspw)

National Conference of State Legislatures. (2022). *Policies for the jurisdiction of the Education Committee.* https://www.ncsl.org/ncsl-in-dc/task-forces/policies-education.aspx

Rivera, A. (2022). *States act to allow student mental health days.* National Conference of State Legislatures. https://www.ncsl.org/research/education/states-act-to-allow-student-mental-health-days-magazine 2022.aspx#:~:text=The%20department%20published%20its%20 guidelines,distr icts%20may%20set%20specific%20policies

Whinnery, E. (2019). *Student mental health* [Policy snapshot]. Education Commission of the States.

13

STATE REGULATIONS

Learning Concepts

In this chapter, readers will learn:

- What state regulations are.
- Who passes state regulations.
- How to align statutory and regulatory efforts.
- That advocacy does not end at the statutory level.
- Regulatory tips for SBMH workforce development and mental health services in schools.

Chapter Keywords

- State regulations
- State board of education

Once statutes are passed into law, there are often corresponding *state regulations* that must be set. This chapter reviews the role of regulation in

DOI: 10.4324/9781003308515-16

supporting access to mental health supports in schools. Advocacy does not end with the legislative session. Following the policy through to implementation means tracking it across the various policy levers. It is important that educators, stakeholders, and other advocates continue to share their voice and help shepherd policies as they work their way through the regulatory process.

What are State Regulations?

Remember from the previous chapter that there are two main types of policy change at the state level: statutory and regulatory. State statutes are passed by state legislatures while regulations are passed by state governing bodies such as state boards of education. In general, a state statute is the overarching law and regulations are the rules to support implementation of the law. These rules help eliminate ambiguities and provide guidance as to what structure must be put in place.

As an advocate, it is important to stay on top of statutes that are passed that also contain a regulatory component. These regulations will need to be developed and passed by their designated regulatory body. There will also be regulation hearings, workshops, and public opportunities for stakeholder feedback. Each step along the way is an opportunity to voice your position, offer research, or promote a specific outcome.

In speaking with colleagues and advocates from across the country, one of the most common "ah-ha!" moments relative to regulation making is the process itself. One of the biggest misconceptions about policy making is that once a law is passed by the legislature that is it: the law is done and nothing else needs to happen. Understanding the process and knowing that often regulations will also need to be set can be very powerful. This goes back to the three advocacy action phases of Boomerang Policy Making discussed in Chapter 6. Each level of policy making offers a new chance to throw the Boomerang, construct your message, and advocate using the three phases. Just knowing that regulation work needs to be done is the first step in advocating for a specific change. This is considered awareness and falls under the 3 As of Advocacy in Phase 1. Once an individual or group understands the regulatory process, they can find ways to access pathways for advocacy and can begin planning their actions.

On the front end, if you are working with a bill sponsor while a statute is being drafted, you may be part of the conversation about whether
to include a regulatory component. In some cases, it makes sense to defer
to regulation if a particular piece of the law may be subject to change
or needs to remain nimble. Intentionally including language along the
lines of "as determined by the State Board of Education" provides for this
flexibility. This would indicate that the supplemental rules, or regulations, that correspond to the statute will be created as regulations by the
governing board. This can be especially helpful when the issue at hand
is complex or requires additional research that is beyond the broad scope
of the statute.

Many statutes are never implemented after they are passed by their
state legislatures. They may not get signed by the Governor and enacted
into law. Or, if they do get signed, they may not get prioritized and
implemented. In some cases, the implementation process begins but
stalls and laws are left partially implemented. Several reasons may contribute to these implementation issues. First, governing bodies may lose
track of what statutes were passed in the legislature, and thus fail to
implement or reinforce the changes. Also, governing bodies may not
efficiently track which statutes require supplemental regulation work
and fail to establish regulations or fully implement a law. Or the lack
of implementation may be intentional. Accountability tracking systems
and adequate staff can help remediate these issues and increase the full
implementation of laws.

Depending on your state, implementation may or may not be an issue.
It is helpful to have software systems set up to track implementation of
laws. To go with this type of system, it is helpful to have an individual or
team of people to manage the software and follow up on any laws that
are not being implemented. States that have these types of accountability
and efficiency processes in place are more likely to fully implement the
laws that get passed, laws with and without corresponding regulations.

Regulations must be viewed in the context of their statutes. If any
changes are recommended to modify an existing regulation, it is helpful to know how the current regulation and corresponding statute came
about. History and intent of bills are critical. Changes may be proposed
because the current regulation no longer fits the need of the students, or
the group(s) impacted by the regulation. Ideally, regulations are developed

that will not need to be changed on a regular basis. Good policy captures not only the current environment, but also sets the rules that should apply across a variety of environments or eventualities.

Who Creates Regulations?

In the education realm, regulations are typically passed by the *State Board of Education*. There may also be supplemental boards that target specific components of education, such as licensure, that then get routed up to the state board. Depending on your state, some mental health regulations that impact students in the school setting may come from the Department of Health and Human Services regulatory board.

The beautiful thing about regulations is that they are generally easier to change than statutes. While state legislatures meet annually or biannually, state governing boards meet on a regular basis, usually monthly. This allows for more opportunities to engage with state board members. State boards of education can be comprised of a variety of members. There may be elected members, appointed members, or members assigned based on their role with their state education departments. For example, the Education Commissioner or State Superintendent may be assigned to the board based on their role as the head of the state education department. There may also be a student representative; it all depends on the unique composition of the board in your state.

Each of these member types may or may not be voting members; it will vary depending on how the board is structured. Strategically, advocates will want to prioritize advocacy efforts with voting members first, and non-voting members second. Also, targeting your specific elected official on the board is another good way to amplify your message. Another good strategy is to target a certain appointed individual who aligns with your stakeholder group. For example, if I am an educator and there is an educator on the state board, I can reach out to them to share my position as they can advocate on behalf of all educators. Similarly, if I am a parent and there is a parent on the state board, I can reach out to them as they were appointed to share parent and family perspective.

Nevada State Board of Education Member Tamara Hudson is a special education teacher and a strong voice for educators. She is appointed to the board in the capacity of an educator. She reports that having educators involved in the policy making process is a proactive move and makes educator voice embedded into the policy making process. She says that educators have reported to her that they have more trust in the policy making process because they know that an educator is on the board and is representing their perspective and concerns. She stresses the importance of policy makers needing to know if a policy is actually possible in the classroom before they pass it into law. In her position on the State Board of Education, she is able to help with explaining how a policy being discussed at the state level might actually look like when implemented in the classroom. State board members from outside Nevada have reached out to Member Hudson because they don't have educator voice on their board, and they value the importance of educator voice at the state level.

State boards of education are the entities that pass state education regulations. They are policy making boards that set the vision and goals for the state and establish standards for student achievement and performance (National School Boards Association, 2022). They are also advocates for their constituents, students, families, and educators. State boards of education work very closely with the state department of education who assists with administrative aspects of policy making and often help select the State Superintendent or State Commissioner. Some state boards of education have designated staff members to assist with research, presentations, and liaising with state departments of education. Others do not and rely on the assistance from the state department of education. Also, some Education Commissioners or State Superintendents report to the state board and some report to a different entity, such as the Governor.

It will behoove advocates to determine how their state board is structured and what the relationship is between the state department of education and the board. Understanding these dynamics can help navigate the system and help identify what power struggles may be going on behind the scenes. In a perfect world, state boards and state departments of education are working in alignment toward shared goals.

Depending on how your state is structured and what particular issue you are advocating for, you may need to advocate to the Department of Health and Human Services. Typically, school-based mental health supports can be channeled through the state's Department of Education as they have jurisdiction over the schools. However, if there are community-based partnerships or clinically based services that are being requested, they may need to be approved by the regulatory board for the Department of Health and Human Services. It all depends on the nature of the ask, the services included, and the jurisdiction of the department who is able to grant your request.

What Is the Regulatory Process?

Each state will have its own process and timeframes for how regulations are developed and passed into law. As with any public comment process, share your message with members of the state board and specifically express what you hope to see enacted.

Nevada State Board of Education President Felicia Ortiz offers the following advice for educators and other advocates. She recommends staying solution-focused with your messaging and start by outlining the problem that you are working to solve. Identify the problem, offer your proposed solution, and state how the proposed regulation is going to fill in the identified gap. President Ortiz suggests bringing research and demonstrating how the proposed solution will benefit students. State how and why the policy needs to change from X to Y.

Tips for Workforce Development at the Regulatory Level

The following are policy recommendations to help you begin building a policy foundation for your SBMH workforce. These pipeline efforts will help ensure that your state has enough SBMH providers to deliver the much-needed mental health services that are needed in schools.

As mentioned previously, there is repetition of the recommendations from the statutory level down to the regulatory level. Depending on the unique composition of your state, some of these duties may lie at the regulation level. Alignment to statutory intent will be important. Conducting an environmental scan and exploring what other states have passed into regulation is a good idea as you work to draft your own regulations.

- Establish statewide ratio targets for all school-based mental health professions

- Require ratio improvement plans involving all relevant stakeholders and policy levers
- Define the scope, practice, and licensing for the three school-based mental health professions (this can also be used to support the establishment of ratios and Medicaid billing)
- Establish accountability mechanisms for the ratio improvement plans that are reinforced through regulation
- Create paid internships, offer provisional license to interns, pay psychological services assistants at their support staff salary and benefits, allow re-specialization of teachers, and permit them to maintain their salary and benefits during internships
- Offer state tuition scholarships to incentivize school-based mental health careers with memorandums of agreement to ensure graduates remain in state
- Allow dual-credit opportunities to all institutes of higher education, not just two-year colleges
- Encourage districts to reinvest Medicaid dollars in school-based mental health provider pipelines
- Formalize career paths for school-based mental health providers using a model such as the ARTERY Pipeline Framework

Tips for Mental Health Supports and Services at the Regulatory Level

When exploring school-based mental health supports and services, it is critical to ensure that what is put into regulation is evidence-based. Not all supports and services will work universally across all environments. Make sure that the guardrails you put in place are prescriptive enough to provide structure, but flexible enough to allow for contextual variabilities. Great resources when looking for evidence-based supports and services include:

- National Association of School Psychologists
- National American School Counselor Association
- School Social Work Association of America
- Collaborative for Academic, Social, and Emotional Learning
- Healthy Schools Campaign
- Healthy Minds, Safe Schools

Specific supports and services will align with those recommended at the statutory level:

- Establish a multi-tiered system of support (MTSS) framework for mental health service delivery
- Include a school-based mental health professional on education regulatory boards
- Establish a Safe Voice, or Safe2Tell, anonymous call line
- Require suicide prevention programming
- Align health standards to include social, emotional, and behavioral well-being
- Require trauma-informed practices
- Establish restorative practices and proactive disciplinary procedures
- Establish universal screening and intervention supports
- Provide training for educators on social-emotional competencies, signs of distress, and ways to support students

Model Policy Examples

Once the legislature passes a bill and the governor signs it into law, there may be components that are transferred down to state regulatory boards or departments. These entities will then pass their own provisions to assist with the implementation of the law. From the previous chapter, there are model policy recommendations at the statutory level that may have regulatory components. Consider the following policy categories for any regulatory components that might make sense in your state:

- Allow student mental health days
- Grants for school-based health services
- Establish ratios and ratio improvement plans
- Adopt trauma-informed practices
- Establish suicide prevention programs
- Adverse childhood experiences training
- Connections between physical and mental health
- Funds for safety screenings and services
- Educator trainings on social-emotional well-being

The following are examples of statutes that included policy making responsibilities for their state regulatory boards:

- *Training on impact of trauma on learning.* In Utah, House Bill 373 (2019) requires the state board of education to provide school personnel training about the impact of trauma on learning (Whinnery, 2019).
- *Revise curricular standards and concepts.* South Carolina passed House Bill 3257 (2020) requiring the state board of education to revise standards to address the mental, emotional, and social health of students (Education Commission of the States [ECS], 2020).
- *Establish mental health competencies.* The state of Washington passed Senate Bill 5082 (2019) requiring the Washington Professional Educator Standard Board to create new competencies for educators in the domains of trauma informed practices, adverse childhood experiences, and mental health literacy (Whinnery, 2019).
- *Establish ratios and ratio improvement plans.* In Nevada, recommended statewide ratios were established along with specific reporting mechanisms and pipeline supports to hold districts accountable for their efforts. This work happened across two legislative sessions with Senate Bills 89 and 319 (2019) and Senate Bills 151 and 352 (2021).

Based on the key learning objectives, I can now:

- Identify the role that regulations play in state policy making.
- Explain the type of entities who can pass regulations.
- Describe why alignment of statutes and regulations is important.
- Explain why a policy may need to be followed after passed into statute.
- Identify regulatory tips that can help support expansion of a SMBH workforce or services in my context.

References

Education Commission of the States. (2020). *Education policy approaches to trauma-informed practices.* Author.

National School Boards Association. (2022). *About school boards and local governance.* https://www.nsba.org/About/About-School-Board-and-Local-Governance

Nevada Department of Education. (April 30, 2020). *Non-binding recommended ratios for specialized instructional support personnel.* https://doe.nv.gov/uploadedFiles/ndedoenvgov/content/Boards_Commissions_Councils/State_Board_of_Education/2020/April/Follow-upSISPRatiosperSB%2089.pdf

Whinnery, E. (2019). *Student mental health* [Policy snapshot]. Education Commission of the States.

14

STATE EDUCATION AGENCIES

Learning Concepts

In this chapter, readers will learn:

- The role of state education agencies in policy making.
- What are the key responsibilities of state education agencies.
- How to engage with state education agencies.
- What policy strategies exist for school-based mental health workforce development.
- What policies to implement to facilitate school-based mental health supports and services.

Chapter Keywords

- State education agencies
- Chief state school officer

Once statutory and regulatory policies are passed, they must be implemented. Each state has a Department of Education and a Department of

DOI: 10.4324/9781003308515-17

Health and Human Services to enforce and support ratified mental health laws. This chapter discusses how advocates can engage with state education agencies to support implementation of enacted laws. Being an active contributor and collaborating with the state department of education is critical to ensuring that the mental health supports that were advocated for and achieved at the state legislative level make their way down to the school level as intended.

What are State Education Agencies?

State education agencies, or SEAs, are more commonly referred to as state departments of education or offices of public instruction. They have a tremendous scope of responsibilities and help ensure an equitable education is provided to all public education students across a state. SEAs are the big machines that help support smaller local education agencies with their operations. All states have many local districts to support except for Hawaii. The state of Hawaii has one SEA and only one local education agency.

SEAs are responsible for coordinating the maintenance and operation of education in the state (U.S. Department of Education, 2017). State education agencies also manage a variety of supports and services including educator licensure, special education, and student achievement. They assist state boards of education with policy making and depending on the constitutional and legislative responsibilities assigned to them, they may also assist with drafting regulations.

SEAs all have a *chief state school officer*, frequently called the state superintendent or commissioner of schools. Some are elected and some are appointed; it may be helpful to identify what the dynamic is in your state. Chief state school officers provide leadership to a state education agency as well as to all the local education agencies and their district superintendents.

State education agencies have innumerable duties and responsibilities. In addition to coordinating and overseeing various divisions of education, they also manage budgetary allocations. SEAs can use monies to prioritize and fund mental health initiatives in the school setting. Funds may come from specific state appropriations, school funding models, or earmarked tax revenue depending on what models are established in your state (Rafa et al., 2021). Advocating for state education agencies to increase spending specifically for school-based mental health initiatives at the district and school levels is beneficial as these local entities may then have more funds available to them to increase mental health supports to students.

What Is the SEA Role in the Policy Making Process?

It is imperative that the state education agency have a close working relationship with the state legislature, the state board, and the local school districts. State education agencies manage many policies and can help lead a policy's implementation to ensure it is successful. Within an SEA, there are several different offices or divisions. For example, there may be a division for students with exceptionalities, for student well-being, for educator licensure, or career and technical programs. Identifying the division that aligns with your advocacy efforts is important. Additional responsibilities SEAs may have include:

- Regulation drafting, hearings, and workshops
- Technical assistance and presentations
- Grant applications and fund distribution
- Guidance documents for local education agencies

Nevada State Superintendent Ebert shares that educators are the front-line staff of our education system and are best positioned to tell us what our students need. Her priority is to keep educators at the center of the discussion as they have first-hand experience, and the overall success of a state lies with them. She highlights that at the state level there is opportunity for educators to have a wide reach and to make systemic change. Educators can work at that level alongside lobbyists, legislators, and community members to impact policies.

In addition to influencing legislative policies, there are also opportunities to contribute to policies drafted by the state education agency.

Providing public comment during public meetings and hearings is one way to contribute. Reaching out directly to an individual who is supervising regulatory work at the state education agency is another.

Aside from regulatory influence, you could also request to work on guidance documents or to provide research that could inform such documents. Every state education agency functions slightly differently and learning where there are opportunities to contribute is key. There may be working groups to join, hearings to speak at, or other ways to promote your key message or best practices.

For example, if you are working to promote school counseling services in schools, seek out the division within the department of education that handles these types of services. Email the director or designated contact person and inquire if there are any opportunities to work with the department as a community member, educator, parent, or other stakeholder to move counseling services forward. Usually, SEAs do not know who all the interested stakeholders are surrounding a particular issue. They may know the largest or loudest organizations and include them in the work, but there is no way they can feasibly know everyone who may want to be involved. Reaching out and requesting to be involved is a great first step.

Tips for School-Based Mental Health Workforce Development at the Department Level

Depending on the structure of your state, some of these recommendations may fall under a different agency or policy lever. You will notice as you read through the policy examples in other policy lever chapters that some of the policy recommendations fall under multiple levers. They are listed in multiple places because multiple levers are involved to fully enact the policy. Also, involving multiple levers helps support alignment of the initiative.

Depending on the policies currently in place in your state, some of these may be more applicable than others, and to varying degrees. I encourage you to begin conceptualizing how these recommendations build on current efforts already in motion in your context. Also, what policies are not in place yet that need to be?

- Hire a professional to act as a school-based mental health workforce alignment specialist to ensure statewide implementation of pipeline efforts
- Provide technical assistance on statewide ratio targets for all school-based mental health professions
- Draft guidance documents relative to ratio improvement plans with recommendations for involving relevant stakeholders and policy levers
- Align licensing requirements to statutes relative to each school-based mental health profession
- Support accountability mechanisms for the ratio improvement plans that are reinforced through regulation
- Create workgroups or facilitate a state coalition to get buy-in from multiple stakeholders and better ensure implementation
- Formalize career paths for school-based mental health providers using a model such as the ARTERY Pipeline Framework
- Encourage districts to reinvest Medicaid dollars in school-based mental health provider pipelines
- Work with all institutes of higher education to facilitate dual-credit opportunities
- Create a career and technical education program relative to Health and Social Services, Psychological Services, or similar related professional area
- Offer state tuition scholarships to incentivize school-based mental health careers with memorandums of agreement to ensure graduates remain in state and/or in certain high-needs school districts
- Establish a strong working partnership with the governance board for the state's institutes of higher education, as well as the leadership of each individual institution
- License the psychological services position at the state level to professionalize and distinguish it from other support staff positions
- Fund paid internships and offer a provisional license to interns
- Actively work to remove barriers to licensure and license renewals

Tips for School-Based Mental Health Supports and Services at the Department Level

Building off the recommendations at the statutory and regulatory levels is to establish an equitable mental health service delivery model.

Depending on your state, this can be reinforced at every level with policies and procedures at each lever.

One of the best supports that can be advocated for is the adoption of a multi-tiered system of support (MTSS) framework for mental health service delivery.

The MTSS organizational service delivery framework is described in greater detail in Chapter 17 and is certainly worth further investigation outside the scope of this book. In addition to the adoption of an MTSS framework, SEAs can support districts and students by prioritizing and allocating funds for (Rafa et al., 2021, p. 6):

- School mental and behavioral health professionals
- State grants and pilot programming
- Training for educators
- Resource development
- Community school models
- Trauma-informed services
- Suicide prevention
- Youth mental health first aid

Model Policy Examples

These model policy examples are derived from state statutes that have obligated the SEAs to draft regulations or policies to assist with implementation. They also typically provide guidance for local education agencies to follow and align their efforts to. Building from the previous chapters, revisit statutes set by the state legislature to see how regulations can be developed to support implementation of the work. This may not be warranted, but in some cases, it will be a natural step forward.

- *Allow student mental health days.* While most states have passed policy directly through their legislatures allowing for student mental health days, it can also be passed into policy through regulation. In Virginia, with House Bill 308 (2020), the legislature directed the Department of Education to establish the guidelines for excused absences from school due to mental or behavioral health concerns (Rivera, 2022; Lane, 2020).

- *Collaboration for mental health services.* In Montana, House Bill 671 (2021) was passed directing the collaboration of two departments, public instruction and health and human services, to support local education agencies in seeking reimbursement from Medicaid or assistance from the Children's Health Insurance Program for qualified school-based mental health services (Education Commission of the States [ECS], 2022).
- *Develop statewide plan for mental health.* The Texas Education Agency has been tasked with creating a statewide plan for mental health under Senate Bill 11 (2019) along with resources for training practices, school-based prevention and intervention services, and community-based supports. Locally, schools are to use this plan and rubric to create school environments that support the social, emotional, and academic development of students (Whinnery, 2019).
- *Pilot for stress and anxiety management.* In Mississippi, House Bill 1283 (2019) directs the state department of education to create a pilot program focused on teaching elementary students stress and anxiety management skills. The department was tasked with selecting the evidence-based curriculum to use in implementation (Whinnery, 2019).
- *Innovative community partnerships.* The following states have developed innovative partnerships across agencies, community groups, and policy levers to maximize the scope of their service delivery model. These examples do not fall under any one statutory, regulatory, or state leadership level. Rather, they represent combined efforts across agencies that are worth investigating. Coordination and monitoring of these efforts will generally fall at the state education agency level. By combining resources, these states were able to leverage their combined physical, fiscal, and mental-behavioral health services (ECS, 2022):

    - *Maryland:* Senate Bill 661 (2019) and Blueprint for Maryland's Future
    - *Iowa:* Executive Order 2 (2018) establishing the Children's Behavioral Health System State Board
    - *Colorado:* Creation of School-Based Health Centers through a partnership between Denver Public Schools and Denver Health
    - *Minnesota:* School-Linked Mental Health programs

- *North Carolina*: Leveraged federal Project AWARE grant from SAMSHA to create a school mental health inventory that identifies redundancies, needs, and recommendations
- *Ohio*: Appropriated $675 million in 2019 for the Student Wellness and Success Fund

Based on the key learning objectives, I can now:

- Identify the role state education agencies have in policy making.
- Explain the key responsibilities of state education agencies.
- Frame how I might engage and advocate at the state agency level.
- Describe policy strategies to support workforce development of school-based mental health providers.
- Identify key policies to adopt relative to school-based mental health supports and services in my unique context.

References

Education Commission of the States. (2022). *Elements of student health supports* [Policy outline]. https://www.ecs.org/elements-of-student-health-support/

Lane, J. F. (2020, June). *Guidelines for granting excused absences due to mental or behavioral health.* Memo #142–20. Commonwealth of Virginia Department of Education.

Rafa, A., McCann, M., Francies, C., & Evans, A. (2021). *State funding for student mental health* [Policy brief]. Education Commission of the States.

Rivera, A. (2022). *States act to allow student mental health days.* National Conference of State Legislatures. https://www.ncsl.org/research/education/states-act-to-allow-student-mental-health-days-magazine2022.aspx#:~:text=The%20department%20published%20its%20guidelines,distr icts%20may%20set%20specific%20policies

U.S. Department of Education. (2017). *Sec. 300.41 State educational agency.* https://sites.ed.gov/idea/regs/b/a/300.41

Whinnery, E. (2019). *Student mental health* [Policy snapshot]. Education Commission of the States.

15

INSTITUTES OF HIGHER EDUCATION

Learning Concepts

In this chapter, readers will learn:

- What role institutes of higher education have in school-based mental health provider training and workforce development.
- Why the advocacy pathway is unique.
- How formalizing a workforce pipeline can help with advocacy efforts.
- What alignment is needed for effective training.
- How to support overall statewide school-based mental health provider workforce needs.

Chapter Keywords

- Institutes of higher education
- Stacked degree programs

DOI: 10.4324/9781003308515-18

The higher education lever plays a unique role in providing mental health services to students. Remember the adage: *having adequate mental health services in schools is predicated on having an adequate number of mental health professionals to deliver those services.* Higher education is the training ground for these professionals. This chapter will outline how higher education institutes can help support state priorities, statutes, and regulations through alignment of their programmatic offerings. Higher education institutes can also be directly involved in policy creation and workforce development strategies. Advocates can help facilitate these processes by staying engaged and helping to align efforts. They can reinforce to higher education decision makers how their programmatic offerings directly contribute to the overall mental health of students in the PK–12 school setting.

What Are Institutes of Higher Education?

Institutes of higher education (IHEs) offer post-secondary education opportunities. They offer degree programs starting at the associate degree level, and may be a technical or business school, college, or university. There are several governance models for IHEs and the model will vary state by state. The most common model in use is a single statewide coordinating board/agency or governing board (Pechota et al., 2020). Identifying what the structure is in your state will help as you begin planning your efforts.

In addition to the statewide governance structure, each individual IHE will have their own governance structure. At each institution, this governing structure will typically include individuals such as the institution's President, Provost, and other key leaders. As you begin your advocacy, if your efforts will be more institution specific versus statewide, it will be helpful to identify who the key individuals are on a particular campus.

What Is the Role of Institutes of Higher Education?

Institutes of higher education are unsung heroes of mental health supports in schools. They play a critical role in the services available to school age children, yet often they don't directly deliver those services themselves. If school-based mental health supports and services are to exist, they must be provided by someone. This is where IHEs play a critical role: they train the professionals who provide that support. Without an adequate number of training programs for school psychologists, school counselors, and school social workers, there will never be enough trained professionals to implement mental and behavioral health services in our schools. Period.

Institutes of higher education are often overlooked in the overarching school-based mental health scheme. Professors don't typically interact directly with school-aged children, nor are they located in PK–12 school buildings. However, they do train the professionals who interact daily with students in the school setting. IHEs are critical partners of state education agencies and local education agencies, and much can be gained by creating partnerships across these agencies.

IHEs can partner with the legislature, state agencies, and local agencies in many ways. They can directly advocate for increased workforce development programs for mental health providers. Higher education campuses often have a government relations person whose job is to advocate on behalf of the IHE. The statewide overarching governing board may also have this position and can advocate on behalf of all IHEs in the state. From a workforce perspective, the number of IHE training programs for school-based mental health providers should meet the demands of the state. The legislature can prioritize through policy that additional funding be allocated, or that certain training programs for mental health be emphasized.

There may also be statewide workforce development offices or efforts happening that determine the demand across a variety of sectors such business, agriculture, or mining. Education is often one of these sectors and typically includes the demand for PK–12 teachers. Working with these offices to specifically target workforce needs of school-based mental health providers can be helpful. Identifying what the need is statewide can help IHEs advocate for expanding or adding higher education training programs.

From a licensing perspective, IHEs can partner with state education agencies to ensure alignment of coursework to licensing requirements for school-based mental health providers. In doing so, when students graduate with their graduate degree, they meet the requirements for licensure in their chosen degree field. If the coursework and the licensing requirements do not align, it is possible that students could graduate and not be able to obtain their license to practice. This would then require the student to take additional coursework. This is a huge barrier to getting trained professionals in the schools and delivering the needed mental health supports and services to students.

From a practitioner training perspective, IHEs can partner with local education agencies to provide training opportunities for students who need to complete practicum or internship hours. Expanding service delivery of professionals can include the training they receive during their preparation programs (Hughes et al., 2017). These experiences can be customized to meet the needs of local communities while meeting the requisite expectations of the training program. Alignment of the state's workforce needs to the program training requirements and the needs of the schools, can optimize learning, training, and delivery of services.

The ARTERY Pipeline Framework in Higher Education

Education and educators are at the heart of all professions. Without educators we wouldn't have a literate populace or a workforce full of professions such as doctors, bus drivers, and business owners. In the school setting, amongst other things, mental health providers help keep students safe and well. They identify student risk, intervene, and save lives. As such, they are part of an artery of support necessary to keep students thriving and healthy.

School-based mental health providers do not materialize overnight. They are highly trained professionals who require extensive coursework and preparation in order to practice. The ARTERY Pipeline Framework (Dockweiler, 2019) was specifically designed to build career pathways into the school-based mental health fields and address workforce shortages. This framework helps organize layered ideas, analyze levers of action, and create actionable policy-to-practice solutions.

Through the Active Recruitment, Training, and Educator Retention to Serve our Youth (ARTERY) we can cast a wide net early, frequently, and in different directions to draw students into the career pipeline. Pipeline programs are an effective way for a state to grow their own school-based mental health providers and address shortages in fields such as school psychology (Schmitz et al., 2022). Once in the pipeline, *stacked degree programs* and employment opportunities await to serve as training vehicles. Educator incentives and retention policies can be put in place to retain practitioners once they've entered the career field. In short, the ARTERY is a one-stop shop that answers questions regarding how to successfully recruit, train, and retain school-based mental health professionals using policy and advocacy.

At its earliest entry point, students are strategically exposed to the three school-based mental health careers in middle school, or even elementary school. Once in high school, students can take classes as part of a social and mental health career and technical education career path along with dual enrollment courses for college credit. Depending on the state or district you are in there will be many options for policy advancement within the ARTERY to ensure that these various options are a reality for high school students. Through intentionally recruiting students from our local communities, we increase the likelihood that once they complete their college studies they will come back and serve the communities they came from.

Similarly, while the terminal degree for all three school-based mental health career fields is a minimum of a graduate level degree, there are significant policy-to-practice structures that must be put in place at the undergraduate level to build out and bolster the career pathways for these professions. For example, introductory coursework in school-based mental health at the undergraduate level is a great starting point to introduce college students to these career fields. Even better, a minor or major in school-based mental health is a great way to cast a wide net for recruitment of SBMH professionals. None of these options are possible without very specific and targeted policy actions at various levels within the ARTERY.

With a solid background in SBMH through their undergraduate studies, college students are then well prepared to enter graduate programming for their master's, educational specialist degree, or doctorate degree. Upon successful completion of programming and licensing, there are many retention strategies that districts can use to keep the practitioners they employ. These strategies are often codified in state law to best ensure that they are consistent and viable retention strategies.

The following chapter provides an in-depth overview of the ARTERY Pipeline Framework and how it engages each layer of the education system from middle school through graduate programming. Worksheets are offered to help advocates as they begin to identify their current training program capacity, and the capacity needed to meet the workforce demands of their state or community. Policy opportunities are offered at each of these education levels to address practice and funding.

Tips for Training Your School-Based Mental Health Workforce

The following are policy recommendations to help you begin building a training foundation for your SBMH workforce. Building a training pipeline will help ensure that your state has enough SBMH providers to deliver the much-needed mental health services that schools require.

- Implement the ARTERY Pipeline Framework to align all career pathway initiatives
- Hire a professional to help advocate and align pipeline efforts from the state level to the schools
- Support the establishment of statewide ratios to determine optimal and current supply and demand of providers
- Contribute to ratio improvement planning with the state and districts
- Align and expand training opportunities to meet the identified demand for ratios
- Advocate to the state for funds to align and expand the identified programming
- Apply for state and federal grants to supplement reliable funding streams
- Offer tuition reimbursement or scholarships for students to enter the school-based mental health career programs
- Create partnerships with local districts for your practicum and internship students to gain field experience
- Establish dual-credit opportunities with local districts into school-based mental health pipeline courses

- Support the licensing of the psychological services position and stacked degree programs
- Create Articulation Agreements across IHEs to support course and degree transfers
- Partner with districts to help fund or co-fund professors to grow and expand training programs as an investment in the pipeline
- Create virtual access to all aspects of programming: dual-credit, minor/undergraduate, and graduate

Tips for Training School-Based Mental Health Supports and Services

Institutes of higher education typically don't deliver direct services to PK–12 students. However, they do train the professionals who eventually end up working and delivering those services in the school setting. Higher education recommendations focus on the training of professionals. In this sense, when developing curriculum at the undergraduate and graduate levels, align content to the standards established by the three school-based mental health professions. At the undergraduate level, this may be a combination of all three. At the graduate level, the curriculum will directly align with its corresponding profession. For example, in a school psychology graduate training program, the curricular standards would align with the 10 Practice Domains established by the National Association of School Psychologists (NASP) (2020).

Advocacy Opportunities

There is a critical shortage nationwide of school-based mental health providers and student to provider ratios are abysmal (National Association of School Psychologists, 2021; American School Counselor Association, 2021; School Social Work Association of America, 2013, 2019). There is also a critical shortage in the faculty and programming options available in higher education to train school-based mental health providers (Kim, 2021).

Advocating for expanded or additional higher education training programs can be tricky and confusing. It may also follow a different advocacy pattern than in school districts. Advocacy can be tricky because IHEs often have their own rules, funding sources, and needs. It can be confusing because how one becomes aware of what lever to access and when to do so might be different than in the district setting.

On a higher education campus, advocacy will be needed at many levels. It will be needed at the department level, which will be offering the program and delivering the courses. It will be needed at the school or college level in which the department is housed, and at the institute level that the school is part of. Beyond the individual institute level, advocacy will also be needed at the overall higher education executive cabinet and governing board level.

Find a faculty member or someone who is familiar with navigating the higher education environment as you head down this advocacy path. There will be a learning curve with this work that is different from the local education agency side. Having someone who can help you navigate will reduce learning time and will increase the timeliness of your advocacy efforts.

Based on the key learning objectives, I can now:

- Identify the role of institutes of higher education in workforce development.
- Understand why higher education advocacy differs from local advocacy.
- Identify components of a formal workforce pipeline and why each are critical.
- Align training to national standards and local needs.
- Identify strategies to support overall statewide school-based mental health provider training needs.

References

American School Counselor Association. (2021). *ASCA releases updated student-to-school-counselor ratio data.* https://www.schoolcounselor.org/getmedia/238f136e-ec52–4bf2–94b6-f24c39447022/Ratios-20–21-Alpha.pdf

Dockweiler, K. A. (2019). *School psychologist pipeline framework ARTERY: Active Recruitment, Training, and Educator Retention to serve our Youth.* Nevada Department of Education [Virtual].

Hughes, T. L., Minke, K. M., & Sansosti, F. J. (2017). Expanding school psychology service delivery within the context of national health and mental health reform. *Journal of Applied School Psychology, 33*(3), 171–178. doi:10.1080/15377903.2017.1317139

Kim, J. (October 19, 2021). Higher ed's invisible understaffing epidemic. *Inside Higher Ed.* https://www.insidehighered.com/blogs/learning-innovation/higher-ed%E2%80%99s-invisible-understaffing-epidemic

National Association of School Psychologists. (2020). *Practice model domains.* https://www.nasponline.org/standards-and-certification/nasp-2020-professional-standards-adopted/nasp-2020-domains-of-practice

National Association of School Psychologists. (2021). *Shortages in school psychology: Challenges to meeting the growing needs of U.S. students and schools* [Research summary]. Author.

Pechota, D., Fulton, M., & Broom, S. (2020). 50 state comparison: State postsecondary governance structures. Education Commission of the States. https://www.ecs.org/50-state-comparison-postsecondary-governance-structures/

Schmitz, S. L., Clopton, K. L., Skaar, N. R., Dredge, S., & VanHorn, D. (2022). Increasing school-based mental health services with a "Grow Your Own" school psychology program. *Contemporary School Psychology, 26*, 22–33. https://doi.org/10.1007/s40688-020-00348-z

School Social Work Association of America. (2013). *School social workers helping students succeed: Recommended school social worker to student ratios.* https://www.sswaa.org/_files/ugd/426a18_4050422b3c41478f9eeodb83d1bc1f75.pdf

School Social Work Association of America. (2019). *School social workers: Vital resources for student success.* https://www.sswaa.org/_files/ugd/486e55_076e1bbb0b594c27b57c44d4f6f9a55b.pdf

16

WORKFORCE DEVELOPMENT
ARTERY Pipeline Framework

Learning Concepts

In this chapter, readers will learn:

- The ARTERY Pipeline Framework and its career pathways.
- What the five pillars of the ARTERY are.
- Why early entry points are so critical to building the SBMH workforce.
- How alignment of the ARTERY pillars enforces and strengthens the pipeline.
- Various policy opportunities to support SBMH career pathways and stacked degree programs.

Chapter Keywords

- Workforce development
- Workforce shortages
- The five pillars

DOI: 10.4324/9781003308515-19

This chapter outlines the gold standard for long-term mental health reform in schools. As discussed in the first chapter of this book, *having adequate mental health services in schools is predicated on having an adequate number of professionals to deliver the services.* The ARTERY Pipeline Framework (Dockweiler, 2019) is a novel career pathway model that can be applied to all school-based mental health (SBMH) professions: school psychology, school counseling, and school social work.

Following the framework will ensure that schools have enough professionals to deliver comprehensive mental health supports to students in the school setting. The shortage of SBMH professionals in schools is pervasive across the country and is the number one barrier for accessing mental health supports. If states can remedy their SBMH workforce issues, they can begin to tackle other mental health issues in schools because they will have the requisite staff to do so. This chapter outlines the details of the ARTERY Pipeline Framework including the stacked nature of the pillars and how each stack supports the next. Worksheets are provided at the end of this chapter along with one state's model of how they were able to successfully identify their workforce needs and solutions.

Workforce Needs

One of the core issues we face today surrounding all aspects of mental health services is a lack of providers. There just aren't enough school-based and community-based providers to meet the growing and intense needs of our families. Situating this workforce issue within a greater context leads us to examine the lack of training programs in higher education. How can we begin to have enough licensed mental health professionals if higher education programs are not training them, or if employers are not recruiting or retaining them? Further, how can higher education training programs ever produce enough professionals when they do not have the capacity to do so?

Historically, school-based mental health professionals have not proactively had to advocate for our professions. We've been able to quietly do our jobs, and we don't usually make many waves. Initially, advocating for our role and our professions did not seem necessary. School psychology was an emerging profession a hundred years ago when student attendance became compulsory. Modern psychology was also an emerging field and there was still much to be understood. The profession has evolved over the decades and instead of primarily studying psychology, cognition, and behavior, we are now also studying advocacy and workforce pipelines. Researchers predicted nearly three decades ago that without substantial change to graduate education, research, and practice, the profession of school psychology would never be able to meet students' well-being needs (Conoley & Gutkin, 1995). With the massive workforce issues that we are facing today this continues to be a concern. What steps could or should have been taken in the past century to ensure students sustainably have access to the services and supports we provide? While we can't change the past, we can learn from history to help guide our actions today and into the future.

At its current workforce trajectory, the field of school psychology is successfully working itself into extinction. There are just not enough school psychology training programs regionally distributed to meet the needs of states and local communities. Even within the national context, there are not enough training programs to meeting the needs of the country. In Nevada alone, there are approximately 220 practicing school psychologists. According to national best-practice recommendations of 1 school psychologist to every 500 students, Nevada would require a total of approximately 960 school psychologists. Where is the state going to get an additional 740 school psychologists?

Currently, Nevada has one school psychology training program. In recent years, that program has graduated approximately one dozen practitioners annually, with only about half of these practitioners entering the workforce in our state. Many return to their home states for work opportunities, many pursue advanced doctoral studies, or some enter into a different career field altogether. How can six students a year close a workforce gap of 740 positions? The answer is easy: it can't.

New and different solutions are needed to address the workforce issues related to school-based mental health providers. The story of Nevada is not unique and not isolated to the field of school psychology. School counselors and school social workers also face similar workforce issues. For example, in Nevada, there is a shortage of approximately 819 school counselors statewide and 1,395 school social workers (Nevada Department of Education, 2020). There are just not enough graduate level training programs to meet our nation's needs for school-based mental health providers.

ARTERY Pipeline Framework

On June 3, 2019, we had just come out of Nevada's 80th legislative session. We had achieved some great successes that laid the groundwork to begin strategically identifying and addressing mental health needs in schools. At the forefront was the policies passed to support *workforce development* of SBMH professionals. While the session achieved many successes, it also created unknowns into how the policies would actually be implemented. In my mind, a clear pathway forward outlining next steps was needed. I remember specifically forcing myself to take a mental "day off" and made myself step away from the work to appreciate the wins that were accomplished. Throughout my career I've learned to "make time to take the time" and to adhere to this motto as stringently as possible. While enjoying this 24-hour reprieve from political strategy, the voice in the back of my mind was also telling me, "the brain needs time to regroup and reenergize".

After my one-day mental vacation, I sat down and put to paper all the next steps that were necessary to address the severe *workforce shortages* for SBMH providers. As the list grew, my newly rested mind was able to creatively play with the information before me. I reorganized the list of unique yet connected pieces into a career pipeline framework applicable to all three SBMH professions. In doing so, the ARTERY Pipeline Framework was born. ARTERY stands for Active Recruitment, Training, and Educator Retention to serve our Youth and encompasses implementation layers from high school to graduate school.

The ARTERY does not have a single entry or exit point. However, it does follow a clear pathway. Think of an aspen grove. All the trees are connected underground and share a similar, foundational root system. How the trees grow and flourish above ground is unique, and no two trees make the same way toward the light. Their pathways may be similar, but their journeys are unique.

So is the student's journey through the ARTERY. Foundationally, there are core courses and shared entry points that feed into the ARTERY root system. However, based on the decisions made by the student, each of their career pathways will look different. Three students may enter the ARTERY as dual-credit high school students interested in school-based mental health. They may each take similar core classes in their undergraduate program and all three may even obtain the same minor in School-Based Mental Health. However, their pathway into the light of their chosen graduate degree program may be different. One student may shoot through the soil emerging into the school counseling graduate program. Another student may choose to enter school social work. The third student may choose school psychology. All three share a similar foundational structure, yet all three enter in three different career fields, becoming three uniquely different trees.

Innumerable benefits emerge from the ARTERY Pipeline Framework:

• It casts a net far and wide to recruit as many students a possible, as early as possible, into the three school-based mental health career fields.
• It creates collegiality between the three professions, and students gain an appreciation for the similarities and unique differences between the three.
• It supports stacked degree programs and licensing opportunities to promote economic development and earning potential while progressing through the ARTERY.
• It recruits students locally, trains them within their state or community, and promotes retention of graduates as they return to and serve the communities in which they came.
• It reduces barriers to access and promotes cultural diversity, equity, and inclusivity efforts as more local graduates are being produced and remain to work in their state.

The Five Pillars

There are five pillars of the ARTERY Pipeline Framework: pre-high school graduates, high school graduates, bachelor students, post-baccalaureate students, and graduate students. Advocacy opportunities exist at all five pillars, as alignment of efforts must be supported at each pillar and within each lever, from the state all the way down to the school. The following section will describe each pillar in greater detail and the corresponding advocacy and policy opportunities that align within.

Your state may have some of these pieces in place already. This is great news and will provide a foundation in which to start building. It is doubtful that your state has all these pieces in place, aligned, and functioning as intended. Cultivate the pieces that are in place and develop new pieces that do not yet exist. When all these pieces are in place and working as intended, we can prevent our current trajectory of a crash course toward professional extinction.

Pre–High School Graduates

Middle and high school students are the first pillar of the ARTERY. One of the challenges with current career pathways for school-based mental health professionals is that exposure and recruitment are focused on the graduate level (Bocanegra et al., 2019). This is a huge missed opportunity and has contributed significantly to our present workforce situation. The ARTERY framework flips this dynamic and focuses efforts at the other end of the education ladder, targeting students in middle and high school.

Middle school efforts are in the form of awareness campaigns and career exposure opportunities. While middle school students are too young to participate in dual-enrollment courses or many mental health employment opportunities, they are not too young to be *aware* that the careers exist. If awareness and exposure activities don't begin until students have graduated with their bachelor's degree, we are missing up to ten years of recruitment opportunities.

As part of the awareness and exposure campaigns, middle school students need short-term tangible goals to look forward to. Students need to know that career and technical education (CTE) opportunities exist in high school and that they need to begin thinking about them *now*. The application for CTE programs typically happens at the end of middle school and if students aren't aware of the timeframes and deadlines, then they stand to miss out. In addition to CTE programs, middle school students need to be aware of dual-enrollment and college credit opportunities in high school that exist for the school-based mental health fields.

CTE programs and dual-enrollment courses are the first "stack" in school-based mental health stacked degree programming. It is the earliest and most foundational place for students to earn their first certificate and enter into the mental health workforce. This first stack will evolve into the next layer of the stack, which leads to additional and higher paying work opportunities and so on.

High school efforts include the implementation of human services and mental health CTE programs along with dual-enrollment courses. Dual-enrollment courses are a great option for students. These courses are often offered at a lower per credit cost and might even be paid for by the district or higher education institute; it depends on what type of agreement has been established. Students who take dual-enrollment courses in high school are more likely to enter into higher education and have higher efficacy for their success as a college student. Many high school students, especially first-generation students, do not "see themselves" in college as they do not have close friends or family members who have attended. It seems like a place for other people, not for them. As such, they don't enroll. Dual-enrollment courses allow high school students to test the waters of higher education and to realize that they *can* be successful in that environment. Students who feel successful and have higher rates of self-efficacy for college-level work will persist through a college degree resulting in greater bachelor's degree completion rates.

Policy Opportunities

- Conduct school-based mental health awareness campaigns in middle and high schools; require them as part of career day–type initiatives
- Create human services and/or mental health career and technical education programming
- Create dual-credit and/or dual-enrollment courses between school districts and institutes of higher education
- Align these dual course options to those courses offered in the School-Based Mental Health minor/major
- Offer financial assistance to offset or fully fund tuition for the high school students enrolled in the dual learning courses

High School Graduates

High school graduates are the second pillar of the ARTERY. Students who have earned their high school diploma or equivalent can enter into the

ARTERY at this level. This may or may not include students who have attended human services or mental health CTE programs or participated in dual-enrollment coursework. Remember that there are many entry and exit points to the ARTERY Framework!

The goal at the high school graduate level is active recruitment. We want to actively entice high school graduates to enroll into higher education and persist through the ARTERY toward a bachelor's degree. In doing so, their trajectory will align with the designated, corresponding school-based mental health coursework, certificates, and licensing options. Tangible rewards that can be earned every few years will help keep students motivated and engaged in the pathway. If we keep students moving through the ARTERY with the end goal of eventual licensure as a school-based mental health professional at the graduate level, we will ultimately retain more students than we lose. The key here is "active recruitment".

Policy Opportunities

- Active recruitment of high school graduates into School-Based Mental Health programming
- Create tuition scholarships for students to enroll in a School-Based Mental Health minor or major and corresponding coursework
- Offer preferential enrollment for students who already have CTE certificates or dual coursework
- Create partnerships with TRIO Upward Bound, Sankofa, and other diverse student support groups to recruit students who represent the local communities

Undergraduate Students

The third pillar of the ARTERY is the undergraduate degree level. At this level, there are so many wonderful opportunities to explore and new learning experiences to have. Undergraduate courses are a great place to increase exposure to possible areas of interest (Morrison et al., 2022) and exploring SBMH coursework is no exception. In terms of possible undergraduate degree fields that might funnel into the ARTERY, some might include nursing, psychology, education, sociology, biology, philosophy, finance, interdisciplinary studies, or human services.

The pre-bachelor level is the next stack in the stacked degree concept. At this level, degree and licensing opportunities exist, such as the two-year associate degree, a community-based mental health worker license, a minor in School-Based Mental Health, and a license as a psychological services assistant (PSA). The root system of the aspen grove is wide at this point and there are many entry and exit points to the ARTERY. A specific school-based mental health profession does not need to be declared and nourishing the roots that lead to these professions is the goal. Once students learn more about the three school-based mental health fields, then they can decide which to focus on and target for the next stack of their pathway.

To enhance exposure to the school-based mental health career fields, it is beneficial for higher education institutions to offer an undergraduate minor in School-Based Mental Health. This lends itself to creating interest across multiple degree fields and can be attached to any bachelor's degree. Or institutes could create a separate bachelor's degree in School-Based Mental Health. State departments of education, school districts, and intuitions of higher education can work collaboratively to create and license the PSA position. This position would typically be at the support staff level within the education setting.

The PSA position can work in schools to assist with many aspects of a school-based mental health professionals daily administrative tasks. By taking on many of these administrative office-type tasks, the PSA frees up the school-based mental health provider to engage in direct consultation and assessment with students. For example, in Nevada, the PSA assists school psychologists with scheduling meetings, compliance paperwork, conducting rating scales, and some forms of assessment such as achievement tests. This position cannot interpret assessment results, but they can administer and score, leaving tasks such as interpretation, intervention, and report writing to the school psychologist.

This position is critical to have in place as districts work to improve their ratios. If a school psychologist can free up 50% of their time with the assistance of a PSA, it is almost as if the district hired a .5 full-time equivalent (FTE) school psychologist because more of their time is available to work directly with students. Another upside for districts is that the PSA position is hired at a support staff level, and is thus more cost-effective to employ. Also, since the entry point for a PSA requires less training, there may be a larger pool of individuals available to hire into this type of position. A final benefit of this position is that the PSA is exposed to what school psychologists do on a daily basis and learn many beneficial skills on the job.

Policy Opportunities

- Create formal Articulation Agreements between two-year community colleges and four-year higher education institutes to facilitate transfer of mental health–related coursework and associate degrees
- Work with the state licensing agency to create a license for the PSA position
- Work with local school districts to create and fund PSA positions
- Create a School-Based Mental Health minor and/or undergraduate major
- Create tuition scholarships for students to enroll in a School-Based Mental Health minor or major and corresponding coursework
- Partner with the various colleges or departments across campus to build the School-Based Mental Health minor into their degree sheets for students

Post-Baccalaureate Students

Students with earned bachelor's degrees are the fourth pillar of the ARTERY. At this level, students will most likely have already been employed in their chosen degree field and they may have even taken some school-based mental health coursework. They may currently be working as a teacher, a geologist, or a financial planner. They may be employed by a school district as a PSA and have completed the next step in their education before moving on to a graduate program in school psychology.

At the post-baccalaureate degree level, a shift transpires from exposure to all the school-based mental health professions toward a more focused level of training. At this point, if individuals are looking to move on in their studies, they will need to select a specialization. They will need to select and apply to a graduate program in school psychology, school counseling, or school social work. Many programs will accept students from a variety of undergraduate degree programs. Having a minor in School-Based Mental Health or having taken related coursework can be beneficial.

This post-baccalaureate degree level is also often referred to as re-specialization. It is not uncommon for teachers to want to shift their focus from classroom instruction to overall student well-being. These teachers love working with students and enjoy the educational setting but realize that they want to focus more on student mental health or special education assessment. These teachers already have a bachelor's degree in education and have extensive knowledge of how education systems operate. They are great candidates to enroll in one of the three SBMH graduate training programs that best aligns with their career interests. In this sense, we are able to retain educators, and they don't leave the education workforce all together. Re-specialization into an SBMH career field is a great option for these teachers.

Policy Opportunities

- Create re-specialization pathways for post-baccalaureate students
- Engage with community organizations to recruit working professionals into SBMH graduate programs
- Create scholarships for working professionals to enter graduate training programs

Graduate Students

Graduate students are the final pillar of the ARTERY framework. This is where all the efforts spent recruiting, training, and retaining students within all stacks of the ARTERY pays off. All pathways of the ARTERY ultimately meet up at the graduate level. At this level, students decide which school-based line of graduate study they'd like to pursue, and the aspen saplings begin to emerge! Will students become future school counselors, or school social workers, or school psychologists?

As your SBMH pipeline grows, so will your applicants to graduate training programs. This is a good problem to have. We need more graduates to enter the workforce in schools and admitting more graduate students is one way to do this. Institutes of higher education will need to be aware of this positive consequence and be prepared to fund expansion of their graduate training programs. Early advocacy and forward planning can help lay this groundwork.

Training at the graduate level must also evolve. For example, the traditional test-and-place practice of school psychology must evolve to a more ecological model that address systems change (Conoley & Gutkin, 2020). Professional advocacy, policy making processes, and leadership responsibilities must also be embedded into graduate coursework if we are going to prepare cadres of future professionals who can advocate for the policy changes needed to improve service delivery to students.

Regardless of the end profession chosen, all students entered the ARTERY at some point. It may have been the traditional entry point of post-baccalaureate, or it may have been several levels before that at the high school level. Hopefully, as the ARTERY model gains momentum and there is political will to implement school-based mental health pipeline models, more and more students will enter at the earliest entry points. The concerted efforts to expand the root system and pathways for student enrollment will reap great benefits for students and our communities as a whole.

Policy Opportunities

- Allow teachers who are re-specializing to maintain their district salary and benefits while they complete their internship
- Create state licensing opportunities for students to obtain a provisional license during their internship to ensure competitive pay
- Create tuition scholarships for students enrolled in SBMH graduate programming
- Advocate to expand programs by hiring additional faculty

Intentional Alignment

As mentioned earlier, your state or local community may have a few of these pieces in place. However, the key to the ARTERY Pipeline Framework, and what sets it apart from other initiatives, is the intentional nature to align every layer of the education spectrum. It is not enough to offer a few dual-credit courses in psychology or counseling.

Where do these students then turn as they head into college? Typically, not into the SBMH career ladder because outside the ARTERY, it doesn't exist. Intentional pathways *within the school-based side of mental health* are critical and are what is currently missing. Removing barriers, establishing pathways, and supporting students on their journey through the ARTERY are game changers.

Alignment within each education layer and each policy lever is critical. If the policies are in place, the practices will follow. Similarly, policies can be created based on best practices from the field. Policies can help protect and formalize good practices or support their expansion. To fully support the ARTERY, every education layer must be considered from middle school to graduate study and juxtaposed against each of the policy levers, federal to the classroom. Each of these intersections offers opportunity for alignment to best support an increased mental health workforce and increased mental health supports in schools.

Final Thoughts

The other night my ten-year-old daughter asked me, "What goes up and never goes down?" She looked at me expectantly while I came up with an answer. My tired brain responded, "a bird". She looked at me like I had barely even tried to come up with a good answer. She shook her head and said, "Nope. It's *age!*" Haha, good one, she got me. Not to be outdone, I returned with, "What never goes up and always goes down?" She thought for a minute and responded intently, "I think it's a balloon, you know, one of those balloons without helium that can't stay up anymore". I liked where she was going with her answer and told her so. I then said, "Think about the bigger picture. *Why* can't the balloon stay up without helium? What else is happening that you might not be able to see that is causing it to come down?" Eventually she came to the conclusion that the force of gravity was the big picture answer.

Advocating for mental health supports and professionals requires the same approach. The answer may not be as simple as what you see on the surface. Situate the problem within the bigger picture; continue to ask "why" until you get to the real source of the issue. The bigger picture that is happening behind the scenes will be what you need to address, not the symptoms of what it impacts. This big workforce picture is what the ARTERY Pipeline Framework addresses. Significant shortages in the SBMH career fields will not be solved by continuing to do what we've always done. The larger solution must run deeper and earlier to create long-term systemic change.

Based on the key learning objectives, I can now:

- Explain the ARTERY Pipeline Framework.
- Discuss how the five pillars of the ARTERY build on each other.
- Explain the role that middle and high schools play in creating early entry points to SBMH training programs.
- Recognize when the ARTERY pillars may be misaligned or absent.
- Identify one or more policy opportunities to begin advocating for in my own context.

Figures 16.1 through 16.11 provide advocates with sample worksheets in which to complete their own school-based mental health workforce needs analysis. It provides a real-life example for school psychologists from Nevada, prior to 2021, that aligns with enacted state statutes and corresponding regulations. Open worksheets allow advocates to walk through the same process to identify current realities and to propose solutions for their own state.

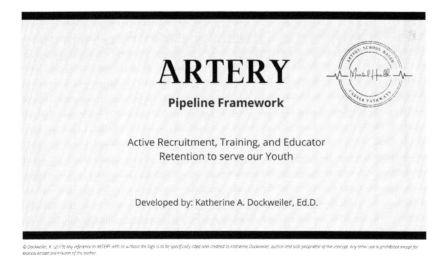

Figure 16.1 ARTERY Title Slide

School Psychologist
Current Career Pathways in Nevada

HS Student	SBMH Minor	PSA	Bachelor's	Master's Plus
No pathway or certificate Opportunity does not currently exist	*No pathway or certificate* Opportunity does not currently exist	*No pathway or certificate* Opportunity does not currently exist	*No pathway or certificate* Opportunity does not currently exist	*Licensed School Psychologist* Ability to work as a practicing school psychologist

Figure 16.2 Current Career Pathways in Nevada

School Psychologist
Current Career Pathways Your State

HS Student	SBMH Minor	PSA	Bachelor's	Master's Plus

Figure 16.3 Current Career Pathways in Your State

School Psychologist

Proposed Career Pathways in Nevada

HS Student	SBMH Minor	PSA	Bachelor's	Master's Plus
High School Student	*Undergraduate Student*	*Undergraduate Student*	*Undergraduate Student*	*Licensed School Psychologist*
Opportunity for dual enrollment courses and/or CTE courses, first entry point to the ARTERY and SBMH professions	Opportunity to work toward a Minor in School-Based Mental Health within the ARTERY career pathway (24 credits)	Ability for district employment and state licensure as a PSA to assist school psychologists with specific tasks	Continued employment as PSA, culmination of BA/BS, and tracked into the Ed.S. in school psychology (124 credits)	Ability to work as a practicing school psychologist with NCSP (minimum 60 graduate credits)

© Dockweiler, K. (2019) Any reference to ARTERY with or without the logo is to be specifically cited and credited to Katherine Dockweiler, author and sole proprietor of the concept. Any other use is prohibited except for express written permission of the author.

Figure 16.4 Proposed Career Pathways in Nevada

School Psychologist

Proposed Career Pathways in Your State

HS Student	SBMH Minor	PSA	Bachelor's	Master's Plus

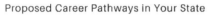

© Dockweiler, K. (2019) Any reference to ARTERY with or without the logo is to be specifically cited and credited to Katherine Dockweiler, author and sole proprietor of the concept. Any other use is prohibited except for express written permission of the author.

Figure 16.5 Proposed Career Pathways in Your State

School Psychologist
Current Higher Education Pipeline in Nevada

HS Student	SBMH Minor	PSA	Bachelor's	Master's Plus
No entry point	No specific entry point	No specific entry point	No specific entry point	Licensed School Psychologist
Annual Openings: 0	Annual Openings: 0	Annual Openings: 0	Annual Openings: 0	Annual Openings: 20
Annual Graduates: 0	Annual Graduates: 0	Annual Graduates: 0	Annual Graduates: 0	Annual Graduates: 12
				Annual Employed: 6

Figure 16.6 Current Higher Education Pipeline in Nevada

School Psychologist
Current Higher Education Pipeline in Your State

HS Student	SBMH Minor	PSA	Bachelor's	Master's Plus
Entry point:	Entry point:	Entry point:	Entry point:	Entry point:
Annual Openings:	Annual Openings:	Annual Openings:	Annual Openings:	Annual Openings:
Annual Graduates:	Annual Graduates:	Annual Graduates:	Annual Graduates:	Annual Graduates:
				Annual Employed:

Figure 16.7 Current Higher Education Pipeline in Your State

School Psychologist

Proposed Higher Education Pipeline in Nevada *

HS Student	SBMH Minor	PSA	Bachelor's	Master's Plus
High School Student	*Undergraduate Student*	*Undergraduate Student*	*Undergraduate Student*	*Licensed School Psychologist^*
Annual Openings: + Annual Graduates: +	Annual Openings: + Annual Graduates: +	Annual Openings: 225 Annual Licenses: 175	Annual Openings: 225 Annual Graduates: 175	Current Openings: 740 Annual Graduates: 125 Annual Employed: 125

*Based on 1:500 ratio (NRS)   + available to all students   ^supported by SB89, SB319, SB151, SB352

Figure 16.8 Proposed Higher Education Pipeline in Nevada

School Psychologist

Proposed Higher Education Pipeline in Your State

HS Student	SBMH Minor	PSA	Bachelor's	Master's Plus
High School Student	*Undergraduate Student*	*Undergraduate Student*	*Undergraduate Student*	*Licensed School Psychologist*
Annual Openings: Annual Graduates:	Annual Openings: Annual Graduates:	Annual Openings: Annual Graduates:	Annual Openings: Annual Graduates:	Current Openings: Annual Graduates: Annual Employed:

Figure 16.9 Proposed Higher Education Pipeline in Your State

School Psychologist
Retention Benefits in Nevada

HS Student	SBMH Minor	PSA	Bachelor's	Master's Plus
High School Student	*Undergraduate Student*	*Undergraduate Student*	*Undergraduate Student*	*Licensed School Psychologist*
Higher education courses paid for via grants, Title I, community supporters, and high school budgets	Stacked degree and PSA program with several entry and exit points	At this entry point, accrue up to 6 years of retirement while working towards degree, fully paid internship during Ed.S.	Potential to begin accruing 3 years of retirement as a PSA while working towards degree at this entry point.	Potential to have accrued up to 6 years of retirement as a PSA and full salary benefits retention during intern year

© Dockweiler, K. (2019) Any reference to ARTERY with or without the logo is to be specifically cited and credited to Katherine Dockweiler, author and sole proprietor of the concept. Any other use is prohibited except for express written permission of the author.

Figure 16.10 Retention Benefits in Nevada

School Psychologist
Retention Benefits in Your State

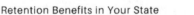

HS Student	SBMH Minor	PSA	Bachelor's	Master's Plus
High School Student	*Undergraduate Student*	*Undergraduate Student*	*Undergraduate Student*	*Licensed School Psychologist*

© Dockweiler, K. (2019) Any reference to ARTERY with or without the logo is to be specifically cited and credited to Katherine Dockweiler, author and sole proprietor of the concept. Any other use is prohibited except for express written permission of the author.

Figure 16.11 Retention Benefits in Your State

References

Bocanegra, J. O., Gubi, A. A., Callan, G. L., Grapin, S. L., & McCall, J. (2019). A lack of exposure to school psychology within undergraduate psychology coursework. *Teaching of Psychology, 46*(3), 208–214. https://doi.org/10.1177/0098628319848876

Conoley, J. C., Powers, K., & Gutkin, T. B. (2020). How is school psychology doing: Why hasn't school psychology realized its promise? *School Psychology, 35*(6), 367–374. https://doi.org/10.1037/spq0000404

Conoley, J. C., & Gutkin, T. B. (1995). Why didn't – why doesn't – school psychology realize its promise? *Journal of School Psychology, 33*(3), 209–217. https://doi.org/10.1016/0022–4405(95)00009-B

Dockweiler, K. A. (2019). *School psychologist pipeline framework ARTERY: Active Recruitment, Training, and Educator Retention to serve our Youth.* Nevada Department of Education [Virtual].

Morrison, J. Q., Davies, S. C., & Noltemeyer, A. (2022). An analysis of the workforce pipeline in school psychology. *Contemporary School Psychology, 26,* 14–22. https://doi.org/10.1007/s40688-020-00319-4

Nevada Department of Education. (April 30, 2020). *Non-binding recommended ratios for specialized instructional support personnel.* https://doe.nv.gov/uploadedFiles/ndedoenvgov/content/Boards_Commissions_Councils/State_Board_of_Education/2020/April/FollowupSISPRatiospersSB%2089.pdf

17

LOCAL EDUCATION AGENCIES

Learning Concepts

In this chapter, readers will learn:

- What role local education agencies have in district level policy making.
- How districts can align policies and procedures to state level policies.
- How to support timely implementation of state level policies.
- What strategies districts can use to help recruit, train, and retain school-based mental health professionals.
- What school-based mental health supports and services districts can implement.

Chapter Keywords

- Local control
- Local education agencies

DOI: 10.4324/9781003308515-20

How do policies that are passed at the state level make their way down to the local level? Do policies get translated into practice immediately? Who is in charge of implementation? These are all common questions as policies work their way down to the local education agency and then into schools. There often seem to be so many layers between the policy and the students. Some school districts have greater *local control* over their implementation efforts, and advocates are encouraged to stay engaged and advocate at the local level. Within a state, not all policies are enacted uniformly across districts. Equity issues often arise and students who need mental health supports the most may not receive them. Similarly, preventative mental health supports that teach protective factors must be taught to all students in a district.

What Are Local Education Agencies?

Local education agencies (LEAs) control educational decisions at a level close to the school. They are often governed by a school board or other similar governing body. Similar to how state education agencies have a regulatory board, the LEA will also have a governing board. The school board will have responsibility for creating and directing the policies that govern all aspects in an LEA (U.S. Department of Education, 2017). These policies will be wide-sweeping, from catering/food distribution and transportation to academic instruction and school safety. They are also responsible for ensuring that state policies are carried out appropriately. The LEA will have responsibility for policy implementation and day-to-day activities of the school district. Each LEA or school board will have a different relationship and will be structured slightly differently. Understanding this dynamic will help you to determine who to go to and where to start your local advocacy efforts.

What Is the LEA Role in the Policy Making Process?

LEAs can have a significant impact on students through their policies. They can advocate at all levels and their voice can often carry great weight. Depending on the size of your LEA, it may have a government relations person or team who is tasked with advocating to the state department of education, the state legislature, and the congressional delegation regarding what policy changes they'd like to see. If your LEA is smaller, it might advocate as part of a regional coalition of school district who work with a single advocate to voice their collective interests.

At a level close to schools and students, LEAs are responsible for carrying out state-level policies once they are passed. Local school boards can help oversee the enactment of state-level policies by asking for regular reports. For example, if the state legislature passes a statute requiring each LEA to implement a social-emotional learning curriculum, the LEA is required to follow the law. Oftentimes, it can feel like districts can be slow to implement new policies or procedures. However, before any change can be made, they need to first research what program to use, purchase the program, create a new process or procedure, and then roll it out to all the schools. And by slow, I mean it can take *years* to fully implement a law depending on how complex it is. Meanwhile, students are often not benefiting from the programming that could be taking place. School boards can facilitate more timely delivery of the support or service by staying on top of implementation efforts.

Dr. Cosgrove reiterates that each level of policy making plays a different role in developing and enacting policies. The state creates laws to ensure that a process is in place and that desired outcomes must be worked toward. This becomes part of the process that triggers district level leaders to implement the law, as they are required to do so. Advocates must help with writing and passing laws, and with putting pressure on the districts to implement the law. This all needs to happen in the open and there must be public assessment documentation. Dr. Cosgrove shares that knowing Open Meeting Law and Robert's Rules of Order are important to understanding the policy making process at all levels.

Community members, families, and educators can be a great resource to the local school board in terms of keeping them informed of progress and encouraging the board to move the district along. Hold-ups and delays can occur due to the board or due to the district. Regardless, as policies trickle down from the state level to the local level, advocates are encouraged to stay on top of, and ahead of, how the policies get implemented. It is critical that policies are enacted as intended, not as how the district leaders or school board interprets them.

When policies reach the local level, there is another great opportunity to engage in Boomerang Policy Making. Reach out to leaders, offer feedback, provide implementation ideas, and suggest district level practices that could align with the state policy. If you don't speak up, you won't be heard. Also, if the LEA knows that the community is paying attention, they are more likely to move quicker on implementation and they may follow accountability and transparency procedures more closely.

LEAs can also set and carry out their own district level policies. This may be in response to state level policies or not. The local school board is tasked with vetting proposed policies, asking questions, and approving proposed policies. Have voice in all aspects of the local policy making process to ensure that students receive the supports that they need. If there is a specific policy, service, or support that you think all students in the district would benefit from, draft your key message and make your ask of the decision makers.

Tips for School-Based Mental Health Workforce Development at the Local Level

Depending on the structure of your district, some of these recommendations may fall under a different agency or policy lever. As mentioned earlier, you will notice as you read through the policy examples in other policy lever chapters that some of the policy recommendations fall under multiple levers. They are listed in multiple places because multiple levers are involved to fully enact the policy. Also, involving multiple levers helps support alignment of the initiative. Below are some examples districts will want to consider as they work to recruit, train, and retain their school-based mental health workforce and pipeline:

- Offer paid internships to school-based mental health providers along with standard health insurance and retirement benefits
- Create and fund the psychological services assistant position
- If psychological services assistants must complete an internship, allow them to maintain their pay and benefits or offer them the internship pay and benefits, whichever is greater
- Allow teachers to re-specialize and allow them to maintain their teacher pay and benefits while they complete their internship hours
- Use funds recouped from school-based mental health providers to be directly reinvested in school-based mental health pipeline

efforts; this may include partnership with local institutes of higher education

- Align position allocation and funding with nationally (or state) recommended ratios
- Create a ratio improvement plan involving all the key stakeholders to help build and retain your school-based mental health workforce
- Establish accountability mechanisms reinforced through policy or the school board
- Create MOUs with institutes of higher education to place their students into practicum and internship sites
- Provide a stipend or additional pay to practicum and internship supervisors
- Hire designated practicum and/or internship supervisors
- Offer dual-credit coursework to all high school students
- Create strong partnerships with IHE
- Partner with other districts to help fund or co-fund professors at IHE to grow and expand training programs as an investment in the pipeline
- Create virtual access to all aspects of pipeline programming at the high school level including career and technical education courses and dual-credit courses

In order to successfully implement any mental health support, a district must first ensure that it has the school-based mental health providers to carry it out. The following are additional tips that districts can use to support long-term solutions to workforce scarcity.

Create and fund the psychological services assistant (PSA) position. This PSA support staff position is a huge benefit to the school psychologist and frees them up to work directly with students. Much of a school psychologist's time is spent on special education paperwork, scheduling, and other administrative type tasks. Having an assistant to help with this work allows the school psychologist to work directly with students running counseling groups, conducting threat assessments, or helping school teams determine who is at greatest risk for mental health issues.

Foster relationships with higher education training programs. If there are institutes of higher education who graduate school-based mental health providers, build relationships with them. They can help provide your district with interns, practicum students, or PSAs as they progress through their education. Similarly, there could be agreements in place where recruitment for their programs can be prioritized from your district and you can create a grow your own pipeline program like the ARTERY. Similarly, if the district has funds available to help support hiring of faculty at the higher education institute to train additional students, an MOU can be negotiated.

Compensate supervisors assigned to practicum and intern students. Practicum and intern students require extensive hours of supervision. This supervision is critical for the preparation of qualified and trained practitioners upon graduation. One downside is that the time spent on supervising the student takes away time from the supervisor's regular duties. This often results in the supervisor completing their work on their own time or less time is spent working directly with students. This can lead to burn out and feelings of resentment. They may also not consent to supervising a practicum or intern student in the future. To avoid all these potential eventualities, pay the supervisor for their time at a rate that is valuable. Or, hire school psychologists who want to supervise exclusively and create a position for this role.

Assign mentors to early career practitioners. Once a student graduates and is a school-based mental health practitioner, they will still have questions and will require a support network or contact person. Assign early career practitioners a mentor to support them through their first few years on the job. This supports retention efforts and will save the district from having to constantly hire new practitioners because they are better able to retain the ones that they have. Similar to providing compensation to practicum and intern student supervisors, provide compensation to the mentors to further support retention efforts.

Allow school psychologists to practice within all 10 Practice Domains as outlined by the National Association of School Psychologists (NASP) (2020). School psychologists often are relegated to completing special education evaluations. While federally mandated and necessary, special education evaluations are only a fraction of what school psychologists are trained and licensed to do. With appropriate ratios and caseloads, school psychologists can assist with many other school safety and well-being initiatives such as multi-tiered systems of support, restorative practices, counseling services, and mental health risk triage.

Allow school counselors to practice the American School Counselor Association National Model (2012). School counselors are trained mental health professionals and this aspect is often lost on school districts. Oftentimes school counselors are assigned responsibilities that are not directly aligned with their specialized training. For example, they get assigned lunch or hall duty, disciplinary procedures, and scheduling responsibilities. School counselors' time would be better spent working directly with students, actively engaged in counseling sessions, and other student well-being activities.

Allow school social workers to practice the tenets of the National School Social Work Practice Model (2013). Similar to the school psychologists' and school counselors' practice models, the school social workers' model is also grounded in legal, ethical, and socially just practices. Allowing school social workers to promote mental health services at school and in the community provides the wraparound care and services that many students and families need. They are the link between school supports and community-based supports that is often missing in districts.

Allocate and fund school-based mental health positions at the following nationally recommended ratios:

- School psychologists at the 1:500 ratio
- School counselors at the 1:250 ratio
- School social workers at the 1:250 ratio
- School nurses at the 1:750 ratio

School nurses are often an overlooked profession in school-based mental health. However, they are a critical team member, especially at the secondary level. As students grow up, they begin to manifest mental health conditions that often require medication to help keep them stable. Staffing school nurses at the nationally recommended ratio allows them time to consult with their team and offer valuable feedback on any possible interactions the student's medication may have, and any side effects that could explain behavior or performance in the school setting.

Tips for Supports and Services at the Local Level

Schools across the country are facing tremendous safety and well-being challenges. There are many different services and supports that can be put in place at the district level to ensure that students are safe mentally and physically. All the evidence- and research-based supports listed will only be impactful if they are implemented with fidelity. And to implement a mental health support with fidelity, you need to make sure you have adequate staffing of school-based mental health providers. Remember, having adequate mental health services is predicated on having an adequate number of school-based mental health providers.

While these supports could be implemented individually, they should be combined with as many other supports listed to maximize positive impact on students. While not an exhaustive list, below are some suggested supports and services districts can offer to their schools and students:

- Require an MTSS framework for mental health service delivery
- Ensure the safety of educators
- Ensure the safety of students
- Foster protective factors
- Implement restorative justice practices
- Use trauma-informed practices
- Select socially just programs and services
- Integrated social-emotional-behavioral programming
- Require suicide prevention programming and training
- Require a single point of entry on school campuses
- Require students to remain on campuses during school hours
- Offer teachers additional resources and supports for service delivery
- Create community partnerships
- Attempt to hire school-based mental health providers at recommended ratios
- Create school-based health clinics
- Identify and build supports available to the family in the community
- Support building community on campus by creating clubs such as a Black Student Union and a Gay–Straight Alliance
- Offer educator mental health supports and wellness programs
- Have an anonymous reporting line available for mental health concerns
- Trainings for principals on the role of each school-based mental health profession according to national best practice standards and how to effectively utilize each on their campus

Model Policy Examples

Many states will transfer implementation responsibilities of state statute down to the local education agencies. The state education agency may collect data on implementation of a bill as an accountability mechanism, but the local school district is in charge of determining how they will implement the law.

Allow student mental health days. In 2021 the Arizona legislature passed Senate Bill 1097 allowing for students to take mental health days. The law allows for students to be excused but leaves it up to the individual school districts to determine their own policies surrounding the law (Rivera, 2022).

Limit use of restraints and seclusion. The South Dakota legislature passed Senate Bill 46 (2018) limiting the use of restraints and seclusion in the schools. The law requires school districts to adopt or revise their current policies following prescribed provisions including a process for parent notification and a general prohibition on prone restrains and involuntary confinement.

Establish teams to respond to traumatic events reported through anonymous reporting system. In 2019 the Nevada legislature passed Senate Bill 80 requiring school districts to establish school-based teams to respond to calls of students experiencing traumatic events that come through their SafeVoice Program or Handle with Care Program.

Advocacy Opportunities

Innumerable advocacy opportunities exist at the district level. With regard to the local school board, opportunity exists to provide comment at public meetings, to email your board representative (or all the board members) to share your position on an issue, or to meet up with them for coffee to talk about an issue. Depending on the size of your community, you may interact with the school board members and district leaders organically. You may play on the same community basketball league team, see them walking in the park with their dog, or run into them at the local coffee shop. No matter if the encounter is by chance or scheduled, never miss an opportunity to voice your ask.

Consider the following scenario. One day you are at the supermarket, and you happen to see the district superintendent inspecting the quality of the strawberries in the produce isle. You have talked with fellow families, educators, and community organizations and have identified a significant need for more school social workers. Your group has identified how many more the district needs and what the cost would be to the district. One of the community organizations has even offered to share in the costs if the social workers also work in collaboration with their organization. So, what do you do when you see that superintendent looking at the strawberries? You have two options. One, you can do nothing and walk away. Or, two, you can approach the superintendent, politely introduce yourself, thank them for their work, and then proceed to share your ask (problem, action, benefit, and cost solution).

The superintendent won't be able to act on your information while in the supermarket. They will, however, now have the information and you've opened the door for further conversation. As you part, request their email address (if you don't have it already) and offer to send them some more information to support your ask. You can also offer to set up a time for you and other members of your group to meet with the superintendent to discuss this issue further. Be bold. Remember that you are advocating on behalf of students, not on your own behalf.

Living in Las Vegas, there are unique opportunities to interact with local officials. I remember one time I saw a school board member walking through a casino. At first, I was in disbelief and second guessed myself that that is who she was. After I'd convinced myself that I was indeed correct in who it was, I ran after her and called her name. She was incredibly gracious while I introduced myself as the president of the Nevada Association of School Psychologists. I briefly explained the issue we were having in the local district recruiting and retaining school psychologists as the pay was incredibly low. She sympathized with our issue and agreed the pay was too low. From that chance encounter we set up a meeting. From that meeting came additional meetings with the local union, the district superintendent, and other key leaders. These meetings and subsequent advocacy activities led eventually, five years later, to the pay being raised for school psychologists.

Municipal agencies are also great partners for policy advocacy. They can help fund initiatives or offer their own supports and services at no cost, or little cost, to the district. Understanding the dynamics between the municipal government and the local education agency can be very powerful. Leslie Baunach, school psychologist, shares that she's had success advocating at city council meetings, town hall meetings, and other community meetings. She recommends attending these local meetings as a great first step to getting involved in local advocacy.

Overall, there are many advocacy opportunities that exist at the district level as the supports and services requested are so close to the students. It is easier to directly see the link between advocacy at the district level and the supports and services provided to students at the school level because there are fewer layers of policy levers in between.

Based on the key learning objectives, I can now:

- Identify the role local education agencies have in district level policy making.
- Describe why state and local policies should align.
- Explain ways to support local implementation of state level policies.
- Identify strategies districts can use to recruit, train, and retain school-based mental health professionals.
- Identify the school-based supports and services that make the most sense to implement in my local context.

References

American School Counselor Association. (2012). *ASCA national model.* https://www.schoolcounselor.org/About-School-Counseling/ASCA-National-Model-for-School-Counseling-Programs

National Association of School Psychologists. (2020). *Practice model domains.* https://www.nasponline.org/standards-and-certification/nasp-2020-professional-standards-adopted/nasp-2020-domains-of-practice

Rivera, A. (March, 2022). *States act to allow student mental health days.* National Conference of State Legislatures. https://www.ncsl.org/research/education/states-act-to-allow-student-mental-health-days-magazine2022.aspx#:~:text=The%20department%20published%20its%20guidelines,distr icts%20may%20set%20specific%20policies

School Social Work Association of America. (2013). *National SSW model.* https://www.sswaa.org/ssw-model

Senate Bill 46, South Dakota 2018.

Senate Bill 80, Nevada 2019.

U.S. Department of Education. (2017). *Sec. 300.28 Local education agency.* https://sites.ed.gov/idea/regs/b/a/300.28

18

SCHOOL ROLE WITH POLICIES AND IMPLEMENTATION

Learning Concepts

In this chapter, readers will learn:

- The school's role in the policy making process.
- The critical importance of a multi-tiered system of support implementation model.
- The different trainings of each school-based mental health profession.
- What school level workforce strategies can be implemented.
- How to intentionally select and implement school-based mental health supports and services.

Chapter Keywords

- Multi-tiered systems of support
- School psychologists

DOI: 10.4324/9781003308515-21

- School counselors
- School social workers

How can schools effectively implement mental health supports and practices? What types of services are available? Who delivers the services? Whether the policy originates at the school level or is mandated by the state or district, there are a variety of ways to implement it. There is tremendous opportunity for advocates at the school level to have a positive impact on student mental health. As we learn more about what mental health services in schools look like, contextualizing mental health supports within an equity frame of multi-tiered systems of support (MTSS) can help schools as they work to implement a comprehensive service delivery model (Arora et al., 2019; Jimerson et al., 2016).

What Is the School Role in the Policy Making Process?

Depending on the context, school leaders and educators can play a significant role in the overarching policy making process. In alignment with the Boomerang Policy Making Model, these content experts can make or break a policy at any lever based on their professional perspectives. Obtaining stakeholder input is part of this process and the insight school professionals can offer decision makers should never be underrated.

At public hearings, professionals are always allowed to offer public comment as individuals. They may speak as a professional who works in the field, but they represent themselves as an individual, not as an employee of a school or district (unless the school or district has deputized them to do so).

Tamara Hudson, special education teacher and State Board of Education Member, stresses the importance that educators have in the policy making process. She shares that educators can give a hands-on perspective to policy makers about how a policy impacts teachers and students in the classroom. This direct connection can help bridge the policy-to-practice gap that so often exists.

Dr. Oyen, assistant professor and school psychologist, shares a similar perspective. She reports that the impact of storytelling is so powerful with legislators. There is power in telling stories as they help to understand key asks. Building relationships, telling stories, and having conversations with the right people are important efforts for educators and advocates to engage in. She shares that what makes a great school psychologist is not necessarily the same wiring that makes a fierce advocate. Our niceness gets in the way, but there is a way to be fierce and still be nice.

Parents and community members are also powerful voices in the collective advocacy of a school. They can sometimes advocate or say things that the school employees may feel uncomfortable saying. Collective voice can go a long way with advocacy and the more people or groups sharing the same message, the better.

At the school level, principals, teachers, school-based mental health providers, and other school staff can directly influence policies. They are often the ones tasked with writing school policies and procedures.

How Do School Policies Align?

Ideally, state, district, and school policies all align. The further away from the student, such as at the state or even district level, the policy may look more like guardrails, such as what type of components to include. It is at the school level where those individual decisions get to be made. For example, a state or district could mandate that all schools implement a violence prevention program. Unless they are willing to pay for it, they typically won't dictate what that program needs to be. The decision to select and implement the violence prevention program would fall at the school level.

Another mandate might be time. The state or district could mandate that all educators receive one hour a year on how to identify signs of mental health crisis in students. The school could then decide how to spend that one hour of training and what the content will include.

Sometimes state, district, and school policies do not align. When this happens, it is usually a matter of interpretation, or misinterpretation. Sometimes the misinterpretation is intentional, but usually it is not. If there are different interpretations of a policy, track the policy back to the lever or board who passed the policy and ask for clarification regarding the intent. This is the best way to get to the true intent, and to begin pulling the policy back into alignment with the intent.

How Are Mental Health Services Delivered in Schools?

Mental health supports and services are most impactful when they are embedded into the culture and climate of the school. They cannot be implemented or perceived as an "add-on" or a "one-off" to the academic instructional supports that are being delivered to students. Mental health supports, or social-emotional-behavioral (SEB) supports, must be woven into the structure of the school day and the content of core academic material. SEB and mental health are terms often used interchangeably in the school setting. Mental health generally refers to overall health and well-being and includes emotional, psychological, and social well-being. This term is generally used more commonly at the secondary level. Since diagnosable mental health conditions don't typically emerge until after puberty, elementary schools will often refer to mental health supports as SEB supports and services.

While mental health supports are most impactful when integrated and implemented with intentionality, each school is unique. They are each in their own phase of development and have their own readiness in which to deliver mental health supports. Integrating these supports into school culture takes time and will not happen overnight. There are three different levels of mental health MTSS implementation in schools (Clark & Dockweiler, 2020). Some schools are *adept implementors* and may be at a more advanced level of implementation. Other schools may have some mental health supports in place but are still focusing on building their capacity. These are considered *transitional implementors*. Other schools, *developmental implementors*, may have academic instruction and supports but nothing is in place for mental health or SEB. Take a moment to reflect on your local school, what level of mental health and SEB implementation is it at?

Depending on your school's level of implementation, comprehensive mental health services may be available, or services may be emerging with one schoolwide service. Regardless of how many services there are or their level of comprehensiveness, mental health supports and services should be delivered within a *Multi-Tiered System of Support* (MTSS) model. MTSS is an equitable framework in which to offer tiered supports so that all students receive the unique services they need. For a comprehensive MTSS implementation guide, see *Multi-Tiered Systems of Support in*

Secondary Schools: The Definitive Guide to Effective Implementation and Quality Control (Clark & Dockweiler, 2019) for use in grades 6 through 12. For elementary campuses and use in the prekindergarten through 5th grade setting, see Multi-Tiered Systems of Support in Secondary Schools: The Definitive Guide to Effective Implementation and Quality Control (Clark & Dockweiler, 2019).

What Are Tiered Intervention Supports and Services?

MTSS delivers instructional services across three tiers. Depending on where you live, there may be a fourth tier, but the concept and approach is the same. At its most basic level, Tier 1 is for all students, Tier 2 is needed for some students, and Tier 3 is needed for few students. The visualization that goes along with this is that of a triangle, with Tier 1 at the bottom, Tier 2 in the middle, and Tier 3 at the top (see Figure 18.1).

Instruction that is delivered to all students is called universal (Tier 1). Supports that are delivered to some students who are struggling are called targeted (Tier 2). Supports that are provided to a few students are called intensive (Tier 3). A good example to liken this to is from an academic perspective. In the academic realm, all students on a campus are provided reading instruction. Some students are going to struggle and will need help practicing letter sounds, blending, or comprehension. Few students will require even more intensive supports to help reinforce these basic reading concepts.

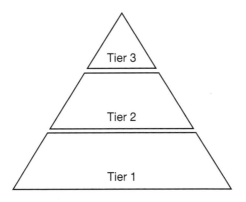

Figure 18.1 MTSS Intervention Tiers

In the mental health and SEB realm, the model is the same. All students on a campus should receive foundation social-emotional learning and positive behavioral interventions and supports. Some students may struggle with self-regulation, friendship seeking skills, or anxiety. Few students will require even more intensive supports to help with feelings of self-worth, thoughts of suicide, or plans to harm others.

The benefits of an MTSS tiered approach are innumerable. Positively impacting all students is at the top of the list. Increasing the likelihood that struggling students are identified, and receiving mental health support, is also a critical benefit. Reducing acts of student violence and self-harm are also key benefits. Decreasing manifestations of depression, anxiety, and somatizations are also significant benefits, as is increasing positive self-regard, decision making, and coping skills. The list goes on. The MTSS framework helps to deliver mental health and SEB supports to students and includes a wide spectrum of benefits, from increased resilience to decreased school shootings.

Who Delivers Mental Health Supports and Services in Schools?

Mental health support and services in schools can be delivered by a variety of people depending on what it is. If it is a counseling service, it needs to be delivered by one of your school-based mental health providers as they are licensed to deliver counseling services. If it is a mental health assessment targeting signs of depression, your school psychologist or school social worker will have the requisite training and licensing to deliver, score, and interpret the results. This will vary depending on how intense the service is. A good rule of thumb is: the more intense the service, the greater the likelihood it will need to be delivered by one of your licensed school-based mental health providers.

School psychologists are trained to help students learn and to support teachers to teach. They have "expertise in mental health, learning, behavior, to help students and youth succeed academically, socially, behaviorally, and emotionally" (National Association of School Psychologists [NASP], 2022, p. 1). They partner with families, schools, and communities to create safe and supportive learning environments where students can thrive. They have specialized training in many domains, including, but not limited to, assessments, behavior management, crisis preparation and response, diversity in development and learning, mental health, and data collection and interpretation. For more information about school psychologists, visit the National Association of School Psychologists' website at www.naspoline.org.

School counselors are trained to help students succeed in school and to plan their career. They help "students learn to develop effective collaboration and cooperation skills, to practice perseverance, to develop time management and study skills, and to learn self-motivation and self-direction habits" (American School Counselor Association, 2022, p. 1). They support inclusive school environments and assist with student academic planning, career and post-secondary planning, school counseling lessons, advocacy for students' needs, short-term supports to students, referral for long-term support for students, and collaboration between school staff, families, and community organizations. For more information about school counselors, visit the American School Counselor Association's website at www.schoolcounselor.org.

School social workers bring social work knowledge and expertise to school systems and school support teams. They are trained to "assist with mental health concerns, behavior concerns, positive behavior support, academic and classroom support, consultation with teachers, parents, and administrators as well as provide individual and group counseling/therapy" (School Social Work Association of America, 2022, p.1). They are hired by schools to provide direct as well as indirect services to students and families. They are the link between the school, home, and community to support a person's social, emotional, and life adjustment. For more information about school social workers, visit the School Social Work Association of America's website at www.sswaa.org.

If the support is more universal in nature or delivered as skill reinforcement to small groups of students, it is probably more appropriate to have a teacher deliver the support. For example, Tier 1 supports that are embedded into the daily instructional content should be delivered by a teacher in the classroom setting. Universal social-emotional learning or SEB screeners are also appropriately delivered by a member of the teaching staff.

Small groups that meet to work on Tier 2 targeted skill development, such as friendship seeking skills, can also be taught be a teacher. If your school has a social studies teacher or some other specialist who has an interest in helping with these types of groups, they may be a good fit. School counselors and the other school-based mental health providers can also certainly run targeted skills groups, but often their time is allocated to more intensive services and supports for students.

School-based mental health providers can assist and provide guidance to staff and school leadership at all three tiers. Their one-on-one interventions with students will fall at the Tier 3 level of support. School psychologists are uniquely trained to support effective MTSS implementation at all three tiers given their training in unique learning patterns, instructional delivery, universal screening, intervention development, and progress monitoring.

Tips for School-Based Mental Health Workforce Development at the School Level

Schools are in a unique position as they directly hire the staff who work in their schools. In some cases, certain positions will be assigned to them from a central or specialized service office. However, in most cases, the school oversees their own hiring. Whether they are directly hiring or are being assigned staff, they can still implement the following strategies to recruit, train, and retain school-based mental health professionals:

- Create and fund a psychological services assistant (PSA) support staff position.
- Foster relationships with higher education training programs.
- Compensate supervisors assigned to practicum and intern students.
- Assign mentors to early career practitioners.
- Allow school psychologists to practice within all 10 Practice Domains as outlined by the National Association of School Psychologists (2020).
- Allow school counselors to practice the American School Counselor Association National Model (2012).
- Allow school social workers to practice the tenets of the School Social Work Practice Model (2013).
- Allocate and fund school-based mental health positions at the following nationally recommended ratios:
  - School psychologists at the 1:500 ratio
  - School counselors at the 1:250 ratio

- School social workers at the 1:250 ratio
- School nurses at the 1:750 ratio

Tips for Mental Health Supports and Services at the School Level

Many of the services or supports shared below can be selected and implemented as stand-alone programs in a school. Remember that the more the services are connected and implemented with intentionality, the greater the likelihood for successful student outcomes. One such program that integrates mental health services and violence prevention within a school following the MTSS framework is *Healthy Minds, Safe Schools* (2022). This program uses an integrated MTSS model that offers tiered intervention services and helps teams place students into intervention bands, reducing ambiguities and increasing timely delivery of supports. For additional information, visit the *Healthy Minds, Safe Schools* website www.healthymindssafeschools.com.

Below is a list of various mental health and SEB supports or services that elementary and secondary schools can implement. This is not an exhaustive list, and some will make more sense than others given your school's unique context. These evidence-based mental health supports and services include:

- Implement MTSS framework for mental health and SEB service delivery

  - Tier 1 social-emotional learning
  - Tier 1 positive behavior interventions and supports schoolwide and classroom
  - Tier 1 Character development
  - Tier 2 Check-in check-out
  - Tier 2 Small group counseling
  - Tier 2 Pressure pass
  - Tier 2 Sticker charts
  - Tier 3 Individualized behavior intervention plan
  - Tier 3 Individual counseling
  - Tier 3 Community-based referrals
  - Tier 3 Family wraparound supports

- Ensure the safety of educators
- Ensure the safety of students
- Implement restorative practices
- Follow trauma-informed practices
- Select socially just programs and services
- Integrated social-emotional-behavioral programming
- Suicide prevention programming and training
- Create a single point of entry on campus
- Require students to remain on campus during school hours
- Offer teachers additional resources and supports for service delivery
- Create community partnerships
- Attempt to hire school-based mental health providers at recommended ratios
- Create school-based health clinics
- Identify and build supports available to the family in the community
- Build community on campus by creating clubs such as a Black Student Union and a Gay–Straight Alliance
- Offer educator mental health supports and wellness programs
- Have an anonymous reporting line available for mental health concerns

Advocacy Opportunities

If advocating for schoolwide delivery of mental health and SEB supports, one of the most impactful practices to advocate for is the MTSS framework. Mental health and SEB supports delivered within this structured service delivery framework will be more impactful, fewer students will inadvertently be overlooked for services, and all students will benefit.

Many states have MTSS policies already in place. If they do, this is a great opportunity to build the framework out in your school. Your district may have a guidance document or supports available to assist with implementation. If they do not, advocacy might be needed at the district level to improve support implementation at the school level.

Advocating for stronger relationships on campus can improve behavior outcomes for students. Dr. Robbins, high school principal, stresses that structures must be in place to create space to address the issues that students and their families face. From a restorative perspective, you can't restore what you don't have. In addition to building strong relationships with students, he also shares that there must be mechanisms in place to divert students from discipline. Most times there are no plans in place to divert students away from engaging in the behavior that resulted in the discipline referral. He recommends being intentional, having a diverting plan, and having therapeutic supports in place. We can't assume that all students have been taught the same things. New structures are needed to address their behavior needs.

State and district level advocacy may be needed for suicide prevention programming, an anonymous tip line, and funding to support additional mental health services and programming on your campus. Walk through the Boomerang Policy Making Model, identify the key levers, the "why" of your audience, and begin constructing your message accordingly. No is never no, and with persistence you will eventually hear a yes in some form.

If you begin to advocate for some of these services and are told they already exist, the issue may not be a policy issue; it is most likely an implementation issue. Revisiting how the policy was translated to practice, and then how the practice was translated into implementation, would be a great advocacy next step.

Schools can be powerful decision makers for students. Oftentimes state or district policy dictates what services are offered in schools; however, this is not always the case. If your district does not have a specific rule about what support or services it cannot offer, then basically any support or service is on the table!

Based on the key learning objectives, I can now:

- Explain the school's role in the policy making process.
- Describe the basic principles of a multi-tiered system of support framework.
- Identify the broad training areas of the three school-based mental health professionals.
- Explain different workforce strategies a school can use.
- Select a variety of school-based mental health supports and services that will benefit students in the school setting.

References

American School Counselor Association. (2012). *ASCA national model.* https://www.schoolcounselor.org/About-School-Counseling/ASCA-National-Model-for-School-Counseling-Programs

American School Counselor Association. (2022). *School counselor roles and ratios.* https://www.schoolcounselor.org/About-School-Counseling/School-Counselor-Roles-Ratios#:~:text=School%20counselors%20are%20highly%20educated,healthy%20goals%2C%20%20mindsets%20and%20behaviors

Arora, P. G., Collins, T. A., Dart, E. H., Hernández, S., Fetterman, H., & Doll, B. (2019). Multi-tiered systems of support for school-based mental health: A systemic review of depression interventions. *School Mental Health, 11,* 240–264. https://doi.org/10.1007/s12310-019-09314-4

Clark, A. G., & Dockweiler, K. A. (2019). *Multi-tiered systems of support in secondary schools: The definitive guide to effective implementation and quality control.* Routledge.

Clark, A. G., & Dockweiler, K. A. (2020). *Multi-tiered systems of support in elementary schools: The definitive guide to effective implementation and quality control.* Routledge.

Healthy Minds, Safe Schools. (2022). www.healthymindssafeschools.com

Jimerson, S. R., Burns, M. K., & VanDerHeyden, A. M. (2016). *Handbook of response to intervention: The science and practice of multi-tiered systems of support.* Springer.

National Association of School Psychologists. (2020). *Practice model domains.* https://www.nasponline.org/standards-and-certification/nasp-2020-professional-standards-adopted/nasp-2020-domains-of-practice

National Association of School Psychologists. (2022). *Who are school psychologists?* https://www.nasponline.org/about-school-psychology/who-are-school-psychologists

School Social Work Association of America. (2013). *National SSW model.* https://www.sswaa.org/ssw-model

School Social Work Association of America. (2022). *Role of school social worker.* https://www.sswaa.org/school-social-work

19

GETTING STARTED

Final Thoughts

Advocating for mental health supports in schools is a vital pursuit. The services sought are needed by students and help to support a healthy school climate. Without your advocacy, how is anyone going to know what your students need?

While persisting in your advocacy, remember to also advocate for more school-based mental health providers. Without them, who will deliver the services that you are advocating for?

As discussed in this book, the students are not okay, and they haven't been for a while. There is a State of Emergency in Children's Mental Health and a State of Emergency in the Workforce Development strategies to help solve the crisis. As change agents, advocates can help to address these emergencies to improve mental health and well-being outcomes for students and our communities.

Students have been experiencing escalated internalized and externalized behaviors for the past several decades. Active shooters on campus

DOI: 10.4324/9781003308515-22

have increased and suicide rates are on the rise. To address these occurrences, we need to proactively provide our students with preventative mental health and wellness care. We need to address adverse childhood experiences, transgenerational trauma, and mental health issues in children and youth. Our students bring these experiences with them to the classroom daily. Many issues are familial and treating the family may be necessary to best treat the student.

In the school setting, structures such as multi-tiered systems of support can help deliver differentiated interventions to students. Advocating for policy change to require this service delivery model is the first step to creating systemic and long-term change. Policies are only as good as their implementation, so following policies through to successful implementation will be key.

While advocating for the mental health services and model policies offered throughout this book, be sure to simultaneously advocate for greater access to school-based mental health providers. This access will generally require workforce development planning and the establishment of a pipeline in which to achieve the number of school psychologists, school counselors, and school social workers needed. Remember that *having adequate mental health services in schools is predicated on having an adequate number of professionals to deliver those services.*

Through it all, remain engaged in the Boomerang Policy Making process. Cultivate relationships, prepare your key messages, deliver your asks. Follow up and be prepared to repeat the advocacy action phases as policies move between levers or boomerang within one lever. Talk stories with policy makers and key decision makers about what students are experiencing in schools and in the community. Your voice matters and the stories, solutions, and recommendations you share can have significant impact. Every day is a new opportunity to advocate!

Tips to Get You Started

1.   Believe in the value you bring.
2.   Ask questions; why is it this way?
3.   Ask to see it in writing.
4.   Find an approach that works for you.
5.   Offer a financial solution.

6.   Do your homework, be a resource, be helpful.

7.   Build relationships and allies.

8.   Listen to both sides of an issue.

9.   Remain professional at all times.

10.   Believe that no is never no.

11.   Engage in active problem solving.

12.   Relationships make change, not just ideas.

13.   Stay flexible and adapt.

14.   Know that you belong.

15.   Know your voice matters.

16.   Start small and stay focused.

17.   Keep showing up.

18.   Just get started.

19.   Don't overthink it.

20.   Never give up!

GLOSSARY

3 As the first of the advocacy action phases and includes awareness, access, and action

Access is having physical or virtual connection to key decision makers

Act is a ratified bill, amendment, or agreement

Action is the communicative delivery of your message or ask

ARTERY Pipeline Framework is the comprehensive workforce development pipeline for school-based mental health career pathways

Adverse childhood experience may include abuse (psychological, physical, sexual), witnessing or experiencing domestic violence, national disasters or terrorism, sudden or violent loss of a loved one, neglect, military family-related stressors, refugees or war experiences, serious accidents or life-threatening illness

Advocacy action phases are three phases that comprise the advocacy action component of policy making, and they rest at the center of all efforts: the Message, the Puzzle, and Puzzle Management

Advocacy plan includes various components of coalition building, message construction, and key asks

Advocacy mismatch is when your advocacy level does not match the level required to make the change you want

Advocate means to promote or support a particular idea

Agendize means to schedule an item onto the established meeting agenda

Agreement in principle means that you agree with the general intent of a proposed initiative

Alignment is when policies, practices, and implementation all support the intent behind an initiative

Awareness is having a sense for what is happening relative to your particular initiative of interest and who the key decision makers are

Boomerang Policy Making Model is multi-directional and relies on a shared responsibility of both decision makers and advocates to engage in the policy making process

Bill sponsor is a legislator who can propose and carry a bill through the legislative session

Change agent is someone working to make change

Chief state school officers provide leadership to a state education agency as well as to all the local education agencies and their district superintendents

Coalition is a group of parties coming together to advocate for a unified cause

Coalition building is when you work to join together individuals or groups toward a common purpose

Content experts are experts from the field who can inform on content to advance best practice policies

Curiosity approach is questioning why something is the way that it is to learn more about it

Earmark funds are federal monies that are set aside for certain projects that fall within priority categories

Elevated pitch is a 30-second window in which you have an opportunity to deliver your key message and/or ask

Epigenetic trauma can impact expressed DNA sequences that can lead to changes in brain development, stress regulation, and how our children learn, problem solve, and respond to their environment

Federal grants that originate from the U.S. Department of Education may be in the form of discretionary grants, student loans or grants, and formula grants

Feedback loop is a process for informing on the implementation of a policy or practice

Grassroots advocacy is the coming together of individuals and groups to make change

Implicit bias are the attitudes, beliefs, or stereotypes about people or groups that we are not aware we hold

Institutes of higher education offer post-secondary education training opportunities

Inter-lever boomeranging is when a policy passes from one lever on to the next and passes through the three core advocacy action phases

Intra-lever boomeranging is when more information or additional advocacy is needed within a specific lever and passes through the three core advocacy action phases

Key messages are high-level sound bites that convey a specific idea

Lever is a level of government or bureaucracy needed to advance a specific initiative

Lobbyists are paid by a group to advance certain policy initiatives

Local control is a term used to describe the scope of a local education agency's power to create policies and make decisions at a level close to students

Local education agencies are responsible for governing the education of all public school students within their jurisdiction

Mentor appointment is when individuals are singled out for their advocacy expertise and are consulted with as part of the learning process

Message expansion is increasing the reach, breadth of content, or impact of a message in response to information learned or progression in the process

Monitor progress is when you keep track of your initiative's progression through the policy making and implementation phases

MTSS Advocacy Model is a conceptual way to envision levels of advocacy support, similar to how we conceptualize instructional support for students

Multi-tiered systems of support is an equitable framework in which to offer tiered supports so that all students receive the unique services they need

No does not truly mean no; it just means not at this time, not in this form, or not with these people

Practice advocacy is needed when there is a policy in place, but it is not being implemented through practice

Public support is when an individual or group goes on the record as publicly supporting, opposing, or being neutral to a proposed policy

Puzzle management is the constant monitoring of levers, of tracking implementation, and of messaging to achieve your desired outcome in the policy advocacy process

Quiet influencer is someone who advocates behind the scenes; interested primarily in making change, not having power

Ratio improvement plans are formalized planning documents that state education agencies or local education agencies create, ideally in concert with institutes of higher education

School-based mental health professionals include school psychologists, school counselors, and school social workers

School counselors support inclusive school environments and assist with student academic planning, career and post-secondary planning, school counseling lessons, advocacy for students' needs, short-term supports to students, referral for long-term support for students, and collaboration between school staff, families, and community organizations

School psychologists have specialized training in many domains, including, but not limited to, assessments, behavior management, crisis preparation and response, diversity in development and learning, mental health, special education evaluation, and data collection and interpretation

School social workers are hired to provide direct as well as indirect services to students and families and to assist with mental health and behavior concerns, academic and positive behavior supports, individual and group counseling, and consulting with teachers and administrators

Scope is the scale of your advocacy efforts, including the target audience that can create the solution

Stacked degree programs are higher education training opportunities that offer degrees that build upon each other

State board of education is a governing board who passes state level policy that acts as rules to support implementation of overarching laws

State education agency is a body with a large scope of responsibilities that helps to ensure coordination and maintenance of an equitable education to all public education students in a state

State legislature (or general assembly) is the governing body who passes laws called statutes that apply to all jurisdictions within a state

State statutes are state-level laws passed by state legislatures

State regulations are state-level laws passed by governing boards or state agencies

Strategize ahead consists of brainstorming different contingencies or eventualities with a planned response or approach to each; solution navigation

Sub-awardee is a subrecipient of a recipient who received a grant

The ask is your message consisting of the identified problem, the specific action or ask requested, potential benefits, and anticipated cost

The Five Pillars are foundational education layers of the ARTERY Pipeline Framework: pre–high school graduates, high school graduates, bachelor students, post-baccalaureate students, and graduate students

The puzzle is every conversation, relationship, revelation, and data in your advocacy efforts

Uncomfortableness is the sense of the unknown or loss of control when advocating

Why is a person's internal motivation for engaging in advocacy work

Workforce development is the systematic creation of professionals to support economic stability and prosperity in designated sectors

Workforce shortages is the difference between supply and demand of designated professions within a specific sector of the economy

INDEX

Page numbers in *italics* refer to figures. Page numbers in **bold** refer to tables.

3 As framework 73, 152; access and 82–84; action and 84–88; awareness and 80–82

access and message phase 79, 82–84
ACE *see* adverse childhood experience (ACE)
action and message phase 79, 84–88
action perspective 67, 68–69
Acts 130
adept implementors, schools as 212
adverse childhood experience (ACE) 6, 49, 148, 159
advocacy 175–176; federal engagement and opportunities for 135–137; mental health 31–32; mismatch 42–43; narrative, controlling 101–102; as personal 26; plan 31; worksheet for planning and action of **39**; *see also specific aspects/types*
advocacy, action phases of 69, 72–74, *80*, 93, 103–105, *104*, 136; access and 82–84; action and 84–88; awareness and 80–82; coalition building and 93–94; continuance of messaging and 106–107; financial solutions finding and 99–101; implementation tracking and 105–106; lever management and 107–111; lever monitoring and 105; message expansion and 95; "no" significance and 96–99; progress monitoring and 94–95; repackaging of ask and 99; repeat of phases and 107; strategizing ahead and 95–96

advocates: care and conviction for 24; meaning and importance of 10–11, 21–23; past as determining 24–26

agendizing 68

agreement in principle 48

alignment 43

American Academy of Child and Adolescent Psychiatry 4

American Academy of Pediatrics 4

American Association of University Women 51

American School Counselor Association Model 22, 59, 204, 215

anonymous reporting system, need for 206

Appropriations Committee 133

ARTERY Pipeline Framework 203; benefits from 182; five pillars of 182–189; in higher education 172–174; intentional alignment for 189–190; sample worksheets for 191–196; significance of 9, 13, 116, 117, 118, 123, 134, 165, 181–182; workforce development and 178–196

ask: message 84, 85–87; repackaging 99

awareness and message phase 79, 80–82

bad timing, in advocacy process 97–98

Barnson, K. 59

Baunach, L. 12, 207

bicameral legislature 142

bill: draft request 143; sponsor 143–144, 153

Board of Examiners for Social Workers 121

Boomerang Policy Making Model: action phases to 72–74; actions and 68–69; iterative revisions and feedback loops and 74–76; levers and 68; local education agencies and 200–201; process of 66–67; public meetings and 83; response from decision makers and 92; significance of 65–66, 70, 69–72, 104, 116, 152, 219

career and technical education (CTE) 183

Centers for Disease Control and Prevention Grants 131

Centers for Medicare and Medicaid Services 131

change agents 9, 12–14, 221

chief state school officers 162

Children's Hospital Association 4

chronic trauma 5

Clark County School District 123

classroom issue and puzzle management 111

coalition building 58–60, 93–94

collective advocacy 56–57

collective voice 211

commissioner of schools see chief state school officers

Commission on Professional Standards in Education 121, 122, 123

community funding projects 133–134
competitive grant process 131
connectors *see* quiet influencers
contact, from decision makers 92
content experts 22, 62, 135, 136, 210
Cosgrove, S. 48, 200
COVID-19 pandemic 32–33
CTE *see* career and technical
    education (CTE)
curiosity approach 36–37
curricular standards and concepts,
    revising 159

decision makers, knowledge of 81
developmental implementors,
    schools as 212
Director of the Legislative Counsel
    Bureau 124
district and school issue and puzzle
    management 111
double feedback loops 75
dual-enrollment courses 183, 184

early career practitioners, assigning
    mentors to 203
earmark funds *see* community
    funding projects
Ebert, J. 26, 163
ECS *see* Education Commission of
    the States (ECS)
education actions, continuing 122
Education Commission of the
    States (ECS) 141
educators: meaning and
    significance of 13; in policy
    making process 210

effective communication 61–62
elevator pitches 84–85, 87–88, 89
emails, importance of 143
epigenetic trauma 5
Every Student Succeeds Act 131
Executive Order 2 (Iowa) 167
experiences, framing as strengths
    26–27

federal engagement 129; advocacy
    opportunities and 135–137; in
    education 130–131; funding
    tips and 131–134; mental health
    services tips and 134–135;
    workforce development tips
    and 134
federal grants and funds 116–117;
    see also federal engagement
feedback loops 74–76, 106
flexibility, in policy making 98
Frisbee policy making 66, 75, 83

general assembly *see* state
    legislatures
graduate students 188–189
grassroots advocacy 54–55

Handle with Care Program 206
Hawaii 162
Healthy Minds, Safe Schools
    program 217
higher education institutes *see*
    institutes of higher education
    (IHEs)
higher education issue and puzzle
    management 110

higher education training programs, fostering relationships with 202–203
high school graduates 184–185
House Bill 308 (Virginia) 166
House Bill 373 (Utah) 159
House Bill 671 (Montana) 167
House Bill 1283 (Mississippi) 167
House Bill 1604 (Virginia) 148
House Bill 2591 (Oregon) 147–148
House Bill 3257 (South Carolina) 159
Hudson, T. 154–155, 210

IHEs see institutes of higher education (IHEs)
imaginary audience 38
implicit bias 27
individual advocacy 55–56
innovative community partnerships 167
institutes of higher education (IHEs) 123–124, 169–170; advocacy opportunities for 175–176; ARTERY Pipeline Framework in 172–174; mental health workforce training tips and 174–175; role of 170–172; supports and service training tips and 175
inter-lever boomeranging 70–71, 75–76
intra-lever boomeranging 69–70
iterative revision 74

key messages 84, 85

layered advocacy 75
LEAs see local education agencies (LEAs)

Legislative Committee on Education 124
lever perspectives 67, 68, 71–72; analysis and management of 107–111; monitoring of 105
licensing actions 123
lobbyists 22
local control 199
local education agencies (LEAs); advocacy opportunities and 206–208; meaning and significance of 124–125, 199; model policy examples and 206; role in policy making process 199–201; supports and service tips at local level and 204–205; workforce development tips at local level and 201–204
Loop, M. D. 30, 32, 59, 143

memorandums of agreement (MOAs) 10
memorandums of understanding (MOUs) 110
mental health competencies, establishing 159
Mental Health Service Professional Demonstration grant program 132
mental health services: collaboration for 167; comprehensive xvii–xviii, xix, 212; delivery in schools 212–216; discretionary grants and 132; higher education for 170; importance of xiv–xvi, xxi, xxiv, 11–12, 108, 121, 130, 166, 204, 205, 219, 222; myths about xvii; and providers, advocate for 14–15; tips

for 134–135, 217–218; training for 174; workforce needs and 179
mentors 61
message expansion 95
message phase 73, 78–80; access and 82–84; action and 84–88; awareness and 80–82; as framework, for core issue 88–89, **90**
MOAs *see* memorandums of agreement (MOAs)
MOUs *see* memorandums of understanding (MOUs)
Multi-Tiered Systems of Support (MTSS) Advocacy Model 11, 166, 210, 212–213, 218, 222; advocacy as 48–49; benefits of 214; intervention tiers 213–214, *213*, 216, 217
municipal agencies 207
municipal issue 110–111

National Association of School Psychologists (NASP) 59, 86, 136, 145, 175, 203, 215
National Conference of State Legislatures 140
National School Social Work Practice Model 204
Nevada Administrative Code 109
Nevada Advisory Committee to the U.S. Commission on Civil Rights 48
Nevada Association of School Psychologists (NVASP) 34, 47, 122, 123
Nevada Department of Education 117, 120, 121, 122, 123

Nevada Educator Performance Framework 121
Nevada Revised Statutes 109, 120
Nevada School Counselor Association 59, 122
Nevada School Nurse Association 122
Nevada School Social Worker Association 122
Nevada State College 123
New York Association of School Psychologists (NYASP) 58
"no", significance in advocacy 96–97; bad timing and 97–98; "not in this form" and 98–99; not with right group of people 99; as response from decision makers 92
NVASP *see* Nevada Association of School Psychologists (NVASP)
NYASP *see* New York Association of School Psychologists (NYASP)

Office for Civil Rights (OCR) 37
Ortiz, F. 156
Oyen, K. 36, 210

Parent–Teacher Association (PTA) 55, 58
physical and mental health, connections between 148
policy advocacy 23, 106, 207
policy issue and puzzle management 108, 109–110
Policy Playbook 145
poorly drafted policies 108
post-baccalaureate students 187–188

practice advocacy 106
practice issue and puzzle
    management 108–109
practicum and intern students,
    supervision for 203
pre-high school graduates 183–184
Project AWARE (North Carolina) 168
psychological services assistant
    (PSA) 125, 126, 186–187, 202
psychological services position 125
PTA see Parent–Teacher Association
    (PTA)
public meetings: access to 83–84;
    importance of 83; knowledge of
    81–82
public support 124, 144–145
puzzle management phase 73–74,
    104; continuance of messaging
    and 106–107; implementation
    tracking and 105–106; lever
    analysis 107–111; lever monitoring
    105; repeat of phases and 107
puzzle solving phase 73

quiet influencers 60–61

ratio improvement plans 118, 122,
    148, 159
Read by Grade 3 law 46, 47
relationship building 53–54;
    coalition building and 58–60;
    collective advocacy and 56–57;
    effective communication and
    61–62; grassroots advocacy and
    54–55; individual advocacy and
    55–56; mentor identification and
    61; quiet influencers and 60–61

relationships, as foundation of
    advocacy xviii
respecialization see post-
    baccalaureate students
restorative practices 94, 219
risk taking 30–32
Robbins, Z. 57, 218

safety screenings and services,
    funds for 148
SafeVoice Program 206
School-Based Health Centers
    (Colorado) 167
school-based mental health
    professionals 8–9
School-Based Mental Health
    Services grant program 133
school counselors 8, 14, 22, 42,
    109–110, 121, 126, 148, 171, 180,
    204, 215, 216
School-Linked Mental Health
    programs (Minnesota) 167
school mental and behavioral
    health services xvii–xviii, xix
school psychologists 34, 203, 214–215;
    see also school counselors; school
    social workers
school psychology 110, 123–125, 175,
    179–180, 187, 189
school role: advocacy opportunities
    and 218–219; in leadership
    building 125–126; policy alignment
    and 211; in policy making process
    210–211; supports and service
    tips at school level and 217–218;
    supports and services delivery
    and 212–213, 214–216; tiered

intervention supports and services and 213–2124; workforce development tips at school level and 216–217

School Safety and Resiliency Act (Senate Bill 1, Kentucky) 109–110

School Safety and Security Fund 148

School Social Work Association of America 59, 215

school social workers 8, 42, 126, 171, 180, 204, 215

scope, of advocacy efforts 42–43; agreement in principle and 48; characteristics and components of 44, 46; considerations in **43**; larger in 45–48; Multi-Tiered Systems of Support (MTSS) Advocacy Model and 48–49; nammer and 51; smaller in 44–45; wellness data and 49–51

SEAs *see* state education agencies (SEAs)

SEB *see* social-emotional-behavioral (SEB) supports

Senate and Assembly Standing Committees on Education 124

Senate Bill 1 (Kentucky) 148

Senate Bill 11 (Texas) 167

Senate Bill 46 (South Dakota) 206

Senate Bill 80 (Nevada) 206

Senate Bill 89 (Nevada) 109, 118, 159

Senate Bill 151 (Nevada) 118–119, 124, 159

Senate Bill 319 (Nevada) 118–119, 159

Senate Bill 352 (Nevada) 119, 125, 159

Senate Bill 661 (Maryland) 167

Senate Bill 953 (Virginia) 148

Senate Bill 1097 (Arizona) 206

Senate Bill 1142 (Pennsylvania) 148

Senate Bill 4990 (New York) 148

Senate Bill 5082 (Washington state) 159

silence, as response from decision makers 92

single feedback loop 75

SISP *see* Specialized Instructional Support Personnel (SISP)

social-emotional-behavioral (SEB) supports 212, 214

social-emotional well-being, educator trainings on 149

solution navigation 95–96

Specialized Instructional Support Personnel (SISP) 34, 120

stacked degree programs 173, 186

State Association Resource Guide 145

State Board of Education 109, 120–121, 122, 124, 154, 155, 159

state-delegated funds, grants from 132–133

state education agencies (SEAs) 121–122, 161–162, 166; education action continuance and 122; licensing actions and 123; meaning and significance of 162–163; mental health support and service tips at department level and 165–166; model policy examples and 166–168; policy making process role of 163–164; ratio improvement actions and 122; workforce development tips at department level and 164–165; *see also* U.S. Department of Education

state legislatures xviii, 58, 123, 130; Boomerang Policy Making Model and 70, 71; local education agencies and 199, 200; puzzle management and 108, 109; scope of advocacy and 42, 47, 49; state education agencies and 163, 166; state regulations and 152–154; state statutes and 140, 141

State of Emergency: in Child and Adolescent Mental Health 4–7; in Workforce Development 8–9

state policy issue and puzzle management 109–110

state regulations 22, 119–120, 141, 151–152; 2019 regulation 120–121; 2021 regulation 121; creation of 154–156; meaning and significance of 152–154; model policy examples and 158–159; process of 156; supports and service tips at regulatory level and 157–158; workforce development tips at regulatory level and 156–157

state statutes 117, 139–140; beginning of process of 142–144; creation of 141–142; meaning and importance of 140–141; model policy examples for 147–149; Nevada State Senate Bill 89 (2019) 118; Nevada State Senate Bill 151 (2021) 118–119; Nevada State Senate Bill 319 (2019) 118–119; Nevada State Senate Bill 352 (2021) 119; public support and 144–145; supports and service tips at statutory level and 146–147; workforce development tips at statutory level and 145–146

state superintendents *see* chief state school officers

statewide plan for mental health, developing 167

storytelling, impact of 210–211

strategizing ahead 95–96

stress and anxiety management, pilot program for 167

student mental health days, allowing 166, 206

Student Wellness and Success Fund (Ohio) 168

sub-awardees, grants to 132

Substance Abuse and Mental Health Services Administration Grants 131

suicide prevention programs, establishing 148

suicide rate, of youths 4–5

support and service tips: at department level 165–166; institutes for higher education and 175; at local level 204–205; at regulatory level 157–158; at school level 217–218

talk stories 12, 15, 144, 222

Teachers and Leaders Council (TLC) 34

Texas Education Agency 167

Thompson, M. 46, 47

TLC *see* Teachers and Leaders Council (TLC)
transgenerational epigenetic inheritance 5, 7
transitional implementors, schools as 212
trauma impact on learning, training on 159
trauma-informed practices, adopting 148

U.S. Department of Education 123, 130, 131, 135, 154; grants from 132; offices for grants within 132; *see also* state education agencies
U.S. Department of Health and Human Services 8, 131, 155, 156
U.S. House of Representatives 130
U.S. Surgeon General xvi
uncertainty, resolving 33
uncomfortableness 29–30, 31; coping strategies for 35–36; imaginary audience and 38; moving past 39; sticking to facts and asking questions to tackle 36–37
undergraduate students 185–187

Washington Professional Educator Standard Board 159
Washington School Counselor Association (WSCA) 58
wellness data 49–51
why process 19–21, 26
workforce development 178–181: at department level 164–165; for federal grants 134; at local level 201–204; at regulatory level 156–157; at school level 216–217; *see also* ARTERY Pipeline Framework
workforce needs 179–181
workforce shortages 181, 191
written policy 37
WSCA *see* Washington School Counselor Association (WSCA)

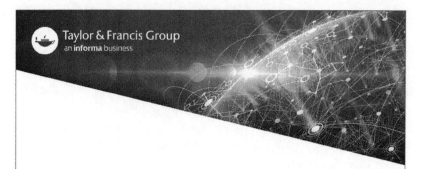

Printed in Great Britain
by Amazon